WHERE THE BUDDHA WALKED

A Companion to the
Buddhist Places of India

Rana P. B. Singh

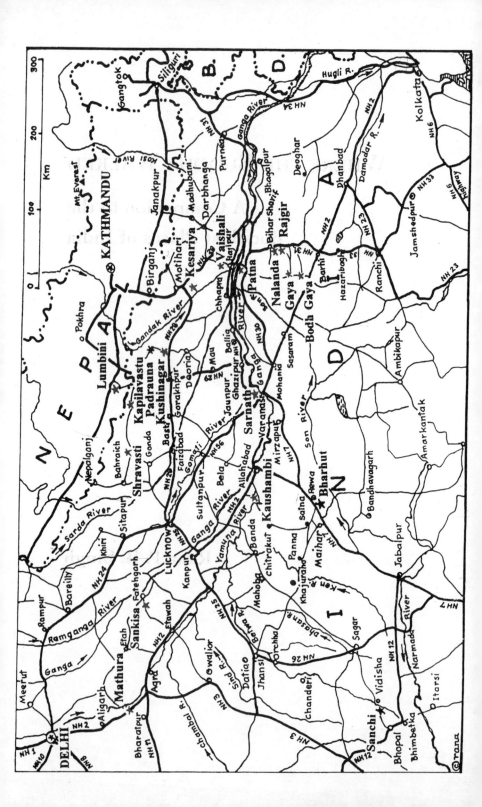

WHERE THE BUDDHA WALKED

A Companion to the Buddhist Places of India

Rana P. B. Singh

INDICA

Pilgrimage & Cosmology Series: 5

Cover illustration: *Footprints of the Buddha*
(from a bas-relief at Amravati, 1ˢᵗ century BCE)

Cataloguing Data:
Singh, Rana P. B. (b. 1950)
Where the Buddha Walked. A Companion to the Buddhist Places of India.
330 pp., 110 Figures/Maps. *Pilgrimage & Cosmology Series 5.*
Indica Books, Varanasi, 2003.
1. Buddhist pilgrimage, 2. Heritage Tourism, 3. Religious Studies

Sponsored by: Society of Heritage Planning and Environmental Health

© Rana P.B. Singh 2003

1st edition 2003
2nd edition 2009

Published by

Indica Books
D 40/18 Godowlia
Varanasi - 221001 (U.P.)
India

Indicabooks@satyam.net.in
www.indicabooks.com

ISBN: 81-86569-36-7

Printed in India : *First Impression*, New Delhi
011-22481754, 09811224048

to

Hsüan-tsang
(CE 603-664)
a great Chinese pilgrim
who followed the Buddha's footprints

Four higher roadways be. Only those feet
May tread them which have done with earthly things
Right Purity, Right Thought, Right Loneliness
Right Rapture. Spread no wings.

Sir Edwin Arnold, 1879: p. 212.

The Message of the Buddha

The Enlightened One saw the four noble truths, which point out the path that leads to Nirvana or the extinction of self:

> The first noble truth is the existence of sorrow.
> The second noble truth is the cause of suffering.
> The third noble truth is the cessation of sorrow.
> The fourth noble truth is the eight-fold path that leads to the cessation of sorrow.

This is the Dharma. This is the truth. This is religion. And the Enlightened One uttered this stanza:

> "Through many births I sought in vain
> The Builder of this House of Pain.
> Now, Builder, thee I plainly see!
> This is the last abode for me.
> Thy gable's yoke and rafters broke,
> My heart has peace. All lust will cease."

There is self and there is truth. Where self is, truth is not. Where truth is, self is not. Self is the fleeting error of *samsara*; it is individual separateness and that egotism which begets envy and hatred. Self is the yearning for pleasure and the lust after vanity. Truth is the correct comprehension of things; it is the permanent and ever lasting, the real in all existence, the bliss of righteousness.

Rhys Davids, *Buddhism* (1890), pp. 106 -107.

CONTENTS

8

PREFACE

In the late 1970s my inner quest mobilised my sight and vision for understanding the *genius loci* of a place or landscape, ultimately trying to interpret and understand the meanings, messages and milieus preserved there. Further along on that march, I don't know when I became a traveller, a wanderer, who always carried the familiarity and ordinary while moving in search of much more powerful settings, scenes, and sacredscapes. On this road while walking, people from different parts of the world joined and made our group a companion of seekers, a mosaic of culture, thought and vision. The American philosopher David Appelbaum in his seminal book, *Everyday Spirit* (1993: p. xv), says that "The idea of a guidebook exposes a treachery in the language. ... Such guidance exists only in a moment when the two worlds achieve contact: '*the physical world of existence and metaphysical world of meanings*'" (italics added).

Since the first stage of human evolution, the idea of the mystical power of place has been part of human consciousness. The identification of a place as sacred is never essentially one of individual recognition; actually, the place is never 'chosen' by humans, it is merely discovered by them. In some way or another the 'spirit of place' attracts and reveals itself to a human, and that is how he or she merely 'finds' it, though the process of discovery becomes easier when one follows the **spiritual path**. The quality of the sacred place depends upon the human context that has been shaped by it, with respect to memories, experiences, miracles and expectations.

To every place, there is a *key* — direct communication with the inherent meanings and messages of the place. When the key is lost, the place is forgotten. Mythologies, folk tales, continuity of cultural traditions, the quest to understand what is beyond — all are the facets of *crossings*. To cross is to be transformed. On the ladder to cross from one side, the physical, to the other end, the metaphysical, the sacred places serve as rungs. The ladder provides the way of ascent through care and deeper quest. A spiritual walk is the ladder, sacred ways are the steps, and human understanding is the destination. Pilgrimage is a self re-discovery. The modern way of pilgrimage is an experiential

11

bridge linking the modernism of the West and the mysticism of the East. Thinking together is a new vision. Going together is a new start. Walking together is a real march. Realising together is the final destination — enlightenment. Without a pilot, one gets lost in madness, illness, or death. Without a way a pilgrim or traveller gets lost in the route. The way is a 'spirit' — spirit is an eternal sight for passing on the path in the right order. The process of understanding a place is a pilgrimage in search of interrelationship between the physical milieu and its metaphysical values.

This book is an attempt to serve as a key, a way and a companion on this march towards crossing and soul healing. This is a humble attempt to narrate almost all the important sites and scenes of the Buddhist places where once the Buddha walked, with a view to experiencing the deeper meanings and messages. It is our wish that you and we will either meet in the Buddhist places, or, even better, that we will perform co-pilgrimage in and around these sites.

Among the friends who accompanied me on several sacred journeys in and around the Buddhist places and those who supported me in various ways include the American art historian Fredrick Asher, the Buddhist co-pilgrims and co-authors Allan Badiner and Stephen Batchelor, the Dutch Indologist Hans Bakker, the President of the Naropa (Buddhist University) University at Boulder Thomas B. Coburn, the Indo-Italian activist Vrinda Dar, the Australian Buddhist monk Ven. S. Dhammika, the established British scholar Mark Dyczkowski, the Indian peregrinologer D.P. Dubey, the Italian Indologist Gian G. Filippi, the Japanese Indologist Masaaki Fukunaga, the American scholar of mysticism Roxanne Gupta, the Vietnamese Buddhist Zen Master Thich Nhat Hanh, the Japanese Buddhist scholar Taigen Hashimoto, the British organiser of meditative and sacred journeys Roger Housden, the American scholar of Hinduism and Buddhism Sandy Huntington, the American art historian couple Susan & John Huntington, the Belgian scholar of Hindu pilgrimages Bermijin Isabelle, the Norwegian Indologist Knut Axel Jacobsen, the Swede Indologist Marc Katz, the American art historian Robert Linrothe, the American scholars of Buddhism Pat Masters and Robert Pryor of Antioch College Program of Buddhist Studies, the British art historian George Michell, the novelist and travelogue writer Pankaj Mishra, the Japanese Indologist Hisayoshi Miyamoto, the ex-director of the Tibetan Institute and prime minister of the exiled Government of Tibet Rev. Samdong Rinpoche, the Japanese Hindi professor Teiji Sakata, the Danish Indologist Eric Sand, the Dutch scholar Irma Schotsman, the organiser of Buddhist pilgrimages Shantum Seth, the geographer of sacred places Ravi Shankar, the scholar of ancient Indian history Arvind Singh, the teacher of Buddhist literature Siddharth Singh, the American site producer and editor Pam Strayer, the historian of ancient India Vibha Tripathi, the Austrian student of Vipassana Robert Wagner, and the Swiss tour organiser Hans Wettstein. The Indian professor of Buddhist philosophy Hari Shankar (Delhi University) needs special thanks as he has helped me in several ways to understand and to read sources and materials on the various facets of Buddhism. I am thankful to my friend Rakesh Singh of Harmony Bookshop (Assi Ghat, Varanasi), for his kindness in making accessible to me many of the relevant publications that helped the writing, and also encouraging me in several ways.

For the last one decade my involvement as Co-ordinator/ President to look after the Banaras segment of the NYSICCSI (New York State Independent Colleges Consortium for Study in India, USA), Friends of the World Programme (Long Island University, USA), Danish Association of Teachers of Religious Studies, Nordic Association of Teachers of Religious Studies, Karlstad University (Sweden) Programme of Indian Studies, Indo-Japanese Friendship Association, and Indo-Nordic Cultural Association, has helped several groups of scholars to get an insightful experience of the sacred journey to Buddhist places. Additionally, my association as President of the Society of Heritage Planning and Environmental Health and of the Society of Pilgrimage Studies has also been beneficial in understanding and experiencing the messages of pilgrimages.

I express my special thanks to the American art historian Robert Linrothe (Skidmore College, NY), a friend and a fellow co-pilgrim, who so kindly edited some portions of the manuscript. In the whole journey his insights are always with us. Alvaro Enterria and Dilip Jaiswal, the publishers and partners of Indica Books (Varanasi), have been a spirit behind the contract, progress and the final product. It is thankless to thank them because they are the companions along the sacred path and writing. However, above all I express my special gratitude to Mr Alvaro, the man *par excellence*, who has been a rational and constructive critic and serious editor, together with raising so many pertinent questions which I enjoyed to answer and add.

From the family side, how can I express my deep gratitude to my wife Manju 'Usha' who sacrificed so many good days in order to keep me free from the family duties and warned me to take care of health. She has always been a source of inspiration and a silent observer! My sons, Pravin and Prashant have assisted me in different ways, sometimes in a very tense situation, to complete this work. Our daughters

Pratibha and Prabha took care to keep up my spirits awakened and keep me on time. Ravi Shankar, a co-pilgrim, my old student and now son-in-law, is a companion on the sacred march; to him I express my deep sense of appreciation for his rational criticism and inspiration. My brother-in-law Dr R.P. Singh, a noted eye surgeon and director of the Buddha Eye Hospital has taken all the care for physical health and strain and stresses on my eyes during the course of writing and preparing the architectural designs; I'm very much thankful to him.

More than anybody else, I humbly express my gratitude to the Buddhist Monk Ven. S. Dhammika (Buddha Dhamma Mandala Society, Balestier Road, Singapore), for being so kind on the path of Buddhist compassion to allow me to directly use several passages from his fascinating and first-hand experiences of the spirit of Buddhist landscape narrated in his famous book *Middle Land Middle Way* (Buddhist Publication Society, Kandy, 2nd ed. 1999, © the author); the extensively used pages include: 10-19, 33-34, 37-43, 69-71, 88-91, 100-103, 114, 117, 120-123, 134-136, 179, 181, 200-203, and 237-239. In a way, the present book is an offering to him.

Remember, no one can write the last saga! This is a first and small attempt and certainly needs constructive criticism and suggestions for incorporation and change in the future.

Rana P.B. Singh
Varanasi: 20 May 2008
Vaishakha, Shukla (light-half)-15th, Samvata 2065
Buddha Purnima, the day of his birth, enlightenment and nirvana

No. : 3848

Name .... Date 14|12|14

Address ....

Qnty.	PARTICULARS	Amount
1.	Where Dhe Buddha Walked	395
	Total	395

Signature

THE BUDDHA AND HIS MESSAGE

Siddhartha Gautama, who was after enlightenment given the title of 'Buddha', was born a prince into the warrior caste (*Shakya clan*) in 563 BCE. On the birth of the child, named Siddhartha, the astrologers predicted to his father Suddhodana: "The child, on attaining manhood, will become either a universal monarch (*Chakravarti*), or abandoning house and home, will assume the role of a monk and become a Buddha, a perfectly enlightened soul, for the salvation of mankind". He was married at the age of 16. At the age of 29 years he left home and started wandering as a beggar and ascetic. After about six years he spent some time in Bodh Gaya. Sitting under the Bo or fig tree (*Pipal, Ficus religiosa*), meditating, he was tempted by the demon **Mara** with all the desires of the world (Fig. 3). Resisting these temptations, he received enlightenment.

Fig. 3: Shakyamuni Buddha. Victory over Mara (Kushana period)

His face shone with divine splendour and effulgence. He got up
from his seat and danced in divine ecstasy for seven consecu-
tive days and nights around the
sacred Bo-tree. His footprints
found at all the important sites
(e.g. at Amravati; Fig. 4) mark this
incidence. After his enlightenment his heart was filled with
profound mercy and compassion. He wanted to share what he
had got with humanity. He travelled all over India and preached
his doctrine and gospel. He became a saviour, deliverer and re-
deemer. These scenes are com-

Fig. 4: Footprints of the Buddha
(from a bas-relief at Amravati, 1st century BCE)

mon motifs of Buddhist art (Fig. 5). After enlightenment at Bodh Gaya,
the Buddha gave his first sermon on "The Foundation of Righteousness" (known as "*Turning the Wheel of Law*") in the Deer Park of Sarnath,
near Banaras. By the time he died he had established a small congrega-
tion of monks and nuns known as the *Sangha*, mostly in north India.

Fig. 5. Six life incidents of the Buddha
(Gandhara and Sanchi)

His body was cremated, and the
ashes, regarded as precious relics,
were divided among the peoples to
whom he had preached. Some have
been discovered as far west as
Peshawar, in the northwest frontier
of Pakistan, and at Piprahwa
(Kapilavastu), close to his birthplace. The *Vaishakha Purnima* (Full-
Moon day of April-May) is connected with three important events
in the life of the Buddha — birth,
enlightenment and *parinirvana*. It is
the most sacred day in the Buddhist
calendar. In the near future the
dates for the *Buddha Purnima* are:
**16 May 2003, 4 May 2004, 23 May
2005, 13 May 2006, 2 May 2007, 20
May 2008, 9 May 2009, and 27 May
2010.**

While preaching and performing pilgrimages, the Buddha at the request of his father had paid a visit to Kapilavastu. Respecting and honouring the chastity of his wife, Yashodhara, a lady endowed with 'discrimination' (*viveka*) and 'dispassion' (*vairagya*), the Buddha went at once to see her. By her inspiration the Buddha established an order of female ascetics, and Yashodhara became the first of the Buddhist nuns. When his son Rahula insistently and repeatedly asked the Buddha for his heritage: "Dear Father, I am your son; give me my birthright, my heritage", the Buddha said to one of his disciples, "I give this boy the precious spiritual wealth I acquired under the sacred Bo-tree. I make him the heir to that wealth". That is how Rahula was initiated into the order of monks.

The Buddha '*Gautama*' (563-483 BCE) was in his childhood confronted by three disturbing facts of life: old age, sickness, and death, and had an intense urge to overcome them. Leaving home, he performed extremely rigorous and tortuous practices, but was disillusioned by them, as these means did not cause any ethical and spiritual transformation within him. Hence he revolted against such practices. Ultimately on his own he attained Enlightenment whose essence was Wisdom and Compassion. This was for him a transforming experience where he learnt the true nature of the universe as containing dependently arising and impermanent things, as well as the true nature of his own being. It was Wisdom because it revealed every being as a conditioned or dependently arising being, and Compassion because it aroused concern for other fellow beings to be enlightened and liberated. These two together, according to the Buddha, cause a revolution in one's attitude and behaviour, and set him on the path of progress in terms of personal and social morality. The Buddha says that the position of a person in the social hierarchy is determined by the level of ethical and humanitarian consciousness he achieves in his moral practices through personal effort. He realised and preached the Four Noble Truths: that life is painful; that suffering is caused by ignorance and desire; that beyond the suffering of life there is a state which cannot be described but which he termed *nirvana*; and that *nirvana* can be reached by following the *Noble Eightfold Path*.

The Buddha's *Noble Eightfold Path* (*ashtanga-marga*) is devised for the above-said purpose and is essentially the perfection of morality, wisdom, and meditation. The first three, based on moral precepts (*shila*), are: *Right Speech* (*samma-vacha*), refraining from speaking falsehood, malicious words, harsh and frivolous talk; *Right Deeds* (*samma-kamanta*), refraining from killing, stealing, and misconduct; and *Right Means of Livelihood* (*samma-ajiva*), refraining from earning livelihood by improper means, such as immoral or illegal trades or professions. The next three, associated with mental development (*chitta*), are: *Right Exertion* (*samma-vayam*), exertion to remove the existing evil thoughts, to keep the mind free from being polluted by fresh evil thoughts, and to preserve and increase the good thoughts; *Right Mindfulness* (*samma-sati*), mindfulness of all that is happening within the body and mind including feelings, and being observant of the things of the world, at the same time suppressing covetousness and avoiding mental depression; and *Right Meditation* (*samma-samadhi*), realisation of the *Four Noble Truths*. The final two, based on knowledge (*prajna*), are: *Right Resolution* (*samma-sankalpa*), resolution for renunciation, and resolution for refraining from hatred and injury to other beings; and *Right Vision* (*samma-ditthi/ dristhi*), realisation of the truth that worldly existence is misery, and its root, its end and its path all lead to an end in such misery.

At his later discourse at Shravasti, the Buddha told,

"Monks, the teaching is merely a vehicle to describe the truth. Don't mistake it for the truth itself. A finger pointing at the moon is not the moon. The finger is needed to know where to look for the moon, but if you mistake the finger for the moon itself, you will never know the real moon.

"The teaching is like a raft that carries you to the other shore. The raft is needed, but the raft is not the other shore. An intelligent person would not carry the raft around on his head after making it across to the other shore. Monks, my teaching is the raft which can help you cross to the other shore beyond birth and death. Use the raft to cross to he other shore, but don't hang onto it as your property. Do not become caught in the teaching. You must be able to let it go.

"Monks, all the teaching I have given you, such as the Four Noble Truths, the Noble Eightfold Path, the Four Establishments of Mindfulness, the Seven Factors of Awakening; Impermanence, Non-self, Suffering, Emptiness, Signlessness, and Aimlessness, should be studied in an intelligent, open, manner. Use the teachings to help you reach liberation. Do not become attached to them."

At the suggestion of the Buddha and with the request of Ananda, Venerable Bhanda summarised the message of Buddha for the common people as:

"Dwelling in tranquillity,
seeing the Dhamma, returning to the source
without hatred or violence,
joy and peace overflow.

Mindfulness is held perfectly;
True peace and ease are realised.
Transcending all desires
is the greatest happiness."

(Samyutta Nikaya, LIV.9)

At his last discourses at Shravasti, the Buddha continued his *Dhamma* talk by saying, "True happiness can be realised in this very life, especially when you observe the following **Ten Rules**:

1. Foster relations with people of virtue and avoid the path of degradation.
2. Live in an environment that is conducive to spiritual practice and builds good character.
3. Foster opportunities to learn more about the Dhamma, the precepts, and your own trade in greater depth.
4. Take the time to care well for your parents, spouse and children.
5. Share time, resources, and happiness with others.
6. Foster opportunities to cultivate virtue. Avoid alcohol and gambling.
7. Cultivate humility, gratitude, and simple living.
8. Seek opportunities to be close to monks in order to study the Way.
9. Live a life based on the Four Noble Truths.
10. Learn how to meditate in order to release sorrows and anxieties"

(Singala Sutta, D. 31)

At one of his last discourses in the lush forest near Rajgir the Buddha praised a young nun for her courage and clarity, and said, "It is dangerous for nuns to walk alone on deserted paths. That is one of the reasons I hesitated initially to ordain women. Subha, from now on, no bhikkhuni should travel alone. Whether crossing a river, entering a village to beg, or walking through a forest or a field, no bhikkhuni should walk alone. No bhikkhuni should sleep alone, either. Whether she sleeps in a nunnery, a small hut, or beneath a tree, no bhikkhuni should sleep by herself. She should always travel and sleep with at least one other bhikkhuni so they can watch out for each other and protect each other." *(Sammanaphala Sutta, D.2)*

The Buddha proceeded to explain the sixty-two theories and expose their errors. He spoke on the eighteen theories concerning the past — four theories of eternalism, four theories of partial eternalism, four theories on the finitude and infinity of the world, four theories of endless equivocation, and two theories that claim that causality does not exist. He spoke about the forty-four theories that concern the future — sixteen that allege the soul lives on after death, eight that say there is no soul after death, eight that posit there is neither a soul that continues after death nor ceases to continue after death, seven annihilistic theories, and five theories that say that the present is already Nirvana. After exposing all the errors contained in these theories, the Buddha said, "A good fisherman places his net in the water and catches all the shrimp and fish he can. As he watches the creatures try to leap out of the net, he tells them, 'No matter how high you jump, you will only land in the net again'. He is correct. The thousands of beliefs flourishing at present can all be found in the net of these sixty-two theories. My dear Monks!, don't fall into that bewitching net. You will only waste time and lose your chance to practice the Way of Enlightenment. Don't fall into the net of mere speculation."

The Buddha added, "Monks, all these beliefs and doctrines have arisen because people have been led astray by their perceptions and feelings. When mindfulness is not practised, it is impossible to see the true nature of perceptions and feelings. When you can penetrate the roots and see into the true nature of your perceptions and feelings, you will see the impermanent and interdependent nature of all dharmas. You will no longer be caught in the net of desire, anxiety, and fear, or the net of the sixty-two false theories." (cf. *Brahmajala Sutta*, D.1)

While staying in the Ghositarama monastery in Kaushambi, the Buddha said to his successor Ananda, "We must not become discouraged every time we meet with difficulty. Solutions should be sought in the very midst of hardship. Ananda, if we practice equanimity, we will not be bothered by insults and slander. The people who slander us cannot harm us. They only harm themselves. When a man spits at the sky, the sky is not sullied. The spit falls back in the face of the one who spat." (*Kalama Sutta*, A.III.65)

At one of the last ceremonies and discourses at Nalanda, the Buddha told his disciples the following fable:

"Once upon a time, a clever king invited several people blind from birth to visit the palace. He brought out an elephant and asked them to touch it and then describe what the elephant was like. The-blind man who rubbed its legs said that the elephant was like the pillars of a house. The man who stroked its tail said the elephant was like a feather duster. The person who touched its ears said it was like a winnowing basket, and the man who touched its stomach said it was like a round barrel. The person who rubbed its head said the elephant was like a large earthenware jar, and the person who touched its tusk said the elephant was like a stick. When they sat down to discuss what the elephant was like, no one could agree with anyone else, and a very heated argument arose."

The Lord added, "Monks, what you see and hear comprises only a small part of reality. If you take it to be the whole of reality, you will end up having a distorted picture. A person on the path must keep a humble, open heart, acknowledging that his understanding is incomplete. We should devote constant effort to study more deeply in order to make progress on the path. A follower of the Way must remain open-minded, understanding that attachment to present views as if they were absolute truth will only prevent us from realising the truth. Humility and open-mindedness are the two conditions necessary for making progress on the path." (*Udana*, VI.4)

From the Buddha's death, or *parinirvana*, to the destruction of Nalanda (the last Buddhist stronghold in India) in 1197 CE, Buddhism in India went through three phases, often referred as Hinayana, Mahayana, and Vajrayana. The *Hinayana*, or the Lesser Way, insists on a monastic way of life as the only path to achieving *nirvana*. Divided into many schools, the only surviving Hinayana tradition is the *Theravada (Sthaviravada)*, or the Way of the Elders, which was taken to Sri Lanka by the Emperor Ashoka's son Mahinda, where it became the state religion under King Dutthagamini in the 1st century CE. In contrast, the followers of the *Mahayana*, or the Greater Way, believed in the possibility of salvation for all by practising devotional meditation. One of the most notable Mahayana philosophers was the 2nd or 3rd century saint, Nagarjuna. The 3rd school, called the *Vajrayana* or the Thunderbolt Way, resembles magic and yoga in some of its beliefs; it tries to get in harmony with the cosmos so as to be able to manifest the cosmic forces within and without oneself. It developed in the Himalaya region (i.e. Tibet) by the 7th century CE, matching the parallel growth of Hindu Tantrism.

The places visited by the Buddha were interconnected by roads used mostly by caravan traders, in whose company the religious people usually travelled for the sake of food, safety and other conveniences as the monks also were not immune from the hands of highway robbers. Many of the holy places were also famous as economic centres and were linked by trade routes. The area covered by the Buddha's pilgrimages and his missionary activities was confined mostly to the central and eastern parts of India, from Kaushambi in the west to Kushinagar and Rajgir in the east, and from Shravasti in the north to Banaras (Sarnath) in the south. Before the rise of Buddhism the Vedic religion had held its sway in this region for a pretty long time. During the period of Emperor Ashoka (270-232 BCE) Buddhism was transformed into a religious movement and also transcended the boundaries of India. To make it a popular religion Ashoka promoted the prevalent cult of worship of local holy places (*chaitya*) which were easily accessible to everyone without distinction. It was an inexpensive and non-violent religious practice. Obviously, it was against the expensive rituals and animal sacrifices that could be commissioned only by rich people and performed only by the Brahmins who had the exclusive right and expertise to perform them. Although Buddhism got patronage from various ancient kings from time to time, there were a few cases of its persecution by certain rulers like the Brahmin king Pushyamitra Sunga (ca. 2nd century BCE), king Mihirakula of the Huna dynasty in the 6th century, and a Shaivite king of Bengal, Shashanka, who had damaged and tried to uproot the Bodhi Tree at Bodh Gaya. But the most cruel blow came during the 12th and the 13th centuries from the Muslim invaders who brutally massacred monks, demolished monasteries, and destroyed the Buddhist centres of learning and their libraries located at Nalanda, Vikramashila, Odantapuri and elsewhere. After the passage of time Buddhism slowly disappeared from Indian soil. However, above all the symbolic physical presence and the cultural roots have survived.

* For the major historical events in the history of Buddhism, **see Appendix: 1.**

WALKING IN THE BUDDHA'S FOOTSTEPS

> "Ananda, there are four places the sight of which should arouse a sense of urgency in the faithful. Which are they? 'Here the *Tathagata* was born' is the first. 'Here the *Tathagata* attained supreme enlightenment' is the second. 'Here the *Tathagata* set in motion the Wheel of the *Dhamma*' is the third. 'Here the *Tathagata* attained Parinirvana without remainder' is the fourth. And, Ananda, the faithful monks and nuns, while making the pilgrimage to these shrines with a devout heart will, at the breaking up of the body after death, be reborn in a heavenly world..."
>
> *Mahaparinibbana Sutta*, 5.8.

Thus, according to Buddhist tradition, the Buddha spoke to his chief attendant Ananda in the very last discourse he delivered before his death (around 483 BCE). Referring to himself as the *Tathagata*, or Perfected One, the Buddha (Fig. 6) prescribed four places of pilgrimage to his followers. He also gave hints for the celebrations to be performed at his funeral pyre. In doing so, he enshrined the activity of pilgrimage as an important act of the Buddhist's life — an act sanctioned by scriptural recommendation. He tied the Buddhist conception of pilgrimage, at least in its original form, specifically and explicitly to those places that witnessed the most significant events of his life; these are Lumbini (birth), Bodh Gaya (enlightenment; cf. Fig. 7), Sarnath (first preaching), and Kushinagar (*parinirvana*, final release; cf. Fig. 8). The other four sites associated with the Great Miracles performed by the Buddha and

Fig. 6. The Buddha's head

23

Fig. 7. Buddha in Meditation

accepted as places of pilgrimages are Rajagriha (Rajgir), where the Lord tamed a mad elephant, Vaishali, where a monkey offered honey to him, Shravasti, where the Lord took his seat on a thousand petalled lotus and created multiple representations of himself, and Sankisa (Sankasya), where he descended from heaven. Altogether this group of 8 holy places are called *Atthamahathanani* (*ashtamahasthanani*; represented in one of the stone slabs, see Fig. 9). In this list the later additions are the place of his childhood (Kapilavastu), the place of several sermons in the 6th and 9th years of enlightenment (Kaushambi), and the place where the Buddha gave his begging bowl to the people (Kesariya). According to the *Jatakas*, the Buddha visited Nalanda several times; this is the place from where the history of the monastic establishments can be traced back to the days of Ashoka. Altogether these twelve places have become the most revered places of Buddhist pilgrimage. Among these twelve places, Sarnath, Kushinagar, Shravasti, Sankasya, Kapilavastu and Kaushambi are in the state of Uttar Pradesh and are approachable from the central point of Varanasi, or Lucknow. Moreover, the birthplace, Lumbini, is in Nepal at the border of the district of Siddharthnagar. Further, Kesariya and Vaishali are also easily accessible and interlinked with the Buddhist circuit of pilgrimage-tourism, taking Varanasi as centre (see Fig. 1). In the pilgrimage circuit of the Buddha's footprints Gaya, Patna and Mathura are also included because at those places too the Buddha passed some of his stays. Thus, in total the 15 places mentioned above are accepted as the sacred sites in the Buddhist pilgrimage.

Fig. 8. The Buddha's Nirvana

The sequence of the fifteen Buddhist places follows the lifecycle and the journeys performed by the Buddha as narrated in the *Jatakas* and the *Tripitaka*. Accordingly, the Buddha was born (563 BCE) in the garden of **Lumbini** (1), passed his first 29 years (563-533 BCE) in the royal palaces of **Kapilavastu** (2), followed by his march to several places and finally to **Bodh Gaya** (3), where he received enlightenment at the age of 35 (528 BCE), and Gaya (4) where he did arduous austerity. Then he proceeded to give his first preaching at **Sarnath** (5) in 528 BCE. After his success in making mass awakening and teaching in Sarnath he returned to Bodh Gaya. After visiting Rajagriha and Nalanda, he frequently visited **Shravasti** (6), where out of his passing 45 rainy seasons he stayed 24 times there, performed miracles and gave sermons. During the 6th (522 BCE) and 9th years (519 BCE) after enlightenment he stayed at **Kaushambi** (7). While returning to Bodh Gaya, to fulfil his promise at the kind invitation of Bimbisara (ca. 543-491 BCE), he paid a visit to **Rajagriha** (8) together with a thousand monks of his new order, and gave his sermons there. On the request of his two chief disciples Sariputra (Pali: Sariputta) and Madgalyana (Pali: Mogallana), the Buddha visited **Nalanda** (9) several times and mostly stayed at Setthi Pavarika's mango grove. Thereafter, the Lord again visited Rajagriha and Nalanda and further proceeded to **Vaishali** (10), the capital city of the Lichchhavis, where he gave his last detailed sermons and re-interpreted several of his teachings, and before his final march he stopped at the bank of the Ganga river in **Patna** (11), called today as Gautama Ghat. While making his final march he stayed a couple of nights at **Kesariya** (12), followed by his final visit to **Kushinagar** (13) where he passed away at the age of eighty (ca. 483 BCE). In the same year he descended from heaven at **Sankisa** (14) and gave his final preaching there. **Mathura** (15) was also visited by the Buddha occasionally; it developed as the major centre of the Buddhist art and sculpture in the Maurya period.

In the course of his marches and periods of stay during the rains' retreat seasons, the Buddha himself encouraged establishing monasteries. Venuvana monastery in Rajgir, Kutagarasala monastery in Vaishali, and Jetavana monastery in Shravasti had become thriving centres for the practice and teaching of the Way. Other monastic centres had been founded throughout Magadha, Koshala, and the neighbouring kingdoms. Everywhere, the sight of saffron-robed monks (*bhikkhus*) had become familiar. The 'Way of Awakening' had spread far and wide in the first six years after the Buddha's Enlightenment.

Fig. 9. Eight incidents related to
the Buddha's life (Sarnath museum)

The Buddha spent his 6th rainy season retreat on Makula Mountain, and the 7th season on Sankisa Mountain, upstream from the Ganga river. He spent the 8th season at Sumsumaragira in Bhagga, and the 9th near Kaushambi. Kaushambi was a large town in the kingdom of Vamsa situated along the Yamuna river. An important monastery had been built there in a large forest called Ghosira, named after the lay disciple who donated the forest. Senior disciples such as Mahakassapa, Mahamoggallana, Sariputta, and Mahakaccana were not with the Buddha during the 9th rainy season retreat at Ghosira. Ananda, however, was present. Rahula remained with Sariputta.

Ghosira was filled with simsapa/ shishama trees under which the Buddha liked to meditate during hot afternoons. One day after his meditation, he returned to the community holding a handful of simsapa leaves (*Vinaya Mahavagga* 10).

One day while sitting in Bhesakala Park in Sumsumaragiri, the Buddha spoke to the monks, "Monks, I want to tell you about the Eight Realisations of Great Beings. Venerable Anuruddha has spoken about these eight realisations before. They are the realisations taught by Great Beings to help others overcome forgetfulness and attain enlightenment. They are:

"The first realisation is the awareness that all *Dhammas* are impermanent and without a separate self. By contemplating on the impermanent and non-self nature of all *Dhammas*, you can escape suffering and attain enlightenment, peace, and joy.

The second realisation is the awareness that more desire brings more suffering. All hardships in life arise from greed and desire.

The third realisation is the awareness that living simply, having few desires, leads to peace, joy, and serenity. Living simply allows for more time and concentration to practice the Way and to help others.

The fourth realisation is the awareness that only diligent effort leads to enlightenment. Laziness and indulging in sensual desires are obstacles to the practice.

The fifth realisation is the awareness that ignorance is the cause of the endless round of birth and death. You must always remember to listen and learn in order to develop your understanding and eloquence.

The sixth realisation is the awareness that poverty creates hatred and anger, which in turn create a vicious cycle of negative thoughts and actions. Followers of the Way, when practising generosity, should consider everyone, friends and enemies alike, as equal, not condemning anyone's past wrong-doings or hating those who are presently causing harm.

The seventh realisation is the awareness that although we dwell in the world to teach and assist others, we should not become caught up in worldly matters. One who leaves home to follow the Way possesses only three robes and a bowl. He always lives simply and looks at all beings with the eyes of compassion.

The eighth realisation is the awareness that we do not practice for our individual enlightenment alone, but devote our whole being to guiding all others to the gates of enlightenment."

The Buddha repeated, "O Monks!, these are the Eight Realisations of the Great Beings. All Great Beings, thanks to these eight realisations, have attained enlightenment. Wherever they go in life, they use these eight realisations to open minds and educate others, so that everyone may discover the path that leads to enlightenment and emancipation."

(*Anguttara Nikaya* VIII.30; *Samyutta Nikaya* XII.15; *Tripitaka* 779)

THE PILGRIMS

Despite its dry climate and harsh environment the central (Middle) part of the Ganga Valley in India has been one of the great cradles of human civilisation. It is frequently referred in the Buddhist literature as the *Majjhimadesa* (Middle Land), where many of Indian civilisation's greatest ideas and innovations sprang up. The Buddha was born in the Middle Land and spent his whole life walking its dusty roads, meditating in its dry forests, and teaching in its cities, towns and villages. The Middle Land nurtured Buddhism during its first crucial centuries, and although it soon spread all over India and eventually beyond its borders to distant parts of Asia, Buddhists have always looked to the Middle Land as the home of their religion.

Being as it is the sacred land of Buddhism, the Middle Land has inspired pilgrims throughout the centuries to overcome enormous obstacles and to risk their lives to see the places associated with the Buddha. They have come from all the regions of India, from China, Korea, Java and Sumatra (Indonesia), Myanmar (Burma) and Sri Lanka, and also from Kazakhstan and Thailand.

Pilgrims who came from China or Korea had to cross the fearful Taklamakan Desert and then climb over some of the highest mountain ranges in the world. Alternatively they could come by ship, spending months at sea risking storms, pirates and sickness. Pilgrims coming from Sri Lanka, Sumatra or Java would have to take a ship into the Bay of Bengal to the port of Tamralipti (now Tamluk near Kharagpur in West Bengal), proceed up the Ganga river as far as Patna and from there continue on foot. For those coming from Nepal and Tibet, it was not distance but climate which was the greatest obstacle. Descending from the cool clean air of their mountain homelands to the hot dusty atmosphere of the Middle Land often meant sickness or even death for these travellers.

Ashoka (r. 270 – 232 BCE)

The first historical record of performing a pilgrimage is about the great Indian emperor Ashoka, or, as he always referred to himself, Piyadassi, Beloved of the Gods. When he was crowned in 270 BCE, becoming the third emperor of the Mauryan dynasty, he inherited a vast empire that stretched from Afghanistan to Bangladesh and included all of India except the southernmost tip and the present state of Orissa, then known as Kalinga. A war of succession preceded his coronation, during which Ashoka had several of his brothers killed. In 278 he conducted a war against Kalinga, as a result of which hundred thousands of people died. This incident deeply shocked Ashoka and brought about a radical change in him, which was to have a profound effect upon his style of government and, in particular, upon Buddhism. He became a devout Buddhist and then did his best to govern his empire according to Buddhist principles. He gave up an expansionist foreign policy, reformed the administration and judicial systems, took positive steps to promote harmony between different religions, introduced medical herbs into areas where they were unavailable, and banned the hunting of many species of wildlife. But of all his innovations, it was his efforts to spread Buddhism that had the most enduring effect. He held the Third Council in his capital at Patna, united the Sangha, and sent experienced teaching monks to all parts of India and as far away as Syria, Egypt and Macedonia. The most successful of these foreign missions was the one headed by his son, the monk Mahinda, who was sent to Sri Lanka.

Ashoka patronised Buddhism, performed religious tours, *dhammayata* (*dharmayatra*), to all the important Buddhist places with his spiritual master, the monk Upagupta. During these tours at each sacred site the emperor made religious gifts, erected commemorative monuments, installed pillars (Fig. 10) and had discourses with people. The *Ashokavadana* (a poem in Sanskrit, referring to Ashoka's pilgrimages) mentions altogether 32 holy places connected with the Buddha's life. In one of the edicts, Ashoka attested his concern for pilgrimage by improving the roads and building rest houses and watering stations. Ashoka sent missionaries all over India and beyond. Some went as far as Egypt, Palestine, and Greece. The Greeks of one of the Alexandrian kingdoms of northern India adopted Buddhism, after their King Menandros (Pali: Milinda) was convinced by a monk named Nagasena — the conversation immortalised in the book *Milinda Panha*.

Fig. 10. Representing the Ashokan Pillar at Sarnath in the monument of Sanchi.

29

Ancient tales refer that Ashoka opened seven of the eight stupas that were built over the Buddha's ashes, divided the relics into 84,000 portions, and built stupas over each portion. No doubt the number 84,000 is an obvious exaggeration, but it is sure that a large number of the stupas in India were first built during the Mauryan period. In one of his inscriptions Ashoka tells us that he had given up the usual kingly habit of going on pleasure trips and had instead started going on pilgrimages, or what he called Dhamma tours. In 260 BCE he went on a pilgrimage to Bodh Gaya, and ten years later to Lumbini.

The modern pilgrim can still see Ashoka's influence in the Ganga Valley, and indeed in many places throughout India, through the huge pillars he erected. These pillars were used to record the edicts he issued during his 38 years of reign, to mark various sacred sites, and also to mark the pilgrim's route from his capital at Patna to Lumbini. They stand today bearing silent witness to the aesthetic and technological genius of the ancient Indians. Although some of these pillars are now broken, the tallest are up to 15 meters high, and all of them exhibit a remarkably high polish that still remains even after many centuries of exposure to the elements. Each was crowned with a capital, sometimes a noble bull or a spirited lion, some of which are recognised as masterpieces of Indian art. All of the pillars were made in the Chunar quarries south of Varanasi and from there were dragged sometimes hundreds of kilometres to where they were raised.

Fa-hsien (CE 374 – 462)

The first Chinese pilgrim who opened the path to see the Buddha's Land was the monk Fa-hsien (also referred as Fa-Hian or Faxian). Anxious to obtain authentic copies of Buddhist texts and to visit the sacred places in India, 25-years old Fa-hsien and three companions set out in 399 CE on what was to be one of the truly great travel adventures in history. Speaking no language but their own, with meagre resources and knowing only that India lay vaguely somewhere in the west, Fa-hsien and his companions had nothing to guide or sustain them but their faith. Crossing the fearful Taklamakan desert, the only thing that marked the way was the parched bones of less lucky travellers.

When he arrived back in China in 414 CE, he had been away altogether for fourteen years. He wrote an account of his epic journey and spent the rest of his life translating the books he had brought back with him, finally dying in his eighty-eighth year in the monastery of Sin at King-Chow. He lived through two great dynasties of China, viz. 'the eastern Tsin dynasty' (317-419) and 'the Sung dynasty of the House of Lu' (420-478). Since the Great Religion travelled east, there has been no one to equal Fa-hsien in his selfless search for the *Dhamma*. His journey is a message to understand that all things are possible to the sincere of heart, and all things can be accomplished if a man has determination. For is it not true that he succeeded because he disregarded what others value, and valued what others disregarded? Fa-hsien was not only a courageous traveller, he was also a person whose modesty, truthfulness, naive innocence and deep faith in the Three Jewels made him loved by all who knew him.

Fa-hsien's account reveals many of the qualities inherent in Buddhist pilgrimage. He was interested not only in the sites associated with the Buddha, his disciples and the Sangha in general, but also in places that feature in the *Jataka* tales of the Buddha's previous lives. Fa-hsien's pilgrimage to India is not only Buddha's biography inscribed as a map onto the landscape, but a hagiography of past lives in which previous incarnations of the Buddha themselves sanctified the land.

Around 187 other Chinese pilgrims followed Fa-hsien to see the land of the Buddha (India). Among those who left records of their trips were Chih-meng (404–414), Sun-yun (early 6th century) and I-tching (671–695).

Hsüan-tsang (CE 603 – 664)

Another pilgrim who went to India inspired by Fa-hsien's example was Hsüan-tsang (also referred as Huien-tsiang and Yuan-chwang, or Xuan Zhang), a famous monk and the most influential of all the Chinese pilgrims and translators. He had travelled in India during 630-644 (Fig. 11). Hsüan-tsang not only wrote an extensive account of his pilgrimage in twelve books, the Si Yu-Ki or '*Records of the Western World*', but as soon as he died became the subject of a hagiographic account by his students Hwui-li and Yen-thsong.

He was born into a religious family and became a monk while still a child. By his early twenties he had gained a reputation for wide learning, and at the age of twenty six he had already resolved to go to India to collect Buddhist texts, to study the *Dhamma* from Indian masters, and to visit the sacred places. He applied to the imperial court for permission to leave China, and when this was refused he decided to go in secret.

Eventually, Hsüan-tsang arrived at Nalanda and settled down for five years of study and teaching (637-642 CE) during which he visited Bodh Gaya and other parts of India from time to time. His profound learning earned him the respect of the other students and

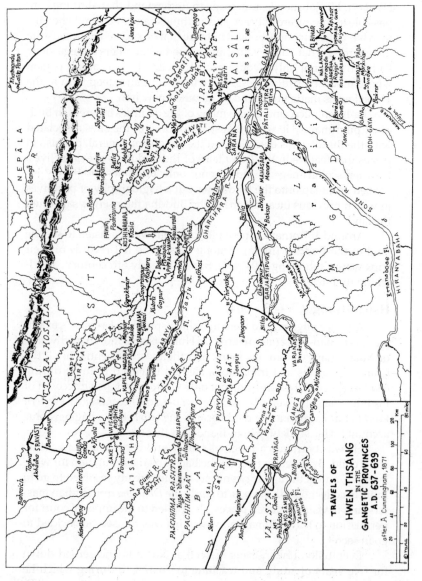

Fig. 11. Hsüan-tsang's travel to the Buddhist Places in north India, CE 637-639 (after A. Cunningham, 1871)

teachers, who were loath to let him go when he finally announced his intention to return to China. All the monks, after hearing about his intentions, came to him and begged him to remain. Unable to dissuade him, the monks took Hsüan-tsang to his teacher, Silabhadra, who likewise asked him why he wanted to leave. Hsüan-tsang answered eloquently and movingly:

"This country is the place of the Buddha's birth; it is impossible not to regard it with affection. My only intention in coming hither was to inquire after the good *Dhamma* for the benefit of our fellow creatures. Since my arrival here, you, sir, have condescended on my account to explain the *Yogacharabhumi Shastra* and to investigate doubtful passages. I have visited and worshipped at the sacred places of our religion and heard the expositions of the different schools. My mind has been overjoyed and my visit here has, I protest, been of the utmost profit. I desire now to go back and translate and explain to others what I have heard so as to cause others also to be equally grateful to you, with myself, in hearing and understanding these things; and for this reason I am unwilling to delay my return and remain here".

Silabhadra was overjoyed with this reply and ordered the monks to help Hsüan-tsang prepare for the long journey that lay before him. When he reached the borders of China, Hsüan-tsang sent a messenger forward to the imperial court to announce his arrival. When he arrived at Loyang, huge crowds turned out to see his entry into the city. He was mildly reprimanded by the emperor for leaving the country without permission and then feted like no monk had ever been before. He had been away for fifteen years and returned with 657 texts bound in 520 cases, carried upon twenty horses, and he had amazing stories to tell about the many things he had seen and the many adventures he had experienced. At the request of the emperor Hsüan-tsang wrote an account of his pilgrimage, a book so detailed and full of facts that it remains to this day one of the most important sources of information about Central Asia and India during the seventh century. Hsüan-tsang spent the remainder of his life translating the books he had brought back from India, twenty four works altogether, and finally died peacefully in 664 CE. In addition to the prodigious translation work — 740 Sanskrit texts of various sizes with the help of amanuenses — Hsüan-tsang also copied scriptures, moulded and painted images of the Buddha, initiated novices into the *Sangha*, instructed the student monks of the monasteries and sometimes the imperial officers who visited him, and even carried bricks and stones for the construction of the Tayen pagoda.

If the myth of Ashoka had been the model for Buddhist pilgrimage within India, that of Hsüan-tsang became the paradigm for pilgrimage to India from China. By the time Wu Ch'eng-en wrote the famous novel *The Journey to the West* (also known as *Monkey*) in the 16th century, the pilgrimage of Hsüan-tsang (now given the name *Tripitaka*) had become a parable which could be read on a number of levels. The *Monkey* consists of the various adventures and experiences of the characters so structured as to represent a picture of the Buddhist doctrine of *karma* (or the relations of cause and effect in one's actions). The progress of the pilgrimage itself was portrayed as an allegory of the progress to enlightenment in the Buddhist tradition: at the end of their journeys both Hsüan-tsang and *Monkey* become Buddhas.

Evidently the central part of the Ganga valley, the heartland of Buddhism, was less Brahmanised and was to a large extent outside the stronghold of Brahmanism, which had its centre in the land of the Kurus (in the far west). There are indications of a few routes that were taken by persons seeking dialogues with the *Tathagata*. One of the important roads joined Shravasti to Rajagriha. Traders were going from Sarnath to Shravasti, Kapilavastu (Piprahwa), Lumbini, Kushinagar/ Kasia, Kesariya, Vaishali, Pataliputa, Nalanda and finally Bodh Gaya.

I-tsing (CE 634 – 713)

I-tsing was about ten years of age when Hsüan-tsang returned to China, but he had prepared himself for the life of a Buddhist monk. He was admitted into the Order when he was fourteen. In CE 672 he came to India and remained here till 685, passing his life in study and pilgrimages. After his return to China in 695, he translated 56 works out of about 400 he had brought back with him, during the years 700–712, and died in 713.

He took the sea route to India both ways. His itineraries lack the variety and scientific interest of those of Hsüan-tsang, but they are full of human interest. On his outward voyage (in 671) he spent eight months in Sumatra, six at Srivijaya, a rising maritime State (now Palembang), and two in Malaya in the neighbourhood. He landed at Tamralipti in 673, and then went to Magadha, the holy land par excellence, and worshipped at Bodh Gaya and other sacred places. He spent ten years at Nalanda, hearing the teaching of the Doctors of the Law and collecting holy books. He had many companions with him of whom he was to write an account later, and from them he took leave, never to see them again, when he left India in 685, again by way of

Tamralipti. He spent four years in Srivijaya with its Sanskrit background in order to translate the sacred works; in 689 he went to China to fetch collaborators for his work, and after another five years at Srivijaya he finally returned to China in 695. Like Hsüan-tsang before him he found the Court interested in his voyages and was given an official reception.

One of I-tsing's works, *A Record of the Buddhist Religion as Practised in India and the Malay Archipelago*, has been translated into English by the Japanese scholar J. Takakusu. More interesting in some ways are his *The Memoirs on the Eminent Monks who Went in Search of the Law in the Western Countries*; of this work a French version by Chavannes is available. It gives us a fair idea of the earnestness and devotion of the pilgrims whose numbers were larger than we are apt to imagine and of the spirit with which they braved the dangers of their enterprises. It is, in fact, a melancholic succession of tales, full of pathetic incidents both on land and sea. I-tsing remarks wistfully: "However triumphal, the path was strewn with difficulties; the Holy Places were far away and vast. Of dozens who brought forth leaves and flowers, and of several who made an attempt, there was scarcely one who bore any fruit or produced any real results, and few who completed their task. The reason for this was the immensity of the stony deserts of the Land of the Elephant (India), the great rivers and the brilliance of the sun which pours forth its burning heat, or else the towering waves heaved up by the giant fish, the abysses, and the waters that rise and swell as high as the heavens. When marching solitary, beyond the Iron Gates between Samarquand and Bactria, one wandered amongst the ten thousand mountains, and fell into the bottom of precipices; when sailing alone beyond the Columns of Copper (South of Tongking), one crossed the thousand deltas and lost one's life. That is how it is that those who set out were over fifty in number, while those who survived were only a handful of men." Several Korean monks had gone to India, the majority across Central Asia, some by the sea route; of them I-tsing says: "They died in India, and never saw their country again." Indeed the Central Asian route was becoming more and more difficult after the weakening of the T'ang empire and the revolt of Tibet, not to speak of the Islamic Arabs who soon appeared on the scene.

On the maritime route the Chinese pilgrims saw India coming out to meet them. The impress of Indian civilisation on Indochina and Indonesia could not escape their notice, and I-tsing recommends that one should stay in Srivijaya and perfect his knowledge of Sanskrit before going on to India. During this period there was a perpetual exchange of ideas, books and art products between India and Ceylon and Java, Cambodia, Campa and the ports of the Canton region of China.

Marpa Chökyi-Lodrö (1012 – 1097)

According to the Tibetan book *The Blue Annals*, Marpa was born in the Water Male Mouse year, 1012, in Lhotrak, and died in the Fire Female Ox year, 1097. The great author, teacher and yogi from Tibet, Tsang Nyön Heruka (1452-1507) wrote the first detailed accounts of Marpa's journeys to the land of the Buddha and his works. Marpa was the most known disciple of the great Buddhist guru Naropa (1016-1100). Marpa was a farmer, householder, a yogi and a great poet too. He was only 12 years old when he began his *dhamma* training, followed by his studies with guru Drogmi for 3 years. He then journeyed to Nepal and stayed at Svayambhunatha for another 3 years. Marpa's coming to India and his worthiness as a disciple had already been prophesised to Naropa by his guru Tilopa (988-1069). Therefore, Naropa immediately welcomed Marpa to assume the role of his regent, the future lineage holder. In fact, Marpa was the sun of the Buddha's teaching, and in particular, he dispelled the darkness in the Land of Snow and was the life tree of the teachings of the secret mantra.

Marpa travelled to India three times and underwent great hardships for the sake of the *dhamma*. Receiving the holy *dhamma* from pandits and enlightened gurus, he brought it back to Tibet. The purpose of his visits was to meet the great Buddhist masters and enlightened gurus. In this search he travelled to most of the important Buddhist places directly associated with the Buddha's life. On his first journey to India, Marpa spent 9 years studying with Naropa and others, and then returned to Tibet. Naropa was one among the four great teachers at Nalanda and Vikramshila universities, where he was serving as director of the programmes, and he was known as the most learned of all. He was also closely attached to other monastic universities of the period, like Bodhgaya and Otantapuri. Naropa had founded a small monastery northwest of Nalanda at Phullahari where Marpa met him the first time. Later Marpa visited all the above mentioned seats of learning with his guru.

In Tibet, Marpa met his students Ngoktön, Marpa Golek, Tsurtön, and Bawacben of Parang. He also married Dagmema with whom he had several sons. On his second journey, Marpa spent 6 years in India. After returning to Tibet he taught more disciples, including Metön Tsönpo and the famous saint-patron of Tibet Milarepa.

On his last journey, Marpa spent 3 years in India. In a song to Paindapa, during his final return to Tibet, Marpa states that he spent one third of his life in India; altogether he spent approximately 18 years in India. He was known as Marpa the Translator due to his great work of translating Buddhist texts into Tibetan [for details see Heruka 1982].

Marpa, the light of wisdom who illumined the day, dispelled the darkness of ignorance among all the sentient beings in Tibet, and exposed himself as the worthy successor of Naropa; he proclaimed this truth in one of his songs:

Since I am the only heart son of Naropa
Why shouldn't the oral instruction be famed,
Since this wish-fulfilling jewel of the hearing lineage
Is the special *dhamma* that no one else possesses.

(Heruka, 1982: 196)

Marpa's chief disciple and successor was Dorje Gyaltsen, known as Milarepa (1052-1135). Despite the many sectarian differences between the numerous sects of Tibetan Buddhism, all Tibetan alike unite in holding Jetsün Milarepa in the highest esteem and reverence. Milarepa, following the advice of his guru Marpa, paid a visit to all the 24 places of pilgrimage in India, including 8 places of cremation described in Buddhist tales, in his invisible subtle body, and so revived the ancient tradition of Tibetan Buddhism of pilgrimages to various places in India. Milarepa died at 84, on the full-moon day of Vaishakha (April-May) of the year of the Wood-Hare, i.e. the day of Buddha's nirvana.

Tilopa was the forefather of the Kagyü lineage, which was successively passed down to Naropa, Marpa and Milarepa etc. The great legacy of special transmissions and oral instructions acquired by Tilopa was handed down to his main disciple Naropa. These four great spiritual teachers of the Vajrayana tradition are described as *mahasiddhas* ('an embodiment of revelation and highest realisation'), of which 84 are known.

Dharmasvamin (1196 - 1263)

Perhaps the last pilgrim to see the sacred places in India before their destruction in the 13th century was the Tibetan monk Dharmasvamin. Buddhists from Tibet had been coming to the Middle Land on pilgrimage and to study for several centuries but Dharmasvamin seems to be the only one who left an account of his journey, the details of which he gave to his biographer, the layman Chos dar.

His biographer tells us that so great was his love of learning that "between the ages of seventeen and forty-five, he had made a vow not to separate himself from his pen and ink." Before leaving Tibet to study at Svayambhu Stupa in Nepal, Dharmasvamin had also made a vow not to return to his homeland until he had also made a pilgrimage to Bodh Gaya. After finishing an eight-year course of study, he announced his intentions to go to India.

And so in 1234 CE, at the age of thirty-seven, Dhamasvamin set off for the Buddha's Land. The whole country was in chaos at that time; the Muslim invaders had destroyed the existing administration and had still not replaced it with one of their own. Bands of robbers and groups of marauding soldiers greedy for loot made lonely roads and even the towns and cities dangerous. Dharmasvamin joined a party of three hundred traders, sixteen of whom, like himself, were headed for Bodh Gaya. Eventually Dharmasvamin reached his destination, only to have to flee straight away to avoid an expected attack. He returned when the danger was over and spent some three months meditating, worshipping, seeing the sights and, being able to speak Sanskrit, acting as an interpreter for groups of visiting monks.

After his stay at Bodh Gaya, Dharmasvamin visited Rajagriha and then Nalanda, where he studied with the great scholar Rahula Sri Bhadra, who was then ninety years old and the abbot of the great monastery. But the quiet studious atmosphere of Nalanda was soon to be brutally shattered. Muslim soldiers had already sacked the monastic University of Odantapuri, one day's march east of Nalanda, and were now using it as a base for their raids. It was only a matter of time before the end came. After burning brightly and shedding its radiance in India for one and a half millennia, the lamp of the *dhamma* was about to be snuffed out.

Dharmasvamin completed his studies and finally began preparing for his return to Tibet. With tears in his eyes, the aged and frail Rahula Sri Bhadra said to his student: "You are a good monk. Go to Tibet. I am old. Tibet is far away and we shall not meet again in this life. We shall meet again in the Stikhavati." Dharmasvamin returned safely to Tibet, but not before he was laid up for months by an illness in Pattata. He died at the age of sixty-seven in the year 1263. Although he spent only a short time in the Buddha's Land, Dharmasvamin's biography is of great interest because it gives us a rare eyewitness account of Buddhism's tragic end in India.

Sir Alexander Cunningham (1814 – 1893)

Of course Cunningham did not come to the Middle Land as a pilgrim, but much of what the modern pilgrim sees at Buddhist sacred sites is due to his efforts. Alexander Cunningham came to India in 1833 as a second lieutenant. He saw active service on several occasions, and later distinguished himself as an administrator, surveyor and engineer. During 1833–1885 he had been in India, and in 1861 when the Archaeological Survey of India, ASI, was founded he became the first Director General which he continued till 1885 when he returned to England, and dedicated his life to revealing and preserving India's past. He himself published 13 volumes of the reports of the ASI, and also supervised many excavations and preparation of reports.

Soon after his arrival, he developed an interest in India's past, and during his extensive trips through the northern plains he never missed the opportunity to visit the thousands of temples, forts and other ancient monuments that dominated the landscape. The archaeology of that time could also be a dangerous and frustrating pursuit. Roads were rough or non-existent, malaria was a constant danger, banditry was widespread, and in many places where Cunningham went, locals would be unhelpful or they would lie to him about the whereabouts of ruins in the area. Worst of all were the Brahmin priests who would claim that any long neglected ruin or statue was 'sacred' as soon as Cunningham showed any interest in it, and who would then demand money before they would allow him to sketch or measure the object.

But despite these difficulties, Cunningham learned to decipher a large number of ancient scripts; he located or visited an enormous number of sites, surveying many of them; and he developed a truly remarkable knowledge of India's ancient geography, its numismatics and the comparative styles of Indian sculpture. So when, in 1861, it was decided to establish an archaeological survey, Alexander Cunningham, who had just retired from the army, was the natural choice to be its first Director General. From then until his return to England in 1885, Cunningham dedicated his life to revealing and preserving India's past.

From the Buddhist point of view Cunningham's importance is due to the personal interest he took in locating places associated with the Buddha's life. As a young man he was, like many Victorians, an evangelical Christian who believed that the quicker his own faith replaced India's indigenous faiths the better. Some of his early writings even indicate that he thought the insights of archaeology could be a useful weapon to help promote Christianity. His poor opinion of Hinduism and Islam never seemed to have changed, but as he got to know Buddhism better he gradually developed a deep respect for its outlook on life and its contributions to Indian civilisation. Drawing on his own vast experience, the research of others, his familiarity with the accounts of the Chinese pilgrims, and a good deal of uncannily accurate guesswork, Cunningham identified or verified the identity of Shravasti, Kaushambi, Kushinagar and several sites at Rajagriha. He also excavated at these places as well as at Mathura, Sarnath and Bodh Gaya.

He seems to have had a particular fascination for the Mahabodhi Temple, and his first act on being appointed head of the Archaeological Survey was to visit the great temple to consider what steps could be taken to excavate in its precincts and preserve its sculptures and inscriptions. On his recommendations, Major Mead dug at the temple in 1863, though he never published an account of his finds. Cunningham visited the site again in 1871 and 1875 and his last book, *Mahabodhi, The Great Buddhist Temple under the Buddha Tree at Buddha Gaya*, contains the sum total of his own and others' research, discoveries and impressions of the temple.

Sir Edwin Arnold (1833 – 1904)

With enthusiasm and deep interest Edwin Arnold came to Bodh Gaya in 1885 as a pilgrim. Arnold already had a reputation as a fine poet when he was appointed principal of the Deccan College in Pune in 1857, and with his liberal attitude and his knowledge of Sanskrit he soon developed an interest in Indian religions, particularly in Buddhism.

On his return to England in 1861, Arnold got a job as a feature writer with the Daily Telegraph, a paper he was later to become editor of, and continued his study of Buddhism. Exactly what he read is not known — there were few reliable books on Buddhism at the time and even fewer translations of Buddhist scriptures. But in 1879 he published his famous poem, *The Light of Asia*, which accurately and sympathetically portrayed the life and teachings of the Buddha. Buddhists in the East, long used to hearing only derogatory comments about their religion from Europeans, were delighted with the poem and made Arnold into something of a hero.

Arnold had long wished to go to Bodh Gaya and Sarnath, and when he received numerous invitations to visit Sri Lanka, Thailand, Burma and Japan, he decided to tour the East and at the same time fulfil his long-cherished wish. On his arrival, he was deeply moved as he stood in the gallery of the Mahabodhi Temple, inspired to think that here the Buddha attained enlightenment, but at the same time saddened by the general neglect of the great temple. He went to the back of the temple and stood quietly under the Bodhi Tree.

Later, Arnold went to Sarnath, saying of the place afterwards: "A more consecrated ground than this could hardly be found anywhere else." Continuing on his journey, Arnold arrived in Sri Lanka to a tumultuous welcome from the island's Buddhists. When he met with Weligama Sri Sumangala, the most erudite scholar-monk of the time and one of the leaders of the Buddhist revival that was rapidly gaining momentum there, Arnold described the woeful state of the Mahabodhi Temple and suggested that something should be done about it. The idea was met with great enthusiasm, and Arnold promised to speak with British authorities in England and India, something he could easily do, being well placed in the British establishment.

While it was Edwin Arnold who conceived the noble idea of restoring the Mahabodhi Temple to Buddhists and set it in motion, others ably took up the task of carrying it through to the end. But even at this time Arnold lent his influence and his pen to the cause. He met with or wrote to the Governor of Ceylon, the Secretary of State for India, General Cunningham, even the Viceroy, and in 1893 he wrote an article for the Daily Telegraph eloquently and passionately arguing for the Buddhist control of the Mahabodhi Temple. When Edwin Arnold died in 1904, the idea he had conceived some twenty-one years before had still not been realised, and indeed would not be realised for nearly another fifty years. But as the pilgrim worships in the Mahabodhi Temple today or wanders in the quiet gardens that surround it, it would be good to remember what modern Buddhist Pilgrims owe to this early western Buddhist.

Anagarika Dharmapala (1864 – 1933)

The man who carried out the idea first initiated by Edwin Arnold was the Sri Lankan Anagarika Dharmapala. Born into an affluent and deeply religious family in 1864, Dharmapala was at an early age influenced by the Buddhist revival that swept through the island from the 1870's onwards. Although he knew that he wanted to dedicate his considerable energy and talents to helping Buddhism shake off centuries of stagnation, it was not until he went on a pilgrimage to Bodh Gaya that he knew exactly how he was going to do it. In 1891 he visited Sarnath and was shocked and saddened by what he saw. The place where the Buddha had proclaimed the *Dhamma* for the first time was being used by local villagers to dump rubbish and graze pigs. The ruins of the once magnificent monasteries, temples and *stupas* were of no interest to anyone except in that they could be pulled down to provide cheap bricks for building.

A few days later, on the 22nd of January, Dharmapala and his friend, the Japanese monk Kozan, arrived in Bodh Gaya. The Mahabodhi Temple had been restored some years before, but there was no one to maintain or care for it, and its environs were overgrown and dirty. As Dharmapala worshipped at the Vajrasana, the 'Diamond Seat' of Enlightenment, a sudden inspiration born of deep devotion occurred to him.

The Mahabodhi Temple had not been functioning as a place of worship for centuries, but some time at the end of the 16th century, a wandering Hindu monk had arrived in the area and settled down nearby, and his successors, who came to be known as the Mahants, gradually came to look upon the deserted and ruined temple as their own. Although supposedly a simple ascetic, the present Mahant was a wealthy and powerful landlord. In the beginning, he had no objections to Dharmapala's presence; he even gave him the keys to a nearby rest house so he could stay. Immediately, Dharmapala wrote letters to friends and Buddhist organisations in Sri Lanka, Burma and India describing the state of the temple and asking for help to maintain it properly. But the little money he had was running out, replies to his pleas for help were slow in coming, and he started to fear that he might have to abandon his promise.

The purpose of his life now became perfectly clear to him. Like much of Buddhism itself, the Mahabodhi Temple had become more of an interesting relic of the past than something vital and living. He would restore and revive them both. He decided he could only do this if he left the temple and tried to arouse public interest and support in Buddhist countries. He founded the Mahabodhi Society to organise and co-ordinate the restoration of the temple and the Mahabodhi journal, the first international Buddhist publication, to inform the Buddhist world about the society's progress. He toured Burma and Sri Lanka, addressing public meetings, and he organised tours for pilgrims from Sri Lanka to India. Unfortunately, the Mahant's desire to cash in on the pilgrims who now started to come, as well as ambiguities about exactly who owned the temple, led to long and bitter court battles and even to violence.

In the following years Anagarika Dharmapala's life was full of events. He addressed the Parliament of Religions in Chicago in 1893 (the first time Buddhism was preached in the West); he founded several Buddhist newspapers in Sri Lanka; he was responsible for the first contact in centuries between Mahayana and Theravadin Buddhists; he built schools, dispensaries and vocational training institutes; and he restored Sarnath and turned it once again into a centre of Buddhism. Due to his efforts, Buddhists were once again able to worship in the Mahabodhi Temple, and although their legal right to do so was not achieved until 1949, it was Anagarika Dharmapala who set the process in motion. Just before he died in Sarnath in 1933, he said "I would like to be reborn twenty-five more times to spread Lord Buddha's *Dhamma*."

THE BUDDHA STATUE

For nearly five hundred years, there were no statues of the Buddha. When the artist wished to indicate the Buddha's presence, he did so with the use of symbols — an empty chair or throne, a tree, a *stupa* or a pair of footprints. At Bodh Gaya, there are three large round stones with such footprints (*pada*) on them, still worshipped by pilgrims. The first Buddha statues (*buddharupa*) began to be produced during the Kushana period, probably under the impact of Greek influence. Over the next thousand years, Indian artists attempted to portray the wisdom and compassion of the Buddha in stone and bronze, and few would doubt that they succeeded brilliantly. From the simple smiling Buddhas of Mathura to the crowned and bejewelled Buddhas of the Pala dynasty, artists expressed their devotion in sculptures that in turn became objects of devotion.

Statues usually depict the Buddha sitting in the lotus posture (*padmasana*) or standing upright, and occasionally, lying down. The lying statue represents the Buddha's final Nirvana. Standing statues like those of the Gupta period are usually in the relaxed 'thrice bent' posture (*tribhanga*), while those of the Pala are somewhat straight and stiff. Statues sitting on a chair or throne are usually not of Gautama Buddha but rather of Maitreya, the Buddha of the next era. Most of the Buddha statues have a lump on the top of the head (*unhisa*), a mark between the eyebrows or on the forehead (*unna*), and sometimes wheels on the palms of the hands and the soles of the feet, these being some of the thirty-two marks of a great being (*mahapurusa lakshana*), auspicious signs that are supposed to appear on the body of all Buddhas. The earlobes are always elongated, and it is very likely

43

that the Buddha actually had earlobes like this due to the heavy earrings that he would have worn prior to his renunciation.

The Buddha's robe (*civara*) is usually depicted in one of two ways, in open style with one shoulder exposed or in closed style with the robe covering the whole upper part of the body. When depicted in this second way the end corner of the robe is usually held in the left hand and the under-robe (*antaravasaka*) can be seen around the ankles. In standing statues from the Gupta period, the outer robe often clings to the body allowing the belt (*kayabandhana*) holding the under-robe to be seen.

Early statues of the Buddha often have a round halo (*prabhamandala*) behind the head, while those from the Gupta and Pala periods have an elongated one behind the whole body. Sometimes, instead of this elongated halo, there are depictions of various events in the Buddha's life.

The hands of the Buddha are always placed in one of several gestures (*mudra*). Both hands resting in the lap is the gesture of meditation (*dhyanamudra*), both raised in front of the chest is the gesture of turning the wheel of the *Dhamma* (*dharmacakramudra*), one hand raised with the palm facing outward is the gesture of imparting fearlessness (*abhayamudra*), while the hand lowered with the palm facing outward is the gesture of bestowing blessings (*varadamudra*). The earth touching gesture (*bhumisparshamudra*) consists of one hand in the lap and the other placed on the knee with the tips of the fingers touching the ground. According to the *Lalitavistara*, just after his enlightenment, the Buddha touched the earth and called upon it to witness his great victory. Sometimes Buddha statues have small figures of devotees at their sides, hands raised to their chest with palms joined in the gesture of worship (*anjalimudra*).

1. LUMBINI
Where the Buddha was born

"After taking seven steps, he speaks with a voice like Brahma's: 'The destroyer of old age and death has come forth, the Greatest of Physicians'. Looking fearlessly in all directions, he pronounces these words rich in meaning: 'I am the first, the best of all beings, this is my last birth'."

Voice of the Buddha

Approach & Historical background

Situated across the border in Nepal, Lumbini is the birthplace of Lord Buddha. Lumbini is easily accessible by road from Gorakhpur (232 km from Varanasi). After travelling 90 km to the north from Gorakhpur one reaches Nautanwa on the Indian border. From there by *auto-rickshaw* or taxi reach Bhairahwa, from where vehicles are regularly plying to Lumbini. It can also be reached by Royal Nepal Air from Kathmandu to Bhairahwa (45 minutes). Buses ply till the Nepalese border from where the remaining 8 km have to be covered by private vehicles or *cycle-rickshaws* to reach Lumbini (Fig. 12). Night buses are also plying regularly to Bhairahwa, taking 9 hrs from Kathmandu, 6 hrs from Pokhara and 7 hrs from Royal Chitwan National Park.

Immediately before his birth, the Bodhisattva was lord of the Tushita divine realm. There he had resolved to be reborn for the last time and show the attainment of enlightenment to the world. Placing his crown upon the head of his successor Maitreya, the Bodhisattva descended from the Tushita to the world of man. During the night of his conception, Queen Mayadevi, who is to be the mother of all the thousand Buddhas of this aeon, dreamt of a great white elephant entering her womb. The earth trembled six times. It is said that in the manner of all Bodhisattvas in their final birth, he remained sitting cross-legged for the whole time within the womb. Furthermore, all Buddhas are born in a forest grove while their mother remains standing. An old sage, Asita Kaladevela, prophesied that the prince would become a world renouncer if he ever experienced suffering. To ward off this possibility, Suddhodana ensconced the prince in the royal luxu-

45

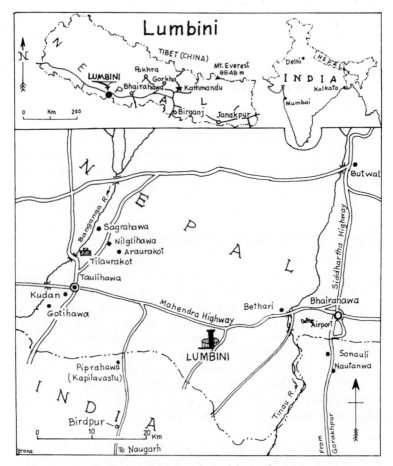

Fig. 12. Lumbini, Location and the nearby area

ries of his palace at Kapilavastu, but to no avail. Destiny took its course and Prince Siddhartha renounced his royal heritage and set off on the course to find a solution to end human misery.

At the appointed time Queen Mayadevi was visiting the Lumbini Garden some 16 km from the Shakya city of Kapilavastu. Emerging from a bath with her face to the east, she leant her right arm on a *shala* (teak) tree. The Bodhisattva was then born from her right side and immediately took seven steps — from which lotus flowers sprang up — in each of the four directions. To each direction he proclaimed as with a lion's roar: "I am the first, the best of all beings, this is my last birth". He looked down to predict the defeat of Mara and the benefiting of beings in the lower realms through the power of his teachings. He then looked up to indicate that the entire world would come to respect and appreciate his deeds. The heavens filled with light and the *devas* (gods) showered flowers on the young Prince Siddhartha who descended from his mother's womb on a lotus pedestal.

After having attained sublime joy giving birth to Siddhartha, Queen Mayadevi (Mahamaya) died eight days later, and the entire kingdom mourned her. King Suddhodana summoned her sister Mahapajapati, also known as Gotami, and asked her to become the new queen. Gotami agreed and she cared for Siddhartha as if he were her own son.

The gods Brahma and Indra then received him, and helped by the four guardian-protectors, bathed him. At the same time two *Nagas*, Nanda and Upananda, caused water to cascade over him. Later a well was found to have formed there, from which even in Fa-hsien's time monks continued to draw water to drink. The young prince was next wrapped in fine muslin and carried with great rejoicing to the king's palace in Kapilavastu.

Many auspicious signs accompanied the Bodhisattva's birth. Also, many beings who would play major parts in his life are said to have been born on the same day: Yashodhara, his future wife; Chandaka, the groom who would late help him leave the palace; Kanthaka, the horse that would bear him; the future kings Bimbisara of Magadha and Prasenajit of Koshala, and his protector Vajrapani. The Bodhi Tree is also said to have sprouted on the day of Buddha's birth.

When Ashoka visited Lumbini two centuries later, his advisor, the sage Upagupta, perceived by clairvoyance and described all these events, pointing out their sites to the emperor. Ashoka made many offerings, built an elaborate *stupa* and erected a pillar surmounted by a horse capital. When Hsüan-tsang saw it, the pillar had already been destroyed by lightning. Nevertheless, when discovered at the end of the last century the inscription that remained on the present ruin was sufficiently legible to clearly identify the site as Lumbini (Fig. 13).

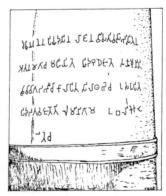

Fig. 13. Lumbini, Ashoka's inscription (249 BCE) that reads "Buddha Shakyamuni was born here, the Blessed One born here."

Legends mention that his mother, Queen Mayadevi had a dream fore-telling his birth. She saw in the dream a white elephant with nine tusks coming down from the heaven and suddenly disappearing into her body. The elephant is a common symbol of royalty. This was interpreted by the royal astrologers as a sign indicating that she would give birth to a noble and renounced soul. During a state visit to her maternal home, she stopped to rest in Lumbini garden under the shadow of a *shala* (teak) tree, as she was pregnant. It was there that Siddhartha (Buddha's name in his childhood) was born. The scene of nativity is distinctly sculptured in one of the stone slabs in the Mahadevi Temple (Fig. 14).

Fig. 14. Scene of nativity sculpted on a stone slab.

The tales narrate that Siddhartha had emerged from his mother's womb while she was resting under a grove of Ashoka trees. After his birth he immediately took seven steps in all the directions. There was a lotus flower at his every step as soon as his foot touched the Earth. The lotus is a symbol of the force of creativity, purity, auspiciousness and wealth. Soon after his birth he declared: "I am the foremost of all the creatures to cross the riddle of the ocean of existence. I have come to the world to show the path of emancipation. This is my last birth and hereafter I will not be born again." He was considered as a celestial being from the very beginning of his childhood. The gods and nymphs also came down in large numbers and enlivened the gorgeous procession arranged to welcome Queen Mayadevi. For seven days at the Lumbini garden the gods and goddesses worshipped the Bodhisattva. It was on the 7th day that the queen, plunging all in dire grief, left the mortal world. Magnificent arrangements were made by the king to bring the Boddhisattva back to the royal city of Kapilavastu. Finally he was entrusted to the care of his mother's sister, Prajapati Gautami. His search and quest for enlightenment was inspired by his realisation of old age, sickness, suffering and death, and at the age of 29 he left home and wandered as a beggar and ascetic.

In the 5th century CE the Chinese pilgrim Fa-hsien visited Lumbini and referred in his account to the sacred lake in which Mayadevi took her bath before the birth of the noble soul. He has also written about the well, the water of which was used by the Naga kings for bathing the child. Hsüan-tsang, another Chinese pilgrim, came to Lumbini in the 7th century CE. He has given a more detailed account of this place. Besides the lake, he has referred to the Ashokan pillar and to the commemorative *stupas*, which were built at the following four places: (i) the site where the Nagaraja appeared, (ii) the place where the two streams of hot and cold water appeared, (iii) Buddha's bathing place, and (iv) the spot where, after birth, the child was taken up by Indra and other gods. Another Chinese pilgrim, Wu-kung, paid a visit to Lumbini in 764 CE. After this we no longer hear about Lumbini. The Khasa King Ripu Malla of Jumla made the last recorded visit to Lumbini in the 14th century before the town's sacredness was forgotten. During the medieval period this area had turned into a dense forest. A team of archaeologists led by Khadga Samsher and the German scholar, Dr. Alois Anten Führer, traced out for the first time in 1895-96 the Ashokan pillar at Lumbini and identified it with the spot where the Buddha was born.

The **Lumbini Development Trust**, supported by 13 nations, was set up in 1970. It created a **Museum** and a library, and made a Master Plan of the area with a view to projecting this as "the creative centre and cultural force to represent the Buddha's life and teaching". A Japanese architect, Kenzo Tange, prepared this plan. This includes the transformation of 4.8 sq. km of land, divided into three sections of 1.6 sq. km each (Fig. 15). All parts will be joined by a 1474 m long pedestrian walkway and canal. The Lumbini complex plan includes the Lumbini village, the Monastic zone and the **Sacred Garden**. The large **yellow temple** opposite to the Sacred Garden was built by King Mahendra in 1953 and contains Buddha statues from Myanmar (Burma), Thailand and Nepal. The wall paintings there depict 'The Turning the Wheel of Law', four Bodhisattvas, and the major Hindu gods welcoming Siddhartha back to Nepal after he had become the Enlightened One. The Lumbini village developing in the extreme north will serve as the gateway to the sacred territory (*sacredscape*). It will include hotels, lodges, motels, restaurants, rest houses, guesthouses, and camping places for the pilgrims. Near the camping ground is the post office and parking blocks. With the help of the Malaysian government and other donors a High School is also running here. In the very near future this sacred complex will have a cultural centre, research institute, library and museum. Near to the sacred garden an eternal flame was lit up on 1st November 1986, the declaration day of the International Year of Peace. *The World Brotherhood of Buddhists Association* (Bangkok, Thailand) has joined her hands to support various development projects in the area.

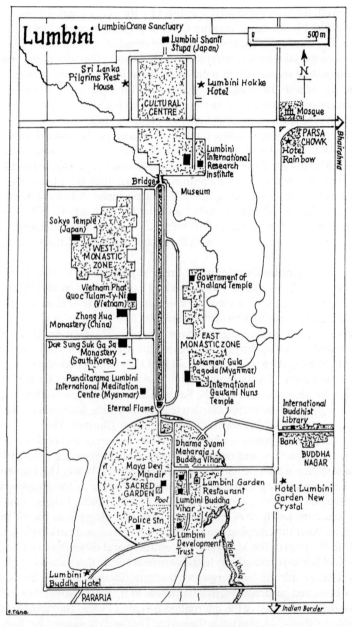

Fig. 15. Lumbini: Master Plan of Development

Ashokan Pillar

The most important monument at Lumbini (modern village of Rummindei), south of the foothills of the Churia Range, is the **Ashokan pillar**, erected in 250 BCE, in the 20th year of the Buddhist Emperor's reign. The inscription in Brahmi script declares that "King Piyadashi, beloved of the gods, 20th years after his consecration, came himself and worshipped saying 'Here Buddha Shakyamuni was born', and he caused to make a stone (capital) representing a horse; and he caused (this) stone pillar to be erected (Fig. 16). Because here the Supreme One was born, the village Lumbini was made religious centre and also liable to pay only one-tenth share (of produce)." This inscription proves the identity of this holy place. Near the top of the pillar the mantra "*Om Mani Padme Hum*" is carved in Tibetan characters. The

Fig. 16. Lumbini: Ashokan pillar

pillar was badly damaged before the 7th century CE due to the effect of lightning. The circumference of the remaining portion of the shaft is 2.21 m and the height 4.11 m. It is believed that a 3.05 m long portion of the pillar is under the ground. Hsüan-tsang saw the figure of a horse on the capital of this pillar, which is no longer to be seen now. Near the pillar there is a small temple, in which an ancient sculpture is preserved. The birth-scene of the Buddha is carved on this stone that shows Mayadevi, the holy mother, standing under a tree facing to the right. With one hand she holds a branch of the tree and with the other she is setting aright her clothes. Beside her is the newly born child. Other people are also shown nearby, including Prajapati Gautami and Indra. This temple has probably been built after the pattern of an ancient temple on the birthplace. Close by is a dried up lake. According to the tradition the Buddha after his birth was given a bath with the water of this lake. The Nepalese government has constructed two new *stupas* and a Monastery-cum-**Buddhist temple** with the old material obtained here. The prayer hall of the Buddhist temple contains a large icon of the Buddha, and medieval-style murals decorate the walls.

The single most important place in Lumbini (and in the entire Buddhist world for that matter) is the stone slab located deep in the **Sanctum Sanctorum**. Existing under the three layers of ruins over the old site of the Mayadevi temple, this site pinpoints the location of the exact spot of the birthplace of Lord Buddha. The sacred site of the Buddha's birth is at the southern end of the Lumbini grove. Excavations have revealed a series of rooms and a stone slab which is now believed to mark the exact location at which the Buddha was born. The place where the miraculous birth took place is today a mound that has been cordoned off for further excavations. The whole place has an air of remoteness except when the occasional busload of pilgrims from different corners of the Buddhist universe arrives.

The **Mayadevi temple** (19th century), sacred to both Hindus and Buddhists, has a stone bas-relief of the Buddha's birth and is thought to have been built over an earlier 5th century temple which itself may have replaced an Ashokan temple (Fig. 17). Enshrined in a small pagoda-like structure, the image shows Mayadevi, supporting herself by holding on with her right hand to a branch of a *shala* tree with the newly born infant Buddha standing upright on a lotus pedestal with an oval halo. To its south, the sacred pool **Pushkarini** with its 3 terraces is where the Buddha's mother Mayadevi is believed to have bathed before giving birth and where Siddhartha Gautama was given his first ritual purification bath. Its sacred water glistens in the faint

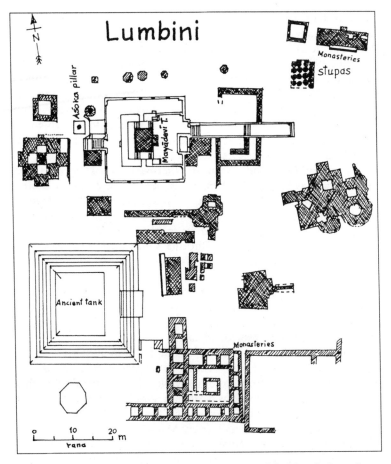

Fig. 17. Lumbini, Ruins and ancient structures around the Mayadevi temple

sun, the gentle breeze creating endless ripples. Architecturally the pool has three projecting terraces in descending order and is reverted with fine brick masonry. The Tibetan style monastery (1975) has old murals and a large bronze image of the Buddha. The other Buddhist Monastery is also modern and contains a large *thangka* and a carved wooden gate. In addition to ruins of ancient walls, a pond and mounds, excavations have shown evidence of *stupas* and a monastery.

New Excavations. Until recently a Hindu temple stood on the top of the large mound next to Ashoka's pillar. Inside the temple was a damaged and much worn sculpture depicting Prince

Siddhartha's birth and dating from the early Gupta period. The image of Mayadevi (Mahamaya) on this sculpture was worshipped by local people as a goddess variously known as Rupadevi or Rummini-devi. In 1997 when this temple was demolished and the ruins beneath it excavated, Nepal's Department of Archaeology announced that they had discovered the exact place where Prince Siddhartha was born. Until epigraphical or other evidence will have been published to back up this startling claim it will be hard to say whether it is genuine or just another attempt to keep Lumbini in the news and thereby attract more visitors.

Lumbini Dharmodaya Samiti Dharmashala, a Theravada Buddhist Vihara, established in 1956, is just outside the complex. Built in the style of modern Nepalese temples, it has intricately carved woodwork in the doorways and windows, and colourful murals depicting events from the life of the Lord in its spacious interiors.

Dharmaswami Maharaja Buddha Vihara, a Tibetan *gompa* belonging to the Shakyapa Order, is also outside the complex. His Eminence Chogya Trichen Rinpoche and the Raja of Mustang established it. Every morning around sixty monks who reside here conduct the *Tara Puja*. At the end of September, two thousand monks congregate for the ten-day peace *puja* and on 13th December each year for the *Mahakala Puja*, which lasts for 10 days.

A couple of kilometres away, a complex of monasteries is being constructed on a grand scale. A little to the east of the ruins are two modern temples; the first was built by Nepal's Theravadin Buddhist community and the second is a Tibetan temple of the Sakyapa sect. About a kilometer beyond Lumbini is a beautiful new *stupa* built by the Burmese government and a new Mahabodhi Society Resthouse. Monasteries in the respective national styles of Myanmar (Burma), China, Japan, Korea and Thailand are among those that are being built. Also in the vicinity are the Lumbini Research Institute, which has an impressive collection of Buddhist literature, and a Museum. Both are open from Sunday to Saturday: 10 am-5 pm, 10 am-4 pm (in winter).

A **Nepalese Buddhist temple** was built in 1956 and a **Tibetan monastery** of the Shakya order was completed in 1975, which, as well as possessing a beautiful and elaborate shrine, is well illustrated within by traditional murals. Here many young monks are studying and practising the Buddha's teachings, thereby aiding to both the revival of Lumbini as a place of Buddhist practice and to the preservation of the great traditions lost in Tibet. The Nepalese temple, which is cared for by a monk of the Theravada tradition, also has rest houses within its grounds, provided by Buddhists from Japan and the former UNO

General Secretary U. Thant. In co-operation with the Nepalese Government, UNESCO is also helping to improve and develop this first of the eight pilgrimage places. About a kilometre beyond Lumbini is a beautiful **new** *stupa* built by the Burmese government and a new Mahabodhi Society Resthouse.

EXCURSIONS

The Taulihawa area, 27 km west from Lumbini and connected by a metalled road, has several Buddhist archaeological sites worth seeing. About 6 km from Taulihawa is **Tilaurakot** (Kapilavastu-1?) which till the 1970s was believed to be the capital of the Shakya republic where the Buddha passed his early twelve years (Fig. 18). There are ruins and mounds of old *stupas* and monasteries made of kiln-burnt bricks and clay-mortar. The remains are surrounded by a moat and the walls of the city are made of bricks. About 10 km northwest of Taulihawa there is a rectangular fortified area, identified as the natal town of Kanakmuni Buddha (the Buddha in his previous life), called **Araurakot**. Remains of ancient moat and brick fortification around the *Kot* (old mound) can still be clearly located.

About 3 km northwest of Araurakot is **Niglihawa**, which has a quadrangular tank surrounded by bushes called Niglisagar. On the western bank of the tank there are two broken pieces of the Ashokan pillar, the longer one laying flat and the shorter one stuck into the ground. The pillar bears two peacocks on the top and an inscription in Devanagari script reading "*Om mani padme hum ripu Mallasya Ciran jaut 1234*".The shorter portion of the pillar, partly buried in the ground, bears four lines of an Ashokan inscription in Brahmi script. The inscription is roughly translated as "King Piyadasi beloved of the gods, after 14 years of his coronation enlarged for the second time the *stupa* of Buddha Kanakmuni, and after 20 years of his coronation he came himself and worshipped (and) he caused (this) stone pillar to be erected". About 5 km further northwest from **Niglihawa** is a forest area called Sagarhawa. In the midst of the forest there is a huge rectangular tank, popularly known as Lambusagar. The ancient tanks' ruins were identified as the "Palace of the massacre of the Shakyas" by the German archaeologist A.A. Führer in 1895.

Kudan, lying 2 km southwest from Taulihawa, consists of a huge structural ruin with a cluster of four mounds and a tank, excavated in

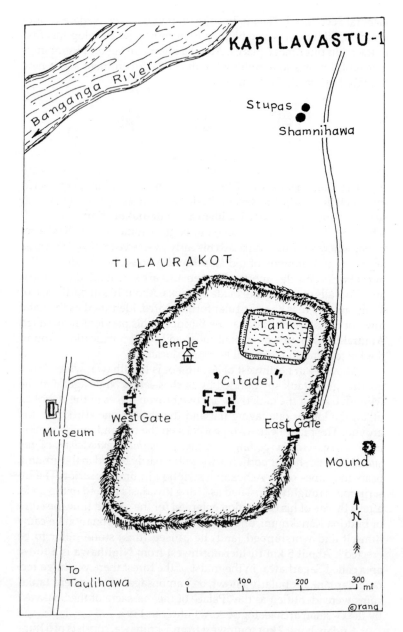

Fig. 18. Kapilavastu - 1: Tilaurakot

1962. About 3 km further south from Kudan is the village **Gotihawa**. In the village there is an Ashokan pillar standing on a slab. The upper portion of the pillar is broken and lost, and only the lower portion of the pillar, 3.5 m high, is still intact. Adjoining the pillar towards its northeast is a huge *stupa* consisting of successive rings of wedge-shaped Mauryan bricks.

Accommodation

The accommodation scene in Lumbini is not so grim. **Lumbini Garden Guest House**, 3 km south, is settled in pleasant gardens, also having a good restaurant serving food at far-from-compassionate prices. **Sri Lanka Pilgrims Rest House** is at a 3 km (45 min.) walk, north of the Sacred Garden. The **Sri Lankan Government Rest House** consists of 188 beds for the pilgrims. Hokke Club of Japan has constructed a 4-star **Lumbini Hokke Hotel** that has 55 rooms for 125 persons. The **Himalayan Inn** at Siddharth Highway, north of the bus stop, has clean and simple rooms with baths. In Bhairahwa **Yeti** at the corner of Siddharth Highway and Bank Road, **Sayapati Guest House** at Bank Road, and **Pashupati Lodge** at the corner of Narayan Path and Market Road are the other places of stay.

LINK SITE: SONAULI

Population: 27,000. STD Tel Code: 05522.

Sonauli is the last destination in the Indian side while marching to Lumbini. This small market village at the Nepalese border is little more than a bus stop, a couple of hotels, a few shops and a 24-hour border post. There's a much greater range of facilities on the Nepalese side, where the environment is more soothing. There are numerous exchange offices on the Nepalese side.

Hotels. Hotel Niranjana (Tel 24901), established by the UP Tourism, 700 m from the border, is a clean and friendly place. **Sanju Lodge** (Tel 24919), closer to the border post, is fairly rudimentary but has pleasant common areas and a bedroom in a clean but crowded dormitary. There are several good, cheap hotels, plenty of open-air restautants and a sudden blitz of beer advertisements on the Nepalese side of the border, where most travellers prefer to stay.

57

2. KAPILAVASTU (PIPRAHWA)

Where the Buddha passed his childhood

When they passed by the palaces of the nobility, Kisa Gotami, a young princess and niece of the king, saw Siddhartha in his manliness and beauty, and, observing the thoughtfulness of his countenance, said: "Happy the father that begot thee, happy the mother that nursed thee, happy the wife that calls husband this lord so glorious."

The prince hearing this greeting, said: "Happy are they that have found deliverance. Longing for peace of mind, I shall seek the bliss of Nirvana." Then he asked Kisa Gotami: "How is Nirvana attained?" The prince paused, and to him whose mind was estranged from wrong the answer came: "When the fire of lust is gone out, then Nirvana is gained; when the fires of hatred and delusion are gone out, then Nirvana is gained; when the troubles of mind, arising from blind credulity, and all other evils have ceased, then Nirvana is gained!" Siddhartha banded her his precious pearl necklace as a reward for the instruction she had given him, and having returned home looked with disdain upon the treasures of his palace.

[...]

Finally one night, the Bodhisattva Siddhartha mounted his noble steed Kanthaka, and when he left the palace, Mara stood in the gate and stopped him: "Depart not, O my Lord", exclaimed Mara. "In seven days from now the wheel of empire will appear, and will make thee sovereign over the four continents and the two thousand adjacent islands. Therefore, stay, my Lord."

The Bodhisattva replied: "Well do I know that the wheel of empire will appear to me; but it is not sovereignty that I desire. I will become a Buddha and make all the world shout for joy."

Thus Siddhartha, the prince, renounced power and worldly pleasures, gave up his kingdom, severed all ties, and went into homelessness. He rode out into the silent night, accompanied only by his faithful charioteer Channa.

Darkness lay upon the earth, but the stars shone brightly in the heavens.

The Jataka Tales, pp. 79-80, 84.

Approach & Historical background

From Gorakhpur, connected by road at a distance of 97 km, is Kapilavastu (Piprahwa). It is linked to important centres by road: Kushinagar 148 km, Varanasi 312 km, Lumbini 95 km, Shravasti 147 km, and Lucknow 308 km. By the Gorakhpur-Gonda loop rail one can approach from Gorakhpur to Siddharthnagar that lies at 30 km from Kapilavastu. The nearest airport is at Gorakhpur, 104 km. For bank (State Bank of India), post & telegraph and Primary Health Centre, the nearest place is the small town of Birdpur which is at a distance of 8 km south of Piprahwa. The earlier scholars like Rhys Davids and P.C. Mukherji identified Kapilavastu with Tilaurakot, lying across the Nepalese border. However the excavations carried out by the Archaeological Survey of India (ASI) in 1971-77 under the direction of K.M. Srivastava have proved that Piprahwa is the site of ancient Kapilavastu (Fig. 19).

Identified today with ancient Kapilavastu, modern **Piprahwa** and **Ganwaria** lie at a distance of 22 km from Siddharthnagar (Fig. 20). Kapilavastu was the ancient capital of the Shakya clan whose ruler was the father of the Buddha, for which reason the Buddha is also referred to as Shakyamuni. The Shakya domain was one of the 16 earliest independent republics (*Janapadas*) of the 6th century BCE. Prince Gautama, or Siddhartha as the Buddha was then known, spent his first twenty-nine years in Kapilavastu, and thereafter left his palace, to re-visit it 12 years later, long after he had attained enlightenment. It was in Kapilavastu's opulent environs that the holy soul of prince Siddhartha spent his childhood. There he performed three of the twelve principal deeds of a Buddha.

Surpassing all the Shakya youths and even his teachers in all fields of learning, skill and sport, he showed that he had already mastered all the worldly arts. One day, while still a child, he was left unattended beneath a tree as his father performed the ceremonial first ploughing of the season. He sat and engaged in his first meditation, attaining such a degree of absorption that five sages flying overhead were halted in mid-flight by the power of it.

As he grew into his teens, Siddhartha came to find palace life stifling, so he began making excursions beyond the city territory to see what life was like outside. He was always accompanied by Channa, his faithful attendant, and sometimes also by his friends or brothers. Channa was responsible for Siddhartha's horse carriage, and he and Siddhartha took turns in holding the reins. As Siddhartha never used a whip, Channa did not either.

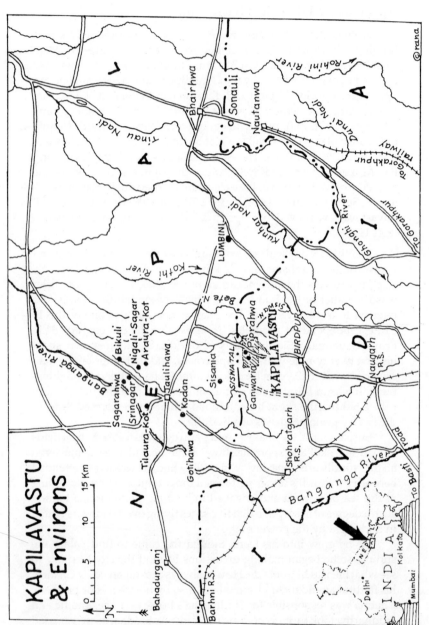

Fig. 19. Kapilavastu and its neighbourhood

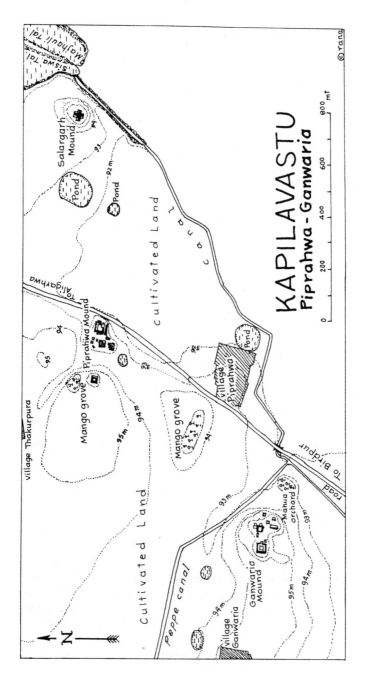

Fig. 20. Kapilavastu: Piprahwa and Ganwaria

61

Siddhartha visited every corner of the Shakya kingdom, from the rugged foothills of the Himalaya mountain in the north to the great plains of the south. The capital, Kapilavastu, was located in the richest, most populated region of the lowlands. Compared with the neighbouring kingdoms of Koshala and Magadha, Shakya was quite small, but what it lacked in area it more than made up by its ideal location. The Rohini and Banganga rivers, which originate in the highlands, flowed down to irrigate its rich plains. They continued southwards and joined the Hiranyavati river before joining the Ganga. Siddhartha loved to sit on the banks of the Banganga and watch the water rush thereby (*Tripitaka*, 186).

Later Siddharta was married to Yasodhara in the autumn, and experienced a life of pleasure in the palace amongst the women of the court. It was an occasion of great joy and celebration for the entire kingdom. The capital, Kapilavastu, was decorated with flags, lanterns, and flowers, and there was music everywhere. Wherever Siddhartha and Yasodhara went in their carriage, they were greeted with resounding cheers. They also visited outlying hamlets and villages, bringing gifts of food and clothing to many poor families.

King Suddhodana supervised the building of three palaces for the young couple, one for each season. The summer palace was built on a beautiful hillside in the highlands, while the rainy season and winter palaces were in the capital city. Each palace had lotus pools, some for pale blue lotuses, some for pink, and some for white. The couple's fine garments and slippers, and the fragrant sandalwood they lit every day, were ordered specially from Varanasi, the capital of the Kashi kingdom to the southwest (*Anguttara Nikaya*, III. 38).

Siddhartha had three other cousins that he liked very much, named Mahanama, Bhaddiya and Kimbila. He often invited them to play with him in the flower gardens behind the palace. Queen Gotami enjoyed watching them play as she sat on the wooden bench beside the lotus pond. Her attendant was always ready to respond to her requests to bring drinks and snacks for the children. With each passing year, Siddhartha grew ever more adept in his studies. Siddhartha was especially gifted in music.

One day when riding in his chariot through Kapilavastu, Siddhartha happened to see a man feeble with age, another struck down with sickness, and a corpse, and tried to understand the sense of sorrow and pain, disease and death. He immediately realised the suffering nature of men's lives. Then finally, when he saw a radiant happy holy man who had conquered all such sufferings, he decided to renounce all worldly riches and pleasures to seek truth and embark on the path of salvation (*nirvana*). It is said that a Buddha renounces the world only after seeing these four signs and when a son has been born to him. Accordingly, seven days before Siddhartha would have been crowned as his father's heir, a son, Rahula, was born to Yasodhara. Without further delay Siddhartha told his father of his resolve to leave the transient luxury of worldly life and live as a renunciate in order to discover the causes of true happiness and the end of misery. Suddhodana was reluctant to let him go. Therefore, riding the horse Kanthaka and accompanied by the groom Chandaka, Prince Siddhartha left Kapilavastu with the aid of the gods. Some distance away he performed the Great Renunciation, cutting off his hair and donning the robes of an ascetic. He sent Chandaka back to the palace with his jewels and horse, and entered into the homeless life.

At the request of his father Suddhodana, the Buddha visited Kapilavastu, some years after attaining enlightenment. The king Suddhodana looked long and hard at the Buddha before saying, "I thought surely you would come to the palace to see your family first. Who could have guessed you would instead go begging in the city? Why didn't you come to eat at the palace?"

The Buddha smiled at his father and replied, "Father, I am not alone. I have travelled with a large community, the community of monks. I, too, am a monk, and like all other monks, beg for my food."

The king in grief said, "But must you beg for food at such poor dwellings as these around here? No one in the history of the Shakya clan has ever done such a thing."

Again the Buddha smiled and said, "Perhaps no Shakya has ever done so before, but all monks have. Father, begging is a spiritual practice that helps a monk develop humility and see that all persons are equal. When I receive a small potato from a poor family, it is no different than when I receive an elegant dish served by a king. A monk can transcend barriers that discriminate between rich and poor. On my path, all are considered equal. Everyone, no matter how poor he is, can attain liberation and enlightenment. Begging does not demean my own dignity. It recognises the inherent dignity of all persons."

King Suddhodana listened with his mouth slightly agape. The old prophecies were true. Siddhartha had become a spiritual teacher whose virtue would shine throughout the world. Holding the king's hand, the Buddha walked with him back to the palace. Nagasamala followed them.

Thanks to a palace attendant who spotted the monks and called out, Queen Gotami, Yashodhara, Sundari Nanda, and young Rahula were able to watch the encounter between the king and the Buddha from a palace balcony. They saw how the king bowed to the Buddha. As the king and the Buddha neared the palace, Yasodhara turned to Rahula. She pointed to the Buddha and said, "Dear son, do you see that monk holding your grandfather's hand, about to enter the palace gates?" (*Khuddaka Nikaya* 1)

During this visit the Buddha admitted Nanda, his cousin, and Rahula, his own son, into the order. Their ordination hurt King Suddhodana, because they were ordained without his permission. Buddha realised this, and laid down the rule that no one should be ordained without his parents' consent (Book of Rules, *Vinaya Pitaka*, I. 83). Later that day, the Buddha said to Sariputta, "From now on, we will not receive children into the community of monks without the approval of their parents. Please note that in our monastic code." Five hundred Shakya youths became monks at this time, including his son, his cousin, and Upali, the barber, who was to later become one of the Buddha's most important disciples.

Time passed quickly. The Buddha and his *sangha* had rested in the kingdom of Shakya for more than six months. New ordinations had increased the number of monks to more than five hundred. The number of lay disciples was too great to be counted. King Suddhodana also gave the *sangha* another place to build a monastery — the former summer palace of Prince Siddhartha, north of the capital, with its cool and spacious gardens. Venerable Sariputta organised a large number of monks to set up monastic living there. The presence of this new monastery helped assure a firm foundation for the practice of the Way in the Shakya kingdom.

King Suddhodana invited the Buddha for a last meal before his departure and asked him to give a discourse on the *Dhamma* for the royal family and all members of the Shakya clan. The Buddha used this occasion to speak about applying the Way to political life. He said, "The Way could illuminate the realm of politics, assisting those involved in governing the kingdom to bring about social equality and justice." He continued, "If you practice the Way, you will increase your understanding and compassion and better serve the people. You will find ways to bring about peace and happiness without depending on violence at all. You do not need to kill, torture, or imprison people, or confiscate property. This is not an impossible ideal, but something which can actually be realised."

And, "When a politician possesses enough understanding and love, he sees the truth about poverty, misery, and oppression. Such a person can find the means to reform the government in order to reduce the gap between rich and poor and cease the use of force against others. My friends, political leaders and rulers must set an example. Don't live in the lap of luxury because wealth only creates a greater barrier between you and the people. Live a simple, wholesome life, using your time to serve the people, rather than pursuing idle pleasures. A leader cannot earn the trust and respect of his people if he does not set a good example. If you love and respect the people, they will love and respect you in return. Rule by virtue differs from rule by law and order. Rule by virtue does not depend on punishment. According to the Way of Awakening, true happiness can only be attained by the path of virtue." (*Mahavagga, Khuddaka Nikaya* 1)

While living there, the Buddha personally trained his disciples and kept a very watchful eye on the new entrants into the order. It is also stated in the *Jataka Tales* that in the 5th year of his ministry, when Buddha was staying at Vaishali, he paid a visit to Kapilavastu to see his father king Suddhodana lying on his deathbed. After the king's death, he returned to Vaishali.

The splendour of Kapilavastu did not last for long, for the city and many of the Shakya clan were destroyed by the rival king Vaidraka even within the Buddha's lifetime. When the Chinese pilgrims visited the area they found nothing but ruin and desolation and merely a handful of people and monks dwelling there. Fa-hsien (399-414 CE) mentioned a *stupa* and a pillar constructed by Ashoka. He mentioned the height of the *stupa* as ca. 10 m, and that it carried the symbol of a lion on its top. The fellow Chinese pilgrim Hsüan-tsang (629-640 CE) further supported his description. Yet all the sites of the events mentioned in the early scriptures were pointed out to them, and several of these were still marked by *stupas*. After this the area was lost in the jungle, and early in the 20th century was still only accessible by elephant.

Today, Kapilavastu comprises of several villages, chief among them being Piprahwa and Ganwaria (Fig. 23). A large *stupa* stands at the ancient site that is said to have housed the bone relics of the Buddha which were preserved by the then rulers, the Shakyas. An ancient Brahmi script inscription discovered at Piprahwa testifies the presence of these relics. The ruins of the place are spread over a large area. Presently there is no trace of the pillar as mentioned by the Chinese pilgrims.

Three groups of seals were found at Piprahwa, dating back to the Kushana period. One of them is inscribed in four lines, which were read as "*Om devaputra vihare Kapilavastu bhikshu anghasa*". The inscription on the second series is limited to three lines, which read as "*Om devaputra vihare Maha Kapilavastu bhikshu sanghasa*". The third group of seals carried the name of monks. The letters on the seals were in Brahmi script of the 1st-2nd century CE. The title 'Devaputra' refers to the Kushana king Kanishka (early 2nd century CE), a great patron of Buddhism who built the biggest *vihara* at Piprahwa and renovated the main *stupa* there. There are also found **stone caskets** containing relics believed to be that of the Buddha's. The recent excavations carried out indicate the ruins of the **palace** of King Suddhodana, the father of Prince Gautama (Lord Buddha). It is said to be the place where Lord Buddha spent the first 29 years of his life. The main archaeological site consisting of a *stupa* was discovered during excavations in 1973-74.

In 1897-98 Mr W.C. Peppe, an Englishman and a landlord of Birdpur (8km south of Piprahwa) had excavated the site extensively. The coffer excavated by him contained five stone caskets. Among the five the smaller one (15.24 cm high and 10.48 cm in diameter), contained an inscription, which provided a clue to the identification of Kapilavastu by its reference to Buddha and his community Shakya (Fig. 21). The inscription was read thus: *Sukiti bhatinam sa-bhaginikanam sa-puta-dalanam iyam salila-nidhane Buddhasa bhagavate Sakiynam*. This was translated by Rhys Davids as: "This shrine for relics of the Buddha, the August One, is that of the Shakyas, the brethren of the Distinguished One, in association with their sisters, and with their children and their wives." Rhys Davids, like G. Buhler and A. Barth (1898), was also of the strong opinion that the *stupa* at Piprahwa is the same which, according to the Buddhist text *Mahaparinibbana Sutta*, the Shakyas of Kapilavastu had raised immediately after the Buddha's nirvana and cremation over their share of relics. There also found two stone caskets carrying the relics of the Buddha (Fig. 22).

Fig. 21. Piprahwa (Kapilavastu): Inscribed soapstone casket found at Piprahwa in 1898.

Fig. 22. Piprahwa (Kapilavastu): Stone caskets with relics of the Buddha, 1898.

Lying to the east of the *stupa* at Piprahwa was the **Eastern Monastery** (44.10 x 42.70 m), that yielded the seals with the legend Kapilavastu (Fig. 23). In all, there were four structural phases in the monastery. The entrance to the monastery was, however, always on the western side facing the *stupa*. The monastery was constructed around a courtyard that was in all likelihood open. Having four cells projected outside, one at each corner, the monastery was square in shape in the first two phases, each side measuring 32.30 metres. The central courtyard was also a square, each side being 21.80 metres. Towards the western side of the monastery a covered veranda, 2.70 m wide, was provided. Immediately after climbing the steps of the monastery, a floor of rammed brickbats and lime mortar was provided. Towards the eastern side, by the side of the steps below the rammed floor there was a burnt brick wall.

The **Northern Monastery** is near the north-western corner to the eastern side of the main *stupa*. It was far smaller in size than other monasteries and also the poorest in its construction. The general layout of the monastery was similar to the eastern monastery, though of course without the veranda around the central courtyard. There was a central courtyard flanked by cells all around.

The **Southern Monastery** was found to be in a very bad state of preservation. The eastern and a part of the southern wing were badly damaged as a result of erosion. The plan of the monastery was also, more or less, similar to other monasteries, with the only exception of two galleries in addition to the cells. In all there were only two structural phases. The monastery was square on plan, with each side measuring 24 metres. The monastery was constructed around a central courtyard and a covered veranda. A drain with a 25 cm wide channel was observed in the southern wing of the monastery running north to south. The drain was constructed to discharge the refuse water of the monastery. Further beyond the drain there was a votive *stupa* with a diameter of 4.80 metres. On the western side of the monastery there was a small *stupa* with a square base.

The **Western Monastery** is about 100 metres to the west of the *stupa*, consisting of another monastic complex. Like the other monasteries, the cells were constructed around a central courtyard and a covered veranda. The monastery was square in plan with one side including outer walls being 25 metres. The thickness of the outer wall was one metre and of the inner one only 75 cm.

A **shrine-like structure** not far from the south-western corner of the eastern monastery was observed close to the *stupa* on the eastern side. In the shrine both plain and moulded bricks were used. The shrine was 3.15 sq m. Towards the southern side of the shrine there was a

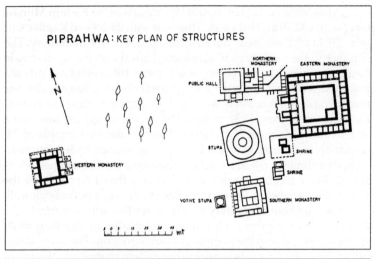

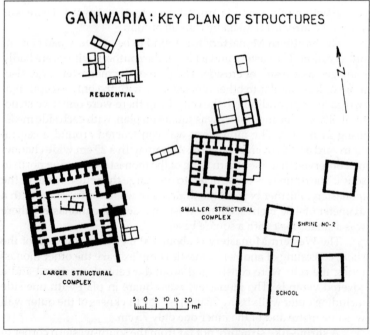

Fig. 23. Kapilavastu: Structural plans of Piprahwa and Ganwaria
(after K.M. Srivastava, 1986: 49 & 63)

small room. The entrance to the room was provided with a flight of steps on the western side. The room, in all likelihood, was meant for occupation by the priest of the shrine. The shrine and the platform belonged to the fourth structural phase.

There was a huge **brick-paved hall** on the north-western fringe of the mound. It was square in shape, with one side measuring 10.60 metres. The hall was enclosed on all sides by a burnt brick wall. Though the hall was constructed in the first structural phase, the enclosure wall was reconstructed in a later phase. The exact purpose of the structure could not be established. No doubt, the location of a school mentioned in the travel documents of the Chinese pilgrim Hsüan-tsang fits in well with this structure.

Shakyan Stupa

The **first** important structure at Kapilavastu is the main *stupa* at Piprahwa, one of the earliest found in India. The *stupa* revealed three stages of constructions. Excavations conducted in 1971 revealed that the *stupa* was first built in the 5th century BCE and enlarged at two later dates. The first and earliest *stupa* was made from baked bricks and consisted of a simple dome with a 5 m wide brick-paved processional path *(pradakshinapatha)* around it. In the first stage a tumulus was raised by piling up natural earth dug up from the surrounding area (Fig. 21). On the top of the mound in the centre two burnt brick chambers were constructed to keep the sacred relics. In the centre of the *stupa*, at ground level, were two brick chambers adjoining each other. The northern chamber contained a beautifully lathed soapstone casket 12 cm high, and two dishes. The southern chamber contained a similar, larger casket 16 cm high, and two more dishes. Both caskets, when opened, were found to contain fragments of charred human bone. The date, location and contents of these caskets make it almost certain that the charred bones are the corporeal remains of the Buddha which had been given to the Shakyas. As of 1990, these precious relics together with the caskets were displayed in a Perspex box at the National Museum in New Delhi.

The second phase referred to compact yellowish clay, not very much different from the natural soil that was filled up above the two brick courses projecting from the structure of the first phase. The entire reconstruction of Phase 2, i.e. dome and projection of the tier, rested on the twelve courses of bricks of the first phase. The massive sandstone coffer containing the inscribed casket found by Peppe belonged to the second phase. In the third phase the base of the *stupa* was converted into a square from a circular one as a result of which the dimensions of the *stupa* were enhanced; one side of the square measured 23.50 m. Rectangular niches at regular intervals of 80 cm embellished the square base of the *stupa*. The plinth of the square base was 1.16 m high including the niches.

The **second** *stupa* was built about 150 years later, after leveling the dome of the first. The dome of this *stupa* was 19 meters in diameter and had a 1.52 m wide projection around its base. It was from this

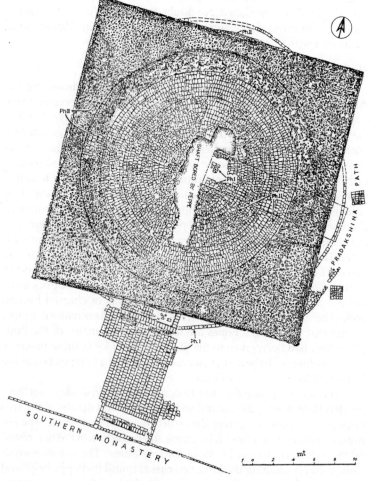

Fig. 24. Kapilavastu (Piprahwa), the site plan of the main *stupa*
(after K.M. Srivastava, 1986: 43)

stupa that Mr Peppe recovered the famous inscribed casket. Having found the huge stone box with the casket in it, he assumed that there were no more relics and thus dug no deeper, and thus missed the other two older caskets only a few metres further down.

The **third** *stupa*, with its dome 23 m in diameter, was considerably larger than the earlier ones and had a square base with 23.5 m long sides added. Mr Peppe found a casket in this *stupa* also, but it had been smashed into tiny fragments. It is this third *stupa* that the pilgrim sees today. Apart from its historical importance, the Shakyan *stupa* is of interest for several other reasons. The earliest *stupa* showed no signs of having been opened after its construction, thus suggesting that the legend about Emperor Ashoka opening all but the Ramagama *stupa* may not be entirely true. It is possible that he left the *stupa* at Kapilavastu untouched out of respect for the Shakyas. The *stupa* also displays the various stages of development that such monuments usually went through. The earliest structure was small and simple, and was added to over time, gradually becoming larger and more complex. Thus *many stupas* display the onion effect — one structure encased within another larger, later one.

Eastern Monastery

A little to the east of the main *stupa* are the ruins of a large monastery. A seal found in this monastery had the words *"Kapilavatthu Bhikkhu Sangha"* on it, proving conclusively that Piprahwa and the surrounding ruins were the site of the Buddha's hometown. It also pointed to the monastery having been built by King Kanishka. The monastery consists of 31 cells built around a courtyard; the larger rooms on either end of the eastern side were probably storerooms, while the others would have provided accommodation for monks. The monastery had steps at its entrance and a drain, probably a urinal, with its outlet on the northeast corner.

At **Salargarh**, about 200 metres east of the ancient site of Piprahwa, another *stupa* and a monastic complex were excavated. The monastery was rectangular on plan with one set of rooms behind the other. The larger axis of the monastery was east-west. The approach to the monastery was from the northern side with the help of a flight of steps. A high plinth was most probably provided to the monastery because of water-logging conditions. This feature was apparent from the number of steps provided in the stair. Traces of an enclosure wall all around the monastery were observed. There were in all three stages of construction in the monastery. The three stages could be dated between 2nd century BCE and 1st century CE.

On the northern side of the monastery, at a distance of about 30 m, are the remains of a *stupa*, which like the *stupa* at Piprahwa, was circular in its initial stages. The maximum diameter was 5.50 metres. In the later stages, most probably during the Kushana times, when image worship was introduced, the base of the *stupa* was converted into a square, each side being 10.85 metres. According to the size of the bricks, the circular *stupa* was of the same date as the second phase of the *stupa* at Piprahwa.

One and a half kilometres from the site there are two excavated mounds. The larger one is a thick walled structure that, according to local belief, was Suddhodana's palace. The excavation at **Ganwaria** reports that at a distance of 6 m from the top there were two niches of 82 x 80 x 37 cm that were made for setting a statue of the Buddha. The remains of metallic pots and coloured plates are testimony of the story as to how the Shakya rulers divided the relics of the Buddha and preserved them. These remains are dated to the early 4th century BCE. On the top of the *stupa* a broken stone box of the size of 132 x 82 x 66.7 cm was found. This box consisted of parts of pots made of wood and silver together with golden garments, small images of lions and elephants engraved on golden plates, golden wheels, pearls wrapped in embroiled cloths, tiny golden boxes. These artefacts and remains are preserved in the Calcutta Museum. The mound marking the town is extensive, although much of it is now used for cultivation. Excavation has shown that the town was occupied from 800 BCE up to the end of the Kushana period, about 300 CE. Today one can see two large monasteries and a collection of secular structures, most of them built after the first century CE.

Other ruins in the area consist of what is believed to be a public hall a little to the north of the main *stupa*, a small votive *stupa* and monastery on its south side, and another monastery some distance to the west.

There is a small Sri Lankan monastery and temple, Mahinda Mahavihara, in the vicinity of the ruins.

Information & Facilities. STD Code 05544. Birdpur, 8 km south, has the facilities of State Bank of India, Post & Telegraph Office, and Primary Health Centre. The nearest Tourist Office is at Siddharth Nagar, 20 km.

Accommodation : Sri Lankan Temple Dharmashala, and UP Tourism Bungalow (UPSTDC).

3. BODH GAYA

Where the Buddha attained Enlightenment

"Here on this seat my body may shrivel up, my skin, my bones, my flesh may dissolve, but my body will not move from this very seat until I have attained Enlightenment, so difficult to attain in course of many *kalpas*."

Voice of the Buddha

The Blessed One having attained Buddhahood while resting under the shepherd's Nigrodha tree on the banks of the river Niranjara at Bodh Gaya, pronounced this solemn utterance:
"How blest in happy solitude
Is he who hears of truth the call!
How blest to be both kind and good,
To practice self-restraint to all!
How blest from passion to be free,
All sensuous joys to let pass by!
Yet highest bliss enjoyeth he
Who quits the pride of 'I am I'.
I have recognised the deepest truth, which is sublime and peace-giving, but difficult to understand; for most men move in a sphere of worldly interests and find their delight in worldly desires".

The Mahavagga, 1, 3 ~4.

Approach and Background

Population : 40,000. Post Code: 824231. STD code: 0631.

Bodh Gaya, east of Varanasi at a distance of 235 km by rail via Gaya and 270 km by road, is located at 12 km south of Gaya City and connected by road from Gaya, the nearest Railway Station. Coming from Varanasi via Sasaram by G.T. Rd (NH 2), from a small township called Dobhi turn towards the north and after 26 km you arrive at Bodh Gaya. If you plan to come by railway, Gaya is the major junction on Delhi-Varanasi-Gaya-Calcutta route. Gaya is at 92 km south of Patna and is well connected by rail and road. From Gaya Railway Station, there are buses, taxis or auto-rickshaws to cover a distance of 16 km for Bodh Gaya. Of course they are phenomenally overloaded.

Airport. On 18 December 2002, air services from Gaya to Kolkata and Bangkok have been started; see Appendix 4 (pp. 298-300).

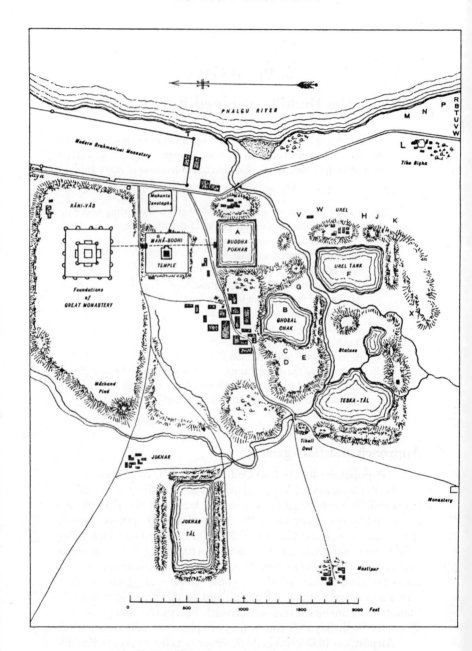

Fig. 25. Bodh Gaya, the area (after A. Cunningham, 1892)

Bodh Gaya

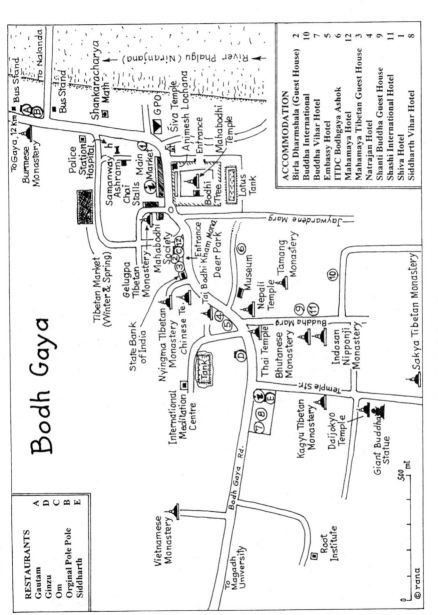

Bodh Gaya

RESTAURANTS

Gautam	A
Ginzu	D
Om	C
Orginal Pole Pole	B
Siddharth	E

ACCOMMODATION

Birla Dharmshala (Guest House)	2
Buddha International	10
Buddha Vihar Hotel	7
Embassy Hotel	5
ITDC Bodhgaya Ashok	6
Mahamaya Hotel	12
Mahamaya Tibetan Guest House	3
Natrajan Hotel	4
Shanti Buddha Guest House	9
Shashi International Hotel	11
Shiva Hotel	1
Siddharth Vihar Hotel	8

Fig. 26. Bodh Gaya, the present map

75

Bodh Gaya is probably all the more interesting a place by virtue of being much more of a working Buddhist centre than an archaeological site (Figs. 25 and 26). It is the most important Buddhist pilgrimage site in the world. Several inscriptions found there refer to Sri Lankan, Burmese and Chinese people who performed pilgrimage to this site in the historical past and patronised repairing and installing images of the Buddha. Bodh Gaya's special character is clearly emphasised in numerous texts and pilgrim records which designate it as the only place where Shakyamuni could have become a Buddha. The famous 7th century Chinese pilgrim Xuanzang (Hsüan-tsang) described Shakyamuni's futile efforts to achieve enlightenment at nearby Pragbodhi Hill (now called Dhongra Hill). Afterwards Shakyamuni found that spot about 3 km south of Pragbodhi Hill, where he was finally successfull. And for centuries since, the Buddhist devotees have journeyed to pay homage to this sacred site of enlightenment.

Hsüan-tsang ascribes the erection of the original Bodhi shrine to Emperor Ashoka. According to one of his rock edicts, Ashoka visited this place, which is called Sambodhi in the inscription, ten years after his consecration, and it is more than probable that the great emperor constructed a shrine on this holy spot. However, no vestige of such a shrine is found here. From the description of Hsüan-tsang it appears that the Mahabodhi temple, essentially in its present shape and appearance, existed already in the 7th century CE. Today this temple which was extensively restored in the late 16th century dominates Bodh Gaya. The Mahabodhi temple in Myanmar (Burma) is a prototype of this grand temple.

The vast majority of sculptures from Bodh Gaya date after the Gupta period and primarily belong to the Pala-Sena period (ca. 8th-12th centuries). The importance of this site after the 6th century is indicated by the fact that the Buddha in *bhumisparsha mudra* (earth-touching gesture) became the most common form for a Buddha image during the Pala period. Although it is a specific reference to Bodh Gaya and a symbol of the achievement of Buddhahood, this form seems to have originated elsewhere at an earlier time. Nonetheless, the first place in eastern India where it became prominent is at Bodh Gaya. Various kings, queens, patrons and visitors repaired, renovated and added to the already existing structures till the 12th century when floods silted the courtyard of the temple complex, which remained buried until 1811.

Although the exact circumstances and date are not known, after the 13th century, despite centuries of activity, Buddhist practices at Bodh Gaya largely ceased. Francis Buchanan-Hamilton, who visited

Bodh Gaya in 1811, reported that the temple was in a dilapidated condition and that much of the immediate area had been greatly disturbed by the extensive removal of bricks and other materials for local building projects. From the beginning of the 19th century, several Burmese missions also travelled to Bodh Gaya, first to find the site and make offerings, and then, in 1877, to renovate the dilapidated structures. In fact, it was the somewhat haphazard renovation by the Burmese that prompted the British Government to undertake a major restoration of the site in the 1880s. Unfortunately, the 19th century changes made at Bodh Gaya have greatly confused the record of earlier activity. Some structures were totally dismantled and many images were moved from their original locations.

In the late 19th century, along with the restoration of the site, attention was focussed on Bodh Gaya by the writings of Sir Edwin Arnold. His famous poem about Shakyamuni entitled *"The Light of Asia"* (1879) and an impassioned newspaper account of the sad neglect of this most sacred Buddhist site proved effective tools for reawakening an interest in Bodh Gaya throughout the world. In 1891 Sir Arnold's writings helped to inspire Anagarika Dharmapala from Sri Lanka to dedicate his life to the struggle to have Bodh Gaya and especially the **Mahabodhi temple** under Buddhist ownership rather than accepting the Hindu Mahant who was in control of the temple at that time. Since 1953, under an act passed by the Government of Bihar, the Bodh Gaya Temple Management Committee, whose members are both Buddhists and Hindus, administers this temple and has made vast improvements to both the temple and its grounds. Existing structures have been repaired and new *stupas* are being erected. With the reintroduction of gilded images in the niches of the Mahabodhi Temple, it begins to regain some of the splendour described by Hsüan-tsang.

The monk Gautama practised austerities in his own way of arduous and austere meditation for six months under the Pipala tree. For the first three of these months, he was alone on the mountain, but during the fourth month, five disciples of Master Uddaka Ramaputta, led by his old friend Kondanna discovered him. Siddhartha was happy to see Kondanna again, and he found out that just one month after Siddhartha left the meditation site, Kondanna himself had attained the state of *neither perception nor non-perception*.

Seeing there was nothing more he could learn from Master Uddaka, Kondanna persuaded four friends to join him in seeking Siddhartha. After several weeks, they were lucky enough to find him, and they expressed their desire to stay and practice with him. Siddhartha explained to them why he was exploring the path of self-mortification, and the five young men, Kondanna, Vappa, Bhaddiya, Assaji, and Mahanama, made their mind to join him. Each monk found a cave to live in, not far from one another, and every day one of them went into town to beg for food. When he returned, the food was divided into six portions so that none of them had more than a small handful each day. In course of time the five friends became tired of hard austerities and fell into doubts, and ultimately lost faith in Siddhartha. The five friends finally left Gautama and departed in search of a powerful place and a great master; however they could not succeed until they met the Buddha.

Gautama abandoned the desire to escape the world of phenomena, and as he returned to himself, he found he was completely present to the world of phenomena. One breathe, one bird's song, one leaf, and one ray of sunlight — any of these might serve as his subject of meditation. He began to see that the key to liberation lay in each breathe, each step, each small pebble along the path.

The monk Gautama went from meditating on his body to meditating on his feelings, and from meditating on his feelings to meditating on his perceptions, including all the thoughts which rose and fell in his own mind. He saw the oneness of body and mind, that each and every cell of the body contained all the wisdom of the universe. He saw that he needed only to look deeply into a speck of dust to see the true face of the entire universe, that the speck of dust was itself the universe and if it did not exist, the universe could not exist either. The monk Gautama went beyond the idea of a separate self, of *atman*, and, with a start, realised that he had long been dominated by a false view of *atman* as expounded in the *Vedas*. In reality, all things were without a separate self. Non-self, or *anatman*, was the nature of all existence. *Anatman* was not a term to describe some new entity. It was a thunderbolt that destroyed all wrong views. Taking hold of non-self, Siddhartha was like a general raising his sharp sword of insight on the battlefield of meditation practice. Day and night he sat beneath the Pipala tree, as new levels of awareness awoke in him like bright flashes of lightning. (*Majjhima Nikaya.* 26)

Ultimately the night of the achievement came. Entering into deeper contemplation, Siddhartha during the first watch of that wonderful night acquired the knowledge of his past lives in various planes of existence; in the second watch he acquired the supernormal divine vision; in the third watch he fathomed the law of cause and effect and gained insight into the destruction of mental cankers; and at sunrise he attained Supreme Enlightenment, Omniscience. Ultimately Siddhartha acquired the rays of enlightenment on the full-moon day of the spring, i.e. Vaishakha (April-May), in 528 BCE. The monk Gautama became the Buddha, 'the Awakened One'; and later also came to be known as Sammasambuddha ('the Perfectly Enlightened One'), Bhagava ('the Blessed One'), Tathagata ('the Perfect One'), Sugata ('the Happy One or the Accomplished One'), and Shakyamuni ('the Sage of the Shakyas'). The fig tree (*Ficus religiosa*) under which he sat became known as the Bodhi Tree, and the area as Bodh Gaya or Buddha Gaya.

Traditions states that Buddha stayed in Bodh Gaya for *seven weeks* after his enlightenment. Each week was spent in a different part of the sacred place or complex. The 1st week was spent under the *Bodhi Tree*. For the 2nd week, he remained standing and gazing uninterruptedly at the tree for having helped him in his quest. *Animeshalochana Stupa* ('unwinking gazing shrine') marks this spot in the northeast to the Mahabodhi temple, and houses a standing figure of the Buddha with his eyes fixed towards the tree. The 3rd week was spent in meditation, walking back and forth from the tree to the unblinking shrine spot, out of gratitude for giving him shelter. Lotus flowers are said to have sprung up in this place which came to be known as *Chankramana Chaitya* (jewel walk) and is marked by a recently made brick platform containing 18 lotus flowers representing the footsteps of the Buddha. The 4th week was devoted by the Buddha to attain higher modes of exposition, i.e. *Abhi Dhamma Naya* (deep meditation). The place where he performed meditation is called *Ratanagraha Chaitya*, which is incorporated in the Buddhist flag of white, yellow, blue, red and orange. The 5th week after enlightenment was again spent in meditation under another tree, called *Ajapa Nigrodha*, where Sujata had offered him a meal of rice-pudding (*khir*). The 6th week takes us to *Muchalinda Lake*, ca. 50 m south of the main temple, where the serpent king Muchalinda, dwelling at the bottom of the lake, rose up to protect the Master from a severe storm created by Mara (the god of chaos) to disturb his meditation. There is a life-size image of the Buddha covered by a cobra at the centre of the Muchalinda Lake. In front of this lake are the remains of an **Ashokan pillar**, which is now about 6 m high. The *Rajayatana tree* marks the 7th and last week, where the Buddha decided to preach and thus save human beings from further sufferings; here two merchants, Tapassu and Bliallika of Utkala (modern Orissa), who by chance had come there in the course of their travelling, offered him cakes of barley and honey as food. From the Rajyatana tree, the Buddha again returned to the Bodhi Tree and paid his finally reverential salute and bowed his head to the sacred Bo tree. After thus spending 49 days meditating, the Buddha left Bodh Gaya on foot to meet the five ascetics, his former associates, at Sarnath (Banaras) in order to turn the First Wheel of *Dhamma*.

Addressing his friend and follower Savasti, a buffalo boy, the Buddha said, "Love is possible only when there is understanding. And only with love can there be acceptance. Practice living in awareness, you will deepen your understanding. You will be able to understand yourselves, other people, and all things. And you will have hearts of love. That is the wonderful path I have discovered".

Savasti asked, "Respected Teacher, could we call this path the 'Path of Awareness'?" Siddhartha smiled, "Surely. We can call it the Path of Awareness. I like that very much. The Path of Awareness leads to perfect Awakening." Siddhartha nodded and accepted Sujata's request that he should be called the 'Awakened One'. Sujata continued, 'Awaken' in Magadhi is pronounced 'budh'; and a person who is awakened would be called 'Buddha'. Now we can call you the 'Buddha'. Fourteen-year-old Nalaka, the oldest boy in the group, spoke, "Respected Buddha, we are very happy to receive your teaching on the Path of Awareness. Sujata has told me how you have meditated beneath this Pipala tree (*Ficus Religiosa*) for the past six months and how just last night you attained the Great Awakening. Respected Buddha, this Pipala tree is the most beautiful and sacred one in all the forest. Allow us to call it the 'Tree of Awakening', the 'Bodhi Tree'. The word '*bodhi*' shares the same root as the word '*buddha*' and also means awakening."

Gautama nodded his head. He was delighted, too. He had not guessed that during this gathering with the children the path, himself, and even the great tree would all receive special names. Nandabala joined his palms. "It is growing dark and we must return to our homes, but we will come back to receive more of your teaching soon." The children all stood and joined their palms like lotus buds to thank the Buddha. They strolled home chattering like a flock of happy birds. The Buddha was happy, too. He decided to stay in the forest for a longer period of time in order to explore ways to best sow the seeds of Awakening and to allow himself, as well, special time to enjoy the great peace and joy that attaining the path had brought him. (*Majjhima Nikaya*. 10)

The Mahabodhi Temple

The **Mahabodhi Temple**, located at the place of the Buddha's enlightenment, is the main site of worship and visit (there is a fee for use of camera) (Figs. 27, 28, 29 and 30). The Mahabodhi Temple has been recently included in the list of **World Heritage Sites** of UNESCO.

Fig. 27. Bodh Gaya, Mahabodhi Temple:
Before and after restoration in the 19th century

Emperor Ashoka (r. 270-232 BCE) paid several visits to Sambodhi, as he preferred to call it, along with his spiritual preceptor Upagupta (Mogalliputta Tissa). His visit is vividly described in a Sanskrit text of the period named *Ashokavandana*. Inspired by his teacher the emperor took a vow and performed special rituals. At this auspicious occasion Upagupta said:
"Here at the seat of enlightenment
the greatest of the sage dispersed
and quickly repelled the forces of Namuci (Mara)
And here that peerless individual
Attained everlasting, exalted,
Supreme enlightenment."
And hearing this the emperor made an offering of one hundred thousand pieces of gold to the Bodhi Tree and finally the construction of a *chaitya* (temple) was started at this sacred place.

Ashoka had built the first *chaitya* (temple) in the 3rd century BCE near the Bodhi Tree. This temple was replaced in the 2nd century CE, which in turn went through several alterations. The present temple, which has been through layers and layers of restorations, dates from

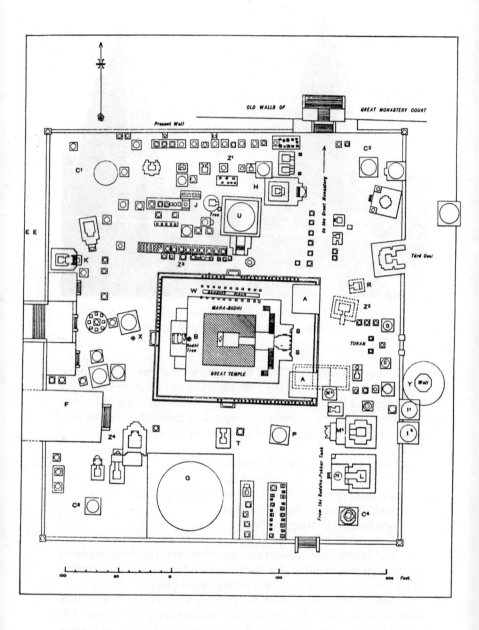

Fig. 28. Bodh Gaya: Mahabodhi Temple's courtyard (after A. Cunningham, 1892)

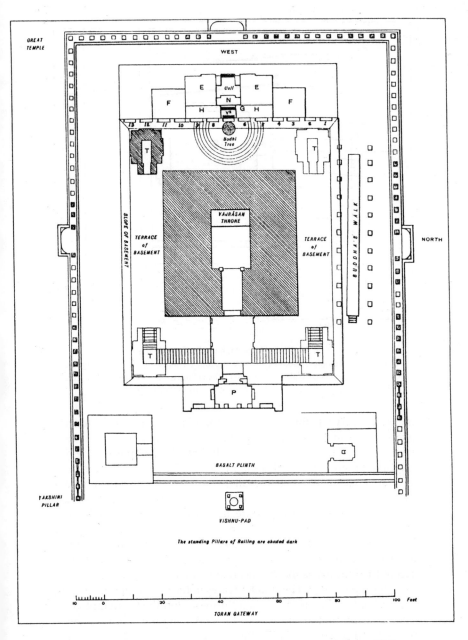

Fig. 29. Bodh Gaya: Mahabodhi Temple plan (after A. Cunningham, 1892)

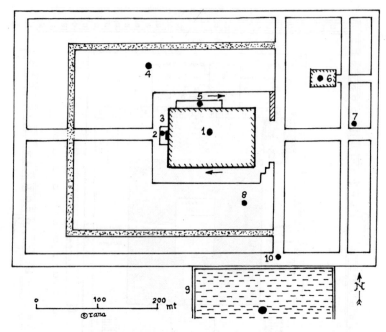

Fig. 30. Bodh Gaya: Mahabodhi Temple map
1 Mahabodhi Temple, 2 Bodhi Tree, 3 Admantine Diamond Throne, 4 Ratnagraha Chaitya, 5 Bejewelled Walk, 6 Animeshalochana Stupa, 7 Ajapala Nigrodha Tree, 8 Rajayatana Tree, 9 Muchalinda (Lotus) Lake, 10 Ashoka Pillar.

the 6th century CE. Burmese monks found the temple neglected and overrun by squatters, and initiated much of the rescue work in 1882. It has been repaired as recently as early 1998. The temple, resting on a high and broad plinth, with a soaring 54 m high pyramidal spire with a square cross-section and 4 smaller spires, houses a gilded image of the Buddha, kept behind glass, in the *bhumisparsha mudra* (earth-touching gesture). This classical gesture, in which the Buddha's right hand touches the ground while the left rests in his lap, signifies enlightenment. In the centre of the temple there is also a **Shiva linga** that was installed in about 860 CE. The temple is also sacred to Hindus, as they accept the Buddha as the 9th incarnation of Vishnu, the preserver in the Hindu pantheon. The smaller spires in the temple appear to have been added to the original when Burmese Buddhists attempted extensive rebuilding in the 14th century. Among the column images, tree worship, especially the Bodhi Tree, and relic casket are the prominent scenes (Figs. 31 and 32).

84

Fig. 31. Columns at Bodh Gaya:
Tree worship (after Fergusson, 1875)

Fig. 32. Columns at Bodh Gaya:
Relic Casket (after Fergusson, 1875)

The original Mahabodhi Temple was destroyed by the Muslims invaders during the 13th century. Parts of the intricately carved railings to the south and west of the temple are very old. Some of the railings are original and parts of the railings are reproductions. Over the last thirty years, many statues have been stolen from the temple's niches. The oldest structure left on the site is a stone railing built in the 1st century CE to keep out wild animals; however, a quarter of it has been whisked away to museums in London and Calcutta. The **entrance** to the Mahabodhi temple is through a *torana*, an ornamental archway, on the eastern side. The lotus pond where the Buddha may have bathed is to the south of the temple. To the north is the *'Chankramana'*, a raised platform, 1 m high and 18 m long, dating from the 1st century with lotus flowers carved on it, which marks the consecrated promenade where the Buddha walked back and forth while meditating on whether he should reveal his Message to the world. This appears to have been later converted into a covered passage with pillars, of which only one survives. On the main walls there still remained the old images (Fig. 33).

Fig. 33. Bodh Gaya, the Mahabodhi Temple: The images on the wall

The Bodhi Tree

At the back of the Mahabodhi temple is the sacred Bodhi Tree (*Ficus religiosa*, holy fig), said to be a descendant of the tree under which the Buddha attained enlightenment. The tree still appears to radiate an aura of abiding serenity, spiritual solitude and peace. It is believed that the original Bodhi Tree sprang up on the day of Siddhartha's birth (Fig. 31). Legend says that Emperor Ashoka, initially hostile to Buddhism, ordered it to be cut down and burned on the spot. But when the tree sprang up anew from the flames his attitude was transformed, then Ashoka revived it and built a protective-enclosing wall, as had previously been done by King Prasenajit of Koshala within the Buddha's lifetime. The legend also says that after his conversion, Ashoka became so devoted to the tree that his queen Tishyarakshita got jealous and had it killed, after which it miraculously grew again. Ashoka's daughter, Sanghamitra, carried a sampling from the original Bodhi Tree to Sri Lanka. The tree that grew from that branch still grows in the ancient Sri Lankan capital at Anuradhapura and is the oldest continually documented tree in the world. Later in turn, a cutting from it was carried back to Bodh Gaya when the original tree here died. History also tells us that King Sashanka destroyed the Bodhi Tree during the time he persecuted Buddhists around 600 CE.

Hsüan-tsang (639) says that every full moon of Vaishakha (April-May), thousands of people from all over India would gather at Bodh

Gaya and bathe the roots of the tree with scented water and perfumed milk, play music and scatter heaps of flowers. Dharmasvamin (mid 13th century) noticed similar expressions of devotion: "The tree stands inside a fort-like structure surrounded on the south, west and north by a brick wall; it has pointed leaves of bright green colour. Having opened a door one sees a large trench the shape of a basin... The devotees worship (the tree) with curd, milk and perfumes such as sandalwood, camphor, and so on. They bring offerings from afar and keep it constantly moist."

The Bodhi Tree originally grew a little further to the east of its present position but was moved when the Mahabodhi Temple was built. The present Bodhi Tree was planted in the 19th century and is probably a distant descendant of the original one.

Later, Nagarjuna is said to have built an enclosure to protect the tree from damage by elephants and, when in time it became less effective, placed a statue of Mahakala upon each pillar. The third destruction, as reported by Hsüan-tsang, took place in the 6th century when a Shaivite king of Bengal named Shasank destroyed the tree. However, even though he dug deep into its roots, he was unable to unearth it completely. It was afterwards revived by Purvavarma of Magadha, who poured the milk of one thousand cows upon it, causing it to sprout again and grow 3 m in a single night. In addition to human destruction, the tree has perhaps perished naturally several times, yet the holy *pipal* (holy fig) is renowned for growing wherever its seeds fall and the direct lineage has continued.

Here are three images of the Bodhi Tree:
The Buddhists look upon the Bo Tree
as most Christians look upon the Cross.
> Rhys Davids, *Life of Gautama*

The Bodhi Tree, thenceforward in all years
Never to fade, and ever to be kept
In homage of the world, beneath whose leaves
It was ordained that truth should come to Buddh.
> Edwin Arnold, *Light of Asia*

Slowly the Prince advanced — beneath his tread,
At every step th' expectant world shook,
Until he rested 'neith the Bodhi Tree —
At once the trembling universe was still
Acknowledging the thronement of its lord.
> Alexander Cunningham, *Mahabodhi*

Vajrashila

The platform between the Bodhi Tree and the temple is a large rectangular stone slab thought to be placed exactly where the Buddha sat. This is the oldest object that can still be viewed at Bodh Gaya. It is called **Vajrashila** ('the rock of diamond'), and some believe that an enormous diamond buried beneath the earth here fuels the site's spiritual power. This stone may have been originally been placed over the oldest Vajrasana inside the temple. This outer Vajrashila is 143 x 238 x 13.5 cm, and is made from polished Chunar red sandstone. The top is decorated with unusual geometrical designs and there is a palmette and goose frieze around the edge. Because of

Fig. 34. Bodh Gaya:
Mahabodhi Temple

its migratory habits, the wild goose (*hamsa*) was used in ancient Buddhism as a symbol of detachment. The Vajrashila was probably made by King Ashoka, and the fact that a similar palmette and goose design is to be found on his pillar capital at Sanchi strengthens this conjecture. Hindus and Buddhists both claim the sign of footprints (**Buddhapada**, cf. Fig. 35) near this rock under the Bodhi Tree as symbol of the feet of Buddha, or Vishnu, respectively.

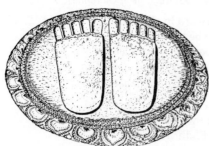

Fig. 35. Mahabodhi Temple, Bodh Gaya:
The Buddhapada

For centuries from the time of Emperor Ashoka (r. 270-232 BCE) there was a Buddhist colony at Bodh Gaya with a number of Viharas and Sangha hermitages where pious Buddhists spent their time in meditation and social service. Then, after the decline of Buddhism in India, this colony ceased to exist, and the holy shrine was desecrated by the Muslims and reactionary Hindus in the 13th century. Later, the Great Temple was occupied by a Shaivite Hindu Mahant who tumbled upon it by chance in the course of his travels in about 1590. And it was only in 1953 that the Mahant was ousted and the management of the Temple was entrusted to the Bodh Gaya Management Committee constituted under the 1949 Act by the Bihar Government. Since then, Bodh Gaya has developed fast and by now a number of Buddhist countries have established their own temples and monasteries at this holy place.

The year 1956 marked the 2500th anniversary of the Buddha's nirvana. It gave impetus to resurgence of activity at Bodh Gaya. A number of foreign temples and monasteries sprang up. However, the earliest among them is the *Mahabodhi Sangharama*, built by the king of Ceylon (Sri Lanka) in the 4th century CE. Presently there are 25 Buddhist Temples, monasteries and organisations functioning at Bodh Gaya in various capacities. The establishment of so many modern temples and monasteries by the World Buddhist Community at Bodh Gaya has enhanced the spirit of the holy land of Buddha's Enlightenment and also transformed it into a Symbol of Buddhist Unity. The sacred and sweet sound of *'Buddham Sharanam Gachchhami, Dhammam Sharanam Gachchhami, Sangham Sharanam Gachchhami'* ('We take refuge in the Buddha, we take refuge in the *Dhamma*, we take refuge in the *Sangha'*) reinforced by *'Om Mani Padme Hum'* and *'Namo Myo Ho Rengo Kyo'* recited daily in these temples certainly adds the serene rhythm of divine echoes promoting spirituality in the congenial environment of modern Bodh Gaya. Verily, the addition of new temples, *gompas* and monasteries have certainly changed the landscape of Bodh Gaya. Additionally, the newly opened international airport at Gaya has opened a new door for the monks and adherent Buddhists from other countries to visit and pay homage to this sacred land.

Most countries with a large Buddhist population have a temple or monastery at Bodh Gaya, usually built in a representative and traditional architectural style.

The Maha Bodhi Society of India

When Anagarika Dharmapala (1864-1933) first came to Bodh Gaya in 1891, the only Buddhist building there was a small rest-house built in 1875 by King Mindon-Min of Burma for housing the Burmese delegation headed by him to carry out repairs in the Maha Bodhi Temple. Naturally, therefore, the Burmese Rest House became the centre of his activities and for the next ten years Dharmapala fought an unequal fight with the mighty Mahant (chief of the temple) from that small rest-house. As the Mahant refused to give any land to the Maha Bodhi Society, it was only in 1900 that a piece of land was allotted to the Society by the Gaya District Board, on which now stands the Maha Bodhi Rest House. This historic building, which has served the cause of the *Dhamma* for about 100 years by now, was constructed by the District Board through the contributions of the Buddhists of Burma and Sri Lanka in response to an appeal by Anagarika Dharmapala. It cost Rs 15,000 at that time.

Ever since its construction in 1901, the Maha Bodhi Rest House served as the office of the Maha Bodhi Society, providing accommo-dation to the Buddhist pilgrims from India and abroad. It also serves as a watchtower to look after the safety and sanctity of the Great Tem-ple. Since 1953, the Bhikkhus of the Maha Bodhi Society have been responsible for performing the traditional form of Buddha's worship and related religious ceremonies at the Maha Bodhi Temple. And, since 1970, duty has been performed with great devotion and dedica-tion by Venerable B. Pannarama, a monk from Sri Lanka. Under his supervision and the sponsorship of the Society, Buddha Jayanti (*Vaishakha Purnima*) and other religious functions are organised in the precincts of the Maha Bodhi Temple. In the near future the dates for the Buddha Purnima are: 16 May 2003, 4 May 2004, 23 May 2005, 13 May 2006, 2 May 2007, 20 May 2008, 9 May 2009, and 27 May 2010.

The historic Buddhist revival movement initiated by Anagarika Dharmapala in 1891 completed its 100th years in 1991. The Centenary Year of the Society was celebrated with great enthusiasm and in a befitting manner by all the Centres of the Society. At Bodh Gaya, where the Society was started, a grand bust of the great Anagarika Dharmapala was installed in the premises of the Maha Bodhi Rest House on 23 September 1991. The bust of Dharmapala was designed and sculpted by Ven. Wipulasara Maha Thera, General Secretary of the Maha Bodhi Society of India, and all expenses thereon were do-nated by R. Premadasa, President of Sri Lanka.

Being ideally located just close to the Great Temple and the Bus Stop, the Maha Bodhi Society at Bodh Gaya is the most convenient contact point for any visitor to Bodh Gaya. The Centre not only pro-vides useful information and guidance to the tourists and pilgrims but also makes available books on Buddhism and Indology.

Burmese Buddha Vihara

The Burmese Vihara is on the old road to Gaya, just beyond the Mahant's Math, and near the Police Station. The shrine in the Vihara has a series of interesting paintings depicting important events from the life of the Buddha. The temple is built in the style of a small pagoda and is reminiscent of Pagan, the city of five thousand pagodas. The old Burmese Rest House was the first building to be built by a Buddhist country at Bodh Gaya in modern times. It was built by King Mindon-Min of Burma (now Myanmar) in 1875 for the Burmese delegation deputed by the pious king to repair the decaying Maha Bodhi Temple. The old rest house was later demolished, and the present Vihara and Rest House built. The Burmese Vihara has a consecrated Seema (sanctum sanctorum) where the monks can be ordained as per the Theravada tradition.

Gelugpa Tibetan Temple

The Tibetan Temple and associated Monastery, right next to the east of the Maha Bodhi Rest House near the centre of the town, is accustomed to sightseers. It belongs to the Gelugpa School of Tibetan Buddhism and was constructed by the famous Lama Khangauwang of Ladakh in 1933. Built in typical Tibetan style, its main shrine on the first floor is stocked with many beautiful images, scriptures and religious objects. Its second-floor chapel has walls painted with *thangka*-style clouds, wheels, and *bodhisattvas*. Visitors are invited to turn the massive cylinder of a prayer wheel downstairs. Its walls are painted in traditional Tibetan style with scenes from the life of the Buddha and the Buddhist saints of the Mahayana and Vajrayana tradition. There is also a huge Prayer Wheel. This temple has assumed greater importance in recent years as His Holiness the 14th Dalai Lama Tenzin Gyatso (earlier name Lhamo Thondup; b. 5 July 1935), who has been living in Dharmashala (India) as an exile since April 1959, stays here whenever he visits Bodh Gaya.

Chinese Temple

A small Chinese Monastery and Temple, built on the pattern of the Buddhist temples in China, is situated further to the south-west of the Maha Bodhi Rest House. It was built in 1935 by a monk named Shih-tih Chen. It contains a fine image of a white marble Buddha, and the walls are fully decorated with the murals depicting scenes of the life events of the Buddha.

Thai Buddhist Temple

Built in a typical Thai pagoda style, the 'Wat Thai' (**Thai Temple**), Bodh Gaya's second-most prominent landmark, is located across from the Chinese Temple, i.e. to the west of the Archaeological Museum, 500 m after the main road. A large colourful *wat*, as the Marble

Temple in Bangkok, with the classic claw-like tips on its orange roof, it was built and opened in 1957. Its eclectic interior includes Thai tourism posters. Side-roads branch off the main road to both sides of the Thai Temple. It was later partially reconstructed in 1970-1972 by the Royal Government of Thailand. The huge Golden Buddha in the main shrine is its primary attraction for the visitors.

The Golden Buddha image was installed at a solemn function on 3 May 1967. Donated by the Prime Minister Thanom Kittikachorn of Thailand, the Golden Buddha Image is 3.60 m high, and was flown from Bangkok to Gaya by a special U.S. military aircraft. From the Gaya aerodrome it was brought to Bodh Gaya by a large number of monks and laymen in a procession led by Venerable Phra Deb Visuddhimoli, Lord Abbot of the Thai Monastery. Before the image was brought to the Thai Temple it was taken three times round the sacred Maha Bodhi Temple, and the Lord Abbot made a special ritual worship before the Vajrasana, near the Bodhi Tree. From 1970 onward the Bhikkhu Sangha of India started holdings yearly meeting at Wat Thai, sponsored by the Thai Monastery.

Bhutanese Temple

Turning to the corner and a little beyond is the newly painted Bhutanese Temple and Monastery. The foundation stone of this Temple was laid on 28 October 1983. The Bhutanese follow Mahayana Buddhism and belong to the Dukpa Kargyu sect of Tibetan Buddhism. Built by the Royal Government of Bhutan, this Temple presents a good picture of the rich spiritual and cultural heritage of Bhutan, the Land of the Thunder Dragon.

Karmapa Tibetan Temple

Across the road and a little further down is the ornately painted Kagyupa Vajrayana Temple and Mahayana Buddhist Monastery (1938), popularly known as Karmapa Tibetan Temple. It belongs to the Kagyupa sect of Tibetan Buddhism. This Temple contains Disneyesque, larger-than-life murals depicting the life of the Buddha and has a large Dhamma Chakra or 'Wheel of Law' which must be turned 3 times when praying for the forgiveness of sins. The paintings inside it are in part copied from the paintings in the Mulagandhakuti Vihara at Sarnath. A large 2 m metal ceremonial drum in red and gold is also on display.

Indosan Nipponji (Japanese Temple)

Beyond this Tibetan Temple and on the right side of the road is the beautiful Japanese Temple, known as Indosan Nipponji. It was built by the International Buddhist Brotherhood Association (Kokusai Bukkyo Koryu Kyokai, **IBBA**), which was founded in 1968 in Japan by various Buddhist sects. The registered office of the Association is at Nakameguro, Meguro-Ku, Tokyo. Its first President was Rev. Shoyu Iwaya, a renowned Japanese Buddhist priest, and this temple was planned and executed under his dynamic leadership. As the first step of the project, the foundation stone of the International Buddhist House was laid in September 1968, and the work was completed in February 1970. The construction of the temple began the same year in December, and it was completed in November 1973. The main door of the temple was formally opened for the public on 8 December 1973 by Mr V.V. Giri, the then President of India. The back wall of the temple has a mural showing a crushing landscape of people flocking to the Buddha. The Indosan Nipponji complex has a free clinic, monastery and Peace Bell that rings with a swinging cadence throughout the morning (06.00-12.00 h) and in the evening. There is a plan to build a Maitreya Buddha statue over 100 m high in Bodh Gaya as a symbol of world peace.

The temple is a replica of an ancient Japanese wooden temple; it emanates natural beauty without any artificial decoration or design. The interior wall of the temple depicts a painting based on some of the important events of the life of the Buddha. In the middle is installed an image of Shakyamuni Buddha which was brought from Japan. The modern two storey, spotless **Japanese Temple** with beautiful polished marble floors has gold images of the Buddha.

A **Japanese Pagoda** was constructed in front of Wat Thai (Thai Buddhist Temple) by the International Buddhist Brotherhood Association (IBBA) in October 1965, on land of the Bihar Government. It has since been shifted within the premises of the Japanese Temple. The stone pagoda, which is unique in India, has been designed and constructed based on ancient Japanese tradition by Japanese architects and engineers.

In front of the temple there is a bell tower (**Bell of Dhamma**) hanging a big bell which weighs about 250 kg. The huge bell was presented by Mr. Kono Suke Motsewhito, Chairman, National Electrical Works Co. Ltd., Japan. Its schedule time of ringing from April to September is 5 a.m. and 6 p.m., and from October to March 6 a.m. and 5 p.m. Additionally, the bell also rings at 12 noon throughout the whole year. The local people are also benefited as they are able to fix their time for daily work according to the timely ringing of the bell.

In the third step of the project, the construction of the **Bodaiju Gakuen** (*Bodhi Tree Kindergarten*), attached to the Japanese Temple, was begun. On 8 December 1975 was held the groundbreaking ceremony, a gift from the children and guardians of All Japan Buddhist Nursery and Kindergarten Association to Indian children. The building was completed in February 1977, and it began running informally with 40 local backward and poor children from 15 September 1977 to 7 December 1977. In 1979, in the third year of its inception the number of children increased to 50. Presently, the total number of children in the school is around 200. Children of three years and a half to four years get admitted after medical examination and psychological test. After completing the two years course, they pass kindergarten for the primary education. As a result of this, almost all local backward and poor caste children, for whom education is not normally within their reach, join primary school after passing kindergarten. During the four hours of daily stay children join *Trisharan, Panchashil* in Nipponji, worship Nono Sama in kindergarten, and listen to pre-lunch talks on various subjects, participate in programmes of language, music and performances, paper work/ painting manual arts, activities in nature and so on. They have the facility of regular medical check-up, uniform dresses, educational materials, tiffin and other perks.

The Japanese Temple also provides medical services to the visitors and local people at its **Komyo Free Medical Centre**, which was inaugurated in December 1983, and has been functioning since then on a regular basis with sufficient staff and equipment.

As per the cherished desire of the late Rev. S. Iwaya, the President of the International Buddhist Brotherhood Association (IBBA) and his associates, since 1975 the IBBA has been holding an **International Buddhist Conference and Seminar** on different aspects of Buddhism every year on 8-10 December at Bodh Gaya. The Organisation provides all the facilities to the participants of the seminar and conference. Every year the number of delegates increases enormously. The papers presented by the scholars are carefully edited and selected by the editorial board for final publication as Proceedings, which are commonly released before the commencement of the following session. Under the patronage of the Japanese Temple, the International Buddhist Conference is invariably presided over by the President of the IBBA, Japan. Presently, Rev. Dr. Arsta Tulku acts as Secretary of the IBBA and the Conference.

Daijokyo Buddhist Temple

Just adjacent to the first Indosan Nipponji, on the other side of the road, is settled another beautiful Buddhist Temple which was built by the Daijokyo Association of Japan. The Daijokyo Sect was founded by Rev. Tatsuko Sugiyama and its headquarters is at Nagoya, Japan. The term *Daijokyo* means the Great Vehicle of the Mahayana. This sect believes in the Lotus Doctrine propagated by St. Nichiren (CE 1222-1282) in the 13th century. The Daijokyo is a lay sect and its rituals are simple and less elaborate, and its priests are also recruited from the lay people only.

The beautiful Daijokyo Buddhist Temple, with a lofty pagoda atop, was declared open by Mr Giani Zail Singh, the then President of India, assisted by Rev. Y. Sugisaki, President of the Daijokyo Sect of Japan, on Sunday 13 February 1983. On this occasion, a special *puja* (*Kalacakra*) was also performed in Japanese style in the main hall where the images of the Lord Buddha and Bodhisattvas are installed.

The First Anniversary of the Daijokyo Buddhist Temple was celebrated on 12 February 1984. On the same day the grand ceremony of the Great Buddha Statue, the erection of which had been announced by Rev. Sugisaki in 1983 at the time of the inauguration of the temple, was also held. The Second Anniversary of the Temple was held on 23 February 1985 and was combined with offerings of prayers on completion of the foundation of the proposed Great Buddha Statue and the inauguration of the Daijokyo Training School. The Third Anniversary was held on 19 January 1986 and was combined with the ceremony of the proposed Daijokyo Rest House. The 6th anniversary of the Daijokyo Temple was combined with the completion of the Great Buddha Statue which was unveiled at a colourful ceremony by His Holiness the 14th Dalai Lama, Tenzin Gyatso, on 13 November 1989. Rev. Y. Sugisaki, President of the Daijokyo Sect of Japan, welcomed the guests present on this historic occasion. The three-day unveiling ceremony, in which hundreds of Buddhist monks drawn from all disciplines performed ceremonial rituals, concluded on 20 November 1989.

The Giant Buddha Statue

Adjacent to the Daijokyo Buddhist Temple at the end of the road, the tallest statue of Buddha in India was installed by the Daijokyo Sect, Japan. The temple area spreads over one hectare of land acquired from the Government of Bihar. This **Giant Buddha** image, in the Japanese Kamakura style, is 24.25 m high and 18.25 m wide. Built of pink and yellow Chunar sandstone, the image is seated on a lotus in the meditation pose with eyes half-closed (Fig. 36). Built on a solid concrete pedestal, the statue is hollow, and has a spiral staircase going from the ground floor to the chest, which makes four storeys. Wooden shelves have been provided in the interior walls in the three storeys of the statue wherein 16,300 small Buddha images from Japan made of

Fig. 36. Bodh Gaya: the Giant Buddha

bronze have been enshrined. The construction of the statue, which was carved and erected by M/s Thakur & Sons of Chunar, took more than five years from 1984 onwards. It was 'opened' by H.H. the 14th Dalai Lama in 1989. The 10th Anniversary of the Daijokyo Buddhist Temple was held on 9 November 1993, when the statues of the two chief disciples of the Buddha, Sariputta and Moggallana, on the two sides of the Great Buddha, were also unveiled.

The Daijokyo Buddhist Temple, in addition to various religious activities, is also running a Sunday school in the temple premises, which is attended by 50 students from the locality. The children are taught to recite the Buddhist prayers, songs, drawing and Origami (Japanese paper art of making flowers, birds, etc.). They are also taught Hindi and English languages. The Temple is also running the Daijokyo Training School since February 1985, which is located in a separate two-storeyed building adjacent to the temple. Here, classes on typewriting (6-months course) and tailoring (one-year course) are regularly held. Training is free and the necessary articles are provided to the students of the tailoring class.

The Daijokyo Buddhist Temple, the Great Buddha Statue, the Rest House and all other activities being run by the Daijokyo Association are presently managed efficiently by Mr. M. Subba, the Manager-cum-Secretary since its inception.

There are also Sri Lankan, Tai Bodhi Kam, Sakyapa, Bhikkhu Sangha, Vietnamese, Korean, Taiwanese, Bangladeshi and Nepali Tamang monasteries with their associated temples.

Adjacent to the Mahabodhi temple is a **Shaivite Monastery** that has a cluster of four temples. Surrounded by enchanting greenery and marked by architectural marvels, these temples have several *samadhis* (commemorative tombs of saints) in their vicinity. Just across are a number of cells for the residence of monks. And don't neglect the **Mahant's Palace**, on the left just before you reach the centre of the town. Now a working Hindu temple, its rear views of the Niranjana (*Lilanjan*) River and the Sujata Mountain beyond make it a great spot for meditation and contemplation. Not far from the Shaivite Monastery is the **Jagannath Temple**, which is dedicated to Shiva and has a statue of the deity carved in glistening black stone.

After attaining enlightenment the Buddha bathed in the nearby **Niranjana** (*Lilanjan*) **River**, which flows outside a quiet hamlet silhouetted against a range of low hills. The Niranjana River is about 250 m east of the Mahabodhi Temple. Prince Siddhartha crossed this river to reach the Bodhi Tree. It is said that the Buddha sent his begging bowl upstream in this river. He made a solemn declaration that if he was to become Buddha the bowl would float upstream and join those of the previous Buddhas. The bowl floated upstream, as he desired. About 2.5 km east across the Niranjana river, on a hill mound overgrown with trees and shrubs, is a hermitage believed to be the site of **Sujata's house**. Others consider it to be the site of the *Ajapala Nigrodha tree*, under which the Buddha spent the 7th week after enlightenment. From its outward appearance, the mound looks like the ruins of an ancient *stupa*.

Archaeological Museum

This museum opened on 28 December 1956 and inaugurated by H.H. the 14th Dalai Lama Tenzin Gyatso, has a fine collection of stone and metal images from the 1st century BCE to the 11th century CE.

Most of the images belong to the Pala-Sena period (8th-12th centuries). There are gold, bronze, and stone sculptures of the Buddha, Hindu deities, two stone images of Yakshis, and fragments of railings and posts from the original temple. As many of the sculptures from Bodh Gaya were either taken to museums during the 19th century or simply disappeared, the Archaeological Museum has only a small collection. The most important exhibit is the stone railing that once surrounded the Mahabodhi Temple, most of it reassembled in the museum's courtyard, with a smaller section inside. The carvings on the railing seem to be illustrations of famous Buddhist shrines, events in the life of the Buddha, scenes from daily life, auspicious symbols, and in some cases, representations of popular Hindu deities and zodiacal signs, composed in no particular order.

Some of the more clearly recognisable carvings on the railing in the courtyard include: (1) an ascetic in a cave; (2) a winged deer; (3) an ascetic in a hut with a lion; (4) a man with a horse-headed female; (5) two men playing chess on a board with 64 squares; (6) a woman and child listening to a goat or deer, perhaps illustrating the *Rohanatamiga Jataka*; (7) a winged elephant; (8) a mermaid. Along the coping stone is a line of mermaids putting their hands in the mouths of sea monsters, a procession of mythological beasts and floral designs.

The carvings on the railing inside the museum include: (1) two figures worshipping at the Indasala Cave; (2) loving couples; (3) a Bodhi Tree surrounded by a railing; (4) a centaur, perhaps Dhanu, the Indian Sagittarius; (5) three elephants worshipping the Bodhi Tree; (6) men in a boat picking lotuses, perhaps illustrating *Sutta Nipatta* V.2; (7) the Hindu goddess Gaja Lakshmi; (8) a temple enshrining a Dhamma Wheel; (9) the purchase of the Jetavana by Anathapindika; (10) a winged horse; (11) a man with wings riding on a sea monster; (12) a warrior carrying a sword and shield. On most of the crossbars are lotus medallions, sometimes with human heads, sometimes with animals in their centers.

The museum is open from 10.00 to 17.00 hr and closed on Fridays; Entrance fee: Rs 5.

Spread over an area of 142 ha of land, the **Magadh University** is situated at ca. 3 km west from the Mahabodhi temple and has an international centre for the study of ancient history, culture and philosophy.

AROUND BODH GAYA

The **Dungeshvari** (also known as Pragbodhi, or **Mahakala**) **Caves**, in remote, almost desert-like surroundings on the far side of the Phalgu, 7 km northeast of Bodhgaya, are the place where the Buddha did a severe penance as an ascetic for six long years after his renunciation of all worldly pleasures. This resulted in the familiar image of him as a skeletal, emaciated figure. After years of extreme self-denial at Mahakala, he came to the conclusion that knowledge could not be gained through mortification of the flesh. Realising this he walked down to Bodh Gaya, where he was offered rice as a gift. The peak is rugged and treeless, and the vultures soaring above only seem to emphasize the silence. Below, the pilgrim will see the foundations of a large monastic complex and on the top of the mountain, the ruins of several ancient *stupas*. The peaceful environment around Pragbodhi, its wild beauty and the powerful presence that can be felt in the cave, make it well worth a visit.

A short climb from the base of the impressive cliff leads to a Tibetan monastery and the small caves themselves. A Buddhist shrine inside the main cave is run by Tibetans, although a Hindu priest has recently set himself up in competition. Few tourists make it here and the occasional car or bus that does arrive gets mobbed by urchins and beggars. Offers by international Buddhist communities to help build roads and some sort of infrastructure have been rejected by the Bihar government.

Meditation Services in Bodh Gaya

Especially during the winter high season (mainly from November to early February), short and long-term **meditation** and **retreat courses** are available in either of the two distinct traditions of Buddhism — Mahayana (the Great Vehicle), epitomized by the various forms of Tibetan Buddhism which spread across China and Japan evolving along the way, and Hinayana (or Theravada), as practised in Sri Lanka, Thailand and other parts of Southeast Asia. Teachers from all over the world jet (or rickshaw) in to provide training to Buddhists and aspiring Buddhists in the spiritual atmosphere of the temple town. A few permanent institutions in Bodh Gaya dedicated to spreading the Buddha's message also conduct lessons. These courses are a major seasonal industry in Bodh Gaya. Check notice boards in the various cafés , and ask at the Root Institute or the Burmese Vihar.

The **Root institute for Wisdom Culture** (Tel: 0631-2400714; web: www.rootinst@nda.vsnl.net.in), located at the edge of the town down a dirty path to the left, is a real haven, a semi-monastic dharma centre 2 km west of the main temple, with pleasant gardens, a shrine room, library and accommodation, all enclosed in its own grounds. It organises in the winter months seven- and ten-day residential courses, focusing on the Mahayana tradition, with guest *lamas* in a quiet and intimate setting. An eight-day course costs Rs 2600 including food. Single rooms, some with bathrooms and verandas, are available from Rs 300-450, and the pleasant dorm is Rs 175 a day. Breakfast is included. Practitioners can take rooms for retreats of up to three months, but these should be booked well in advance. They are also working for the local community with health, agricultural and educational projects, including tree planting during the monsoon, running all-year Leprosy and Polio Projects and a Destitute House. The institute is always looking for volunteers, for general tasks and to help in its charitable school and polio clinic. All are funded by the Foundation for the Preservation of the Mahayana Tradition, FPMT, which runs ninety Buddhist meditation and retreat centres throughout the world including one in Kopan near Kathmandu, Nepal, and is involved in the ambitious Maitreya Project to construct a 128 m Buddha.

The **Dhamma Bodhi International Meditation Centre** (Tel. 0631-2400437), one of the many Vipassana centres in India, lies a few kilometres out of town near Magadha University on Dobhi Road. It organises regular ten- and twenty-day courses throughout the year (except June). They will also house and feed you for no charge — but donations are appreciated. Details of all Vipassana courses are available from the International Academy in Maharashtra (Tel. 02553-284076). Alternatively, you can contact the Dhamma Dipa Centre in England (Harewood End, Hereford HR2 8JS; Tel. 01989-730234).

The **International Meditation Centre** (IMC, Tel.: 0631-2400707), a couple of hundred metres behind the Chinese temple, established by Ven. Dr. Rashtrapal Mahathera, started functioning from 29 January 1970. It is near to the Magadh University, across from the Thai Monastery. It is the first full-fledged meditation centre at Bodh Gaya. Its old centre is situated by the main roadside in an area over 2 hectares of land just opposite the Magadh University. An imposing pillared Entrance Gate fashions its existence. The complex consists of a two-storeyed Meditation Building with seven annexes comprising of an office-cum-library, a Pragyananda Free Primary School, and Taugpulu Sayadaw Free Health Unit. From November 1993, an Orphanage-cum-Welfare Home has also been functioning at this Centre. From April 1990, the International Meditation Centre has established another Complex near the Great Maha Bodhi Temple. The New

Complex has an eight-roomed two-storeyed guest house and a self-contained spacious Meditation Hall along with other annexes. Both the Centres of the IMC have been adorned with two beautiful Lord Buddha images in meditative posture, of enormous value, gifted by the Venerable Bhadant Yanaviriyachan, Lord Abbot of Wat Dhammamongkol, Bangkok, and Ven. Nun Kruapanich of Thailand. It holds ten-day beginners' Vipassana courses and thirty-day courses for the more experienced. A typical day begins at 4.30 am and features six hours of group meditation with various breaks in between. The IMC also offers courses in the Vipassana method of meditation year-round. Donations are accepted, as there are no fixed fees.

Meditation courses on occassional basis are also offered at the **Burmese Vihar**; although not currently running meditation courses they have some useful information and are involved with voluntary social work projects including schools. Western volunteers are always welcome. Tibetan monasteries also run meditation courses. The **Thai temple** also runs occasional meditation courses in the Theravada tradition. Friends of the Lotus Mission just behind the Chinese temple offer Zen instruction.

Accommodation

Pilgrims can stay in monasteries; most of the rooms are very basic. Across from the seasonal New Pole-Pole restaurant, on the left side of Gaya Road, the **Burmese Vihar** (Tel: 0631-2400721), provides basic amenities at a very low price, Rs 100/ 200. During the high season (Nov.-Jan.), 35 students of Antioch College in Ohio (USA) transform the usually serene atmosphere into a temporary American University. The **Bhutanese Temple** (Tel: 0631-2400710), Temple Road, near the statue of Great Buddha, several metres up to the Shanti Buddha Hotel, is a good choice at cheaper rates for singles and family rooms; tariff Rs 200/ 400. **Daijokyo Temple** (Tel: 0631-2400747), near the Giant Buddha statue, is a beautifully maintained Japanese Nichiren Buddhist hotel for pilgrims and tour groups; currently running on a donation basis. The **Tamang Monastery** (Tel: 0631-2400802), Bodh Gaya Rd, near the Archaeological Museum, gives clean but cramped rooms. The **Mahabodhi Society** and **Sri Lanka Pilgrims Rest/ Guest House** (Tel: 0631-2400742, Fax: 0631-2400880), near the main temple provides large dormitories with comfortable beds; tariff Rs 200/ 300. The **Gelugpa Tibetan Monastery**, near the Mahabodhi Society, somewhat more spartan and a bit cheaper, has simple and clean rooms around a Tibetan-style courtyard; charges Rs 200/ 300. The **Kagyu Tibetan**

Monastery, on the road to the Giant Buddha, is a friendly low-cost place; charges Rs 100/ 150. **Ram's Guesthouse** (Tel: 0631-2400644), Hotels **Amar** and **Shashi** on Gaya Road have good valued rooms and are better choice for budget travellers. Apart from these, we can include the **Shakya Tibetan Monastery** and **Nepalese Monastery**. All the religious organisations expect guests to conform to certain rules of conduct and good behaviour. The **Birla Rest House** built by Jugul Kishore Birla is to the northeast of the Mahabodhi Society rest house; also there is an attractive *stupa*.

There is a spate of building going on in Bodh Gaya, mostly of middle and top-price HOTELS. **Bodhgaya Ashok** (Tel: 0631-2400700, at Gaya), near the museum, has comfortable bungalow-type rooms and a pleasant building; tariff Rs 2500 and above. **Buddha International** (Tel.: 0631-2400505), in the south of the town near the Indosan Japanese Temple, is an impressive hotel but pricey; tariff Rs 2000-3000. **Hotel Lotus Nikko** (32 rooms; Tel: 0631-2400789, Fax: 0631-2400788; Email: lotus@del3.vsnl.net.in), near Archaeological Museum at walking distance from the Mahabodhi Temple, has a spacious and comfortable rooms, and garden; tariff Rs 2500-3000. **Buddha Vihar** (Tel: 0631-2400445), Bihar Tourist Complex, provides cheap three-four-and six-bed dormitory accommodation. **Embassy** (Tel: 0631-2400711) passes the white-glove test; tariff Rs 1500-2500. **Mahayana Tibetan Guest House** (73 rooms; Tel: 0631-2400756, Fax: 0631-2400676, Email: mahayanagt@yahoo.com), a new huge hotel at 200 m from the Gelugpa Monastery, has pleasant rooms and a spacious lobby where monks often hold court; the 14th Dalai Lama stayed here in his 1998 visit; tariff Rs 600-1200. **Nataranjana** (Tel: 0631-2400475) is similar to Embassy, and charges Rs 1200 for doubles. **Shanti Buddha Guest House** (Tel: 0631-2400534), south of the museum, is one of the most established mid-price options with en-suite rooms; tariff Rs 1500-2500. **Shiva** (Tel: 0631-2400425), opposite Mahabodhi Temple, is centrally located with range of comfortable a/c rooms; tariff Rs 600-1500. **Siddharth Vihar** (Tel: 0631-2400445), Bihar Tourist Complex, has double rooms with attached bath; tariff Rs 400-600.

Food

Restaurants are highly seasonal, and prices become surprisingly high during winter, when pilgrims and tourists arrive. The **Mahabodhi Canteen** at the Sri Lanka Guesthouse serves reasonably good Chinese food. **Shiva Hotel** near the tourist office provides mixed menus, western and Indian. **Fujia Green Chinese Restaurant**, right outside the Tibet Temple provides a huge selection of Tibetan and Indian dishes, including the chicken *momos* and vegetable *thukpa* in both high and low seasons. **Sujata Restaurant** (Tel. 2400725), inside Hotel Bodh Gaya Ashoka, next to the museum, is the only fancy, pricey restaurant. **Om Café** is well established, and is a popular meeting place. The rates in winter include the chocolate chip cookies at the **New Pole-Pole**, across from the Burmese Temple, and **Ginza**, on the opposite side of the town, across from the Thai Temple, which caters to Japanese tourists. Among the seasonal tent-restaurants **Pole-Pole**, **New Pole-Pole** and the **Gautam** are good choices.

4. Gaya

A place visited by the Buddha many times

The Lord stayed near Gaya at Gayasisa together with a thousand monks.

Vinaya, IV.35.

Population: 335,000. Postal Code: 823001. STD Tel. Code: 0631

Gaya is 220 km southeast by rail and 276 km by road from Varanasi, and about 100 km south of Patna, the State Capital of Bihar. Gaya is on the main Delhi to Kolkata railway line and there are direct trains to Delhi, Kolkata, Varanasi, Puri and Patna (cf. Appendices 9 and 10). Gaya is 12 km north of Bodh Gaya.

Mythologically described in Hinduism as the last among the three pillars in "the Holy Bridge to Heaven" and eulogised as the most sacred place to conduct rituals for the ancestors, the city of Gaya and its territory records continuity of tradition at least since the ca. 8th century CE as narrated in the *Vayu Purana*. The *Vayu Purana* mentions 324 holy sites and spots related to ancestors-rites, of which 84 are identifiable at present and are concentrated in the vicinity of nine sacred clusters. At present pilgrims most commonly visit only 12 sacred centres. The cosmogonic hierarchy is marked by three territorial layers — Gaya Mandala, Gaya Kshetra, and Gaya Puri, within which there is a complex interweaving of themes of birth, fertility, Sun, and death. In the symbolic realm of the cosmic triad, Vishnu's footprints in the **Vishnupad** temple serve as the *axis mundi*, and the cardinal and solstitial points are marked by the hills and other sites of the mandala (Fig. 37). The primordial solar symbolism of Vishnupad and its radial solstitial alignments suggest an initial importance of the Sun at the site. The most common ritual period is the 7-day week, each day of which is prescribed for particular rituals and ancestors-rites, combining sacrality with space, time and function. The distinct spatial affinity phenomenon of the holy spots in Gaya is interpreted with reference to the landscape view and the ritual system as described in mythology and tradition. It is obvious that this forms a complex interacting system which in itself converges into an order; the wholeness is transformed into holiness.

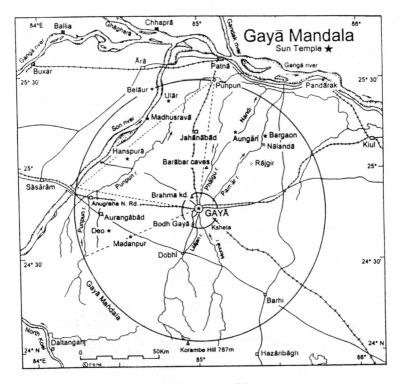

Fig. 37. Gaya Mandala

The *core* area of Gaya Puri ('the sacred city of Gaya'), known as Adi Gaya ('the old Gaya'), may be marked by a radial distance of 0.25 *krosha* (0.8 km) from Vishnupad to Sita Kund across the Phalgu river in the east and referring the edge of Prabhas hill. Gaya Puri can be identified closely to **Gayashirsha** (Gayasisa in Pali); literally '*shirsh*' means 'head', and is conceived as the core area whose edges are marked by Naga Hill in the east and the tank of Uttaramanas in the north (cf. *Vayu Purana*, 111.22). Gaya and Gayashirsha were well known to ancient texts. The Gaya Puri closely corresponds to the present city of Gaya.

According to one of the most authoritative Sanskrit texts on pilgrimage and sacred places, the *Tristhalisetu* ('Bridge to the Three Holy Cities'), dated ca. the 16th century, of the three pillars of the '*bridge to the realm of soul*', Gaya is the easternmost. The other two are Varanasi and Prayaga (Allahabad), both along the Ganga river to the west. The

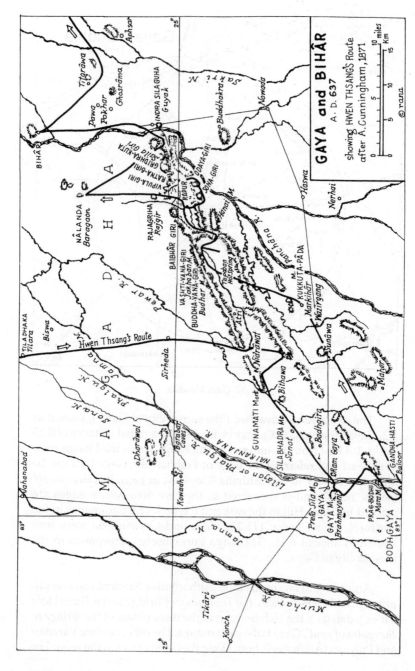

Fig. 38. Gaya and Bihar: Hsüan-tsang's route of journey, ca. 637 (after A. Cunningham)

first clear indication of Gaya as a holy place is metaphorically eulogised in the *Rig Veda* (1.22.17): "Vishnu crossed this and placed his first foot in three ways: the whole of it is encompassed in his steps". The treatise *Nirukta*, ca. the 8th century BCE, explains the "three ways" as the three sacred places in Gaya called Samarohana, Vishnupad, and Gayashisha. The glory of Gaya was already accepted in the period of the *Mahabharata*, especially for ancestors-rites. The Chinese traveller Hsüan-tsang (ca. CE 639), while passing in the Gaya region (Fig. 38), also mentioned Gaya as a sacred place for bathing which possesses the power to wash away sins.

The name *Gaya* is derived from a demon-king, Gayasura, who by his arduous austerity pleased the gods and got the blessing that the spirit of all the divinities would reside in his body, i.e. the territory of Gaya marked by his reclining body. By his power of great meditation the divine spirit met the earth spirit, resulting in the formation of a very powerful holy place. To commemorate the glory and spiritual power of the demon Gayasura, his city is called Gaya.

Prof. Asher (1989) suggests that the special sacred ritual of ancestors' worship and pilgrimage to Gaya since the Mahabharata period "probably drew Shakyamuni to the outskirts of Gaya where he engaged in meditation that resulted in the attainment of Buddhahood". According to inscriptional sources, the antiquity of the site and the tradition of ancestral rites in and around the Vishnupad temple goes back to the period of Samudragupta (5th century CE). Queen Ahilyabai Holkar of Indore made a major sculptural and architectural change in the Vishnupad temple and also other temples in the late 18th century.

The three primal objects of nature symbolism described and given ritual connotations are the **Phalgu river** ('flowing water'), **Akshayavata** ('the imperishable Banyan') and **Pretashila** ('the hill of the ghosts'). The river symbolises the fertility by liquidity ('living water') in which life, strength and eternity are contained (Fig. 39). The five hills marking the territory of Gaya Kshetra are Pretashila (northwest), Ramashila (northeast), Prabhas, also called Ramagaya Pahar, across the Phalgu River (east), Brahmayoni (southeast), and Griddhrakuta (southwest). Except Prabhas hill (163 m) and Pretashila (266 m), the rest of the three hill summits record a height of around 218 m. There are 45 active sites, arranged spatially into eight sacred clusters. However, three-fourths of the pilgrims perform their ancestors-rites at three places — Phalgu River, Vishnupad and associated sacred centres.

The **Phalgu river** ('the merit giving river') forms the eastern boundary of Gaya City. The Puranic mythology explains that the name Phalgu is a combination of *Phala* ('merit') and *go* ('wish-giving cow'); by con-

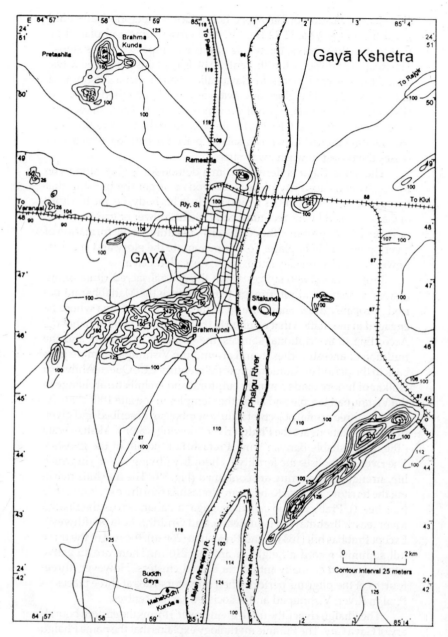

Fig. 39. Gaya Kshetra

notation it means that the river manifests the highest power of piety and merit. The two streams Lilajan and Mohana, both originating from Korambe Pahar/ hill (767 m), about 75 km south of Gaya, meet about 5 km south of Gaya and are then named Phalgu. Lilajan is a corrupt form of the old name Niranjana, a river in which the Buddha bathed and finally released his begging bowl. Flowing about 82 km north from Gaya, the Phalgu turns to the east and finally meets the Ganga. Of course, for the greater part of the year the Phalgu River remains dry. Presently there are eleven *ghats* at the left bank of the Phalgu river used for rituals, bathing and performing ancestral rites. The **Shmashan** ('cremation') **Ghat** is at the southernmost and is used only for crema- tion rituals. The area between **Gadadhara** and **Sangat Ghats** is most intensively used for various types of rituals, oblations and festivities (Fig. 40). On the right bank, facing west to Vishnupad, is the **Sita Kund** sacred cluster; the stairway to the bank is known as **Ramagaya Ghat** and is used for religious purposes associated with this cluster. The an- cestors' dark-fortnight, *Pitripaksha,* falling in *Ashvina* (September-Oc- tober), close to the autumn equinox (21st September), is the main pe- riod to perform ancestral rites. On this occasion a hundred thousand pilgrims from all parts of India come here and almost all perform vari- ous rites of different degrees at the bank of the Phalgu river.

Vishnupad ('Vishnu's footprint'). Lying in the crowded central part, in the southeast on the bank of the Phalgu, Vishnupad is a domi- nant place in Gaya. The mythology narrates the story of the demon Gayasura; his meditation and austerity endowed him with great strength and vigour. Later Brahma and Vishnu requested him to pro- vide his body to serve as an altar on which all the gods stood under the direction of Vishnu. The commemorative *Vishnu's footprint* (ca. 10 x 40 cm), imprinted on a solid rock in an octagonal basin, ca. 1.1 m in diameter, is the central point of attraction in the temple. A silver- plated basin surmounts this.

Visitors not belonging to Hinduism are not allowed to enter the temple. Until the 1950s even low caste people were not allowed to enter. The 30 m high temple of Vishnupad has 8 rows of beautifully carved pillars which support the *mandapa* (pavilion) which were re- furbished in 1787 by queen Ahilyabai Holkar of Indore, central India. King Krishna Deva and his wife Tirumala Devi in CE 1521 made a *gateway* that lies between the Vishnupad temple and the Surya tem- ple. Ranjit Pandey, minister of the king Rana of Nepal, presented the main *bronze bell* in the compound. Another bell that hangs at the entrance is a gift presented by a British Officer, named Gillander, in January 1790. Around the Vishnupad temple the Lodging House Com-

109

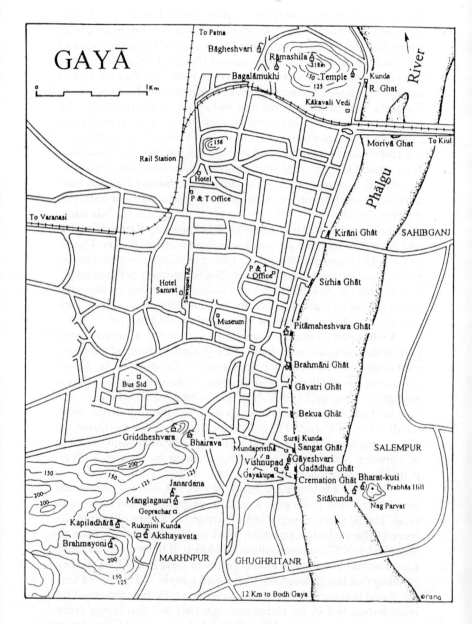

Fig. 40. Gaya Puri

mittee constructed a *dharmashala* during the 1960's, a pilgrims' rest house, a monument consisting of a park in honour of Shankaracharya, and two other parks named Vishnu and Tulasi at the back of the temple. The lack of proper maintenance and civic sense all around the temple creates an obnoxious scene. Many of the old houses and religious buildings are presently in a dilapidated condition, and some of the old spots have already been lost.

Vishnupad and the Buddha's Footprints

The Vishnupad Temple, which was rebuilt in the closing years of the 18th century by Ahilyabai Holkar, a Maratha queen, has a Vishnu footprint engraved in basalt. Now there are no distinguishing marks on it as centuries of washing and scrubbing have obliterated the usual Buddhist symbols. The majority of scholars believes that Vishnu's footprint was originally a Buddhist emblem, which was appropriated by the Hindu devotees as part of the transformation of Gaya into a Hindu site after the decline of Buddhism. Based on rigorous researches, the following conclusions will prove the point:

(i) The Buddha's footprints were carved on stone and served as an object of veneration at many Buddhist shrines as early as the 2nd century BC. In the sculptures of Bharhut (in Madhya Pradesh) we find that on the bas-relief representing Ajatashatru's homage to the Lord two footprints marked by a wheel are visible, symbolically indicating the presence of the Lord. The footprints of the Buddha were also a popular object of veneration in South India. And this is much before Vishnu's footprint was found at any Hindu site.

(ii) The city of Gaya was elevated to its present status in the Hindu world only after the downfall of Buddhism in India. Not much is known about its history before the 8th or 9th century, nor of its earlier monuments.

(iii) In order to make the Hinduised Gaya popular with the masses and to create a halo around its sanctity, the Hindus had to invent the fantastic and incredible legend of Gaya Asura.

(iv) Nowhere else in India has the worship of footprints received such a high place and honour in the cult of Hindus.

(v) The fact that the Vishnupad was once a Buddhist shrine has also been confirmed by the findings of L.P. Vidyarthi, who carried out extensive field researches at Gaya in 1951-1956.

Attached to the Vishnupad temple are many other important shrines and temples adorned with antiquities and beautiful images. In the compound of Vishnupad the **Gadadhar temple** enshrines a 1.6 m

111

standing image of Vishnu, possibly dating to the mid 11th century. Of
the same period another 1.8 m tall image of Vishnu in the **Krishna
Dvaraka temple**, with finely articulated jewellery and crisply deline-
ated features, elevates the mace and lotus above his left and right shoulders respectively.

In the **Surya Temple**, close to Vishnupad, there is a Sun image of
1.5 m in grey stone, dating to the mid 11th century. This tautly modelled erect figure stands against a black slab carved with flying figures and the seldom found images of planets (*grahas*) above his head.
The largest image of the Sun god (Surya) in Gaya, 2.44 m in grey stone,
is in a shrine at *Brahmani Ghat*, facing the Phalgu river and popularly called as Narayana by devotees.

Akshayavata ('imperishable Banyan tree'). A little over 1 km from
the Vishnupad Temple, in the southwest, at the foothill of Brahmayoni
is Akshayavata. The mythology relates that at the time of the cosmic
flood (*pralaya*) when the earth was submerged into the ocean, Lord
Vishnu ('the Preserver') took the form of a child and went into deep
sleep on a branch (or leaf) of the Banyan tree. The present Banyan
symbolises that mythic tree. The *puranic* literature describes this story
in different ways, however they all indicate its location at Gaya. Like
the mountain, such a unique tree is also symbolised as a pillar or post
serving as a link between the heavens and the earth; this sense justi-
fies its attribution to the ancestral rites. Presently, its spreading
branches shade a small shrine whose exterior walls carry many sculptures and also an inscription at the right of the doorway. Attached to
the Akshayavata is a water pool filled with lotus flowers, called
Rukminikunda.

Less than a half km to the northeast of the Akshayavata is a temple of the goddess **Mangalagauri**, believed to be one of the *Shaktipithas*,
where the breast of the corpse of Shiva's wife, Sati, fell down. The
image of the goddess is housed in a squat, cavernous mausoleum,
and on the front are inscribed the epic verses of Sati's destruction.
This shrine is also approached from the main market side by a narrow
crowded lane, after climbing 125 steps. Following a zigzag path towards the north from Mangalagauri there is an ancient temple of
Janardana (Vishnu) in a dilapidated form, containing several sculptures, which may be assigned to the 9th century. While returning from
this temple on the western slope one meets a hilly scratch containing
a rock-cut Vishnu carved on a boulder in a shrine called **Gau Prachara**,
dating to the 5th-6th centuries. About 300 m west from Akshayavata,
there is a hermitage and shrine called **Kapiladhara**. Here exists a seasonal spring believed to be a source having an underground link with

the confluence of the Ganga river in the Bay of Bengal. The hermitage of the mythical sage Kapila, called *Kapiladhara*, lies there.

Pretashila ('the rock of ghosts'). The Pretashila hill, lying at a distance of 8 km northeast of Vishnupad, was perhaps originally a site of the folk religion of spirit worship which was transformed in time into a site for ancestors worship, and later the shrine of Pretabhairavi ('the goddess of ghosts') and Vishnu were added. The *Vayu Purana* mentions that one has to offer *pindas* ('grain balls') to his ancestors on its summit (246 m), which can be reached by climbing 400 stone steps. These *pindas* are offered in the name of two forms of the 'god of death', Yamaraja and Dharmaraja and their respective carrier dogs, Shyama and Shabala. Pilgrims take a holy bath in the **Brahmakunda** (*Brahmasara*) at the foot of the hill, and offer water from this water pool to the **Brahmeshvara Shiva**, whose temple is close to the water pool. Legends say that Brahma ('the Creator') had performed his 'horse-sacrifice' ritual near this site.

Ramashila ('the rock of Rama'). About 4 km north of Vishnupad is the Ramashila hill. The old name of this hill was *Pretaparvata* ('the mountain of ghosts'). The Puranic myth suggests that all the rituals and oblations to be performed here are similar to the ones done at other important sites in Gaya. The age-old tradition of non-Brahmin overseers of the shrine still exists, while a close tie with Brahmin priests is maintained. The oblation ritual is performed at the two shrines on the summit (218 m) of the hill, named Paleshvara and Rameshvara, which one reaches after climbing 357 stone steps. At the foothill there is a temple complex; in one of the temples is a crystal-made Shiva linga. Across the dirty road in the east are **Rama Kunda** and **Rama Ghat** where pilgrims offer oblations to their ancestors. About 300 m south along the road, near the fly-over bridge of the railway, is **Kakabali Vedi** ('an altar offering oblations to crows').

Sita Kunda and Ramagaya. Prabhas hill, about 800 m east of Vishnupad, lies at the right bank of the Phalgu river. The meeting point of the hilly part and the waterfront is considered more holy for sacred bath. Pilgrims worship the Prabhas ('light manifested') Shiva *linga* and Rama by offering special rice-balls (*pindas*). The mythology tells us how all the gods were standing on the body of demon Gaya; and in the same way the goddess Lakshmi in the form of Sita, Parvati as Mangalagauri and Sarasvati as Gayatri also took their seat. Sita's image in a tiny shape exists is a small basin, known as Sita Kund. In this basin there is a *stone image of a big hand* carrying a ball, popularly explained as symbolising the right hand of Rama's father Dasharatha, who from the netherworld put his hand out to receive the *pinda* offered by Sita (Rama's wife). The priest and overseer assistants narrate this story to any visitor with elaboration and justification. Rama's brother Bharata was living in a hermitage here, so the shrine and place are now known as Bharatashram.

Uttaramanas. Near **Pitamaheshvara Ghat**, about 1 km north of Vishnupad, the holy tank of Uttaramanas is assumed to be an ancient pool which was renovated, made broader, deeper and reconstructed in the mid 11th century by king Vishvarupa's son, Yakshapala. At the waterpool of Uttaramanas, three other holy spots are manifested, viz. Udichi in the northwest corner, Dakshinamanas in the southwest corner, and Kankhal at the centre. The pilgrims offer rice-balls at all four of the above sites, followed by the bank of the Phalgu River. Altogether these five are known as *Panchatirthi*. Tonsure is a common ritual here. Close to Uttaramanas are many other temples, dedicated to Shiva and Durga, where pilgrims pay a visit but do not perform rites.

The **Mahabodhi tree** (*Ficus religiosa*) was already described in the *puranic* mythologies as a sacred spot for glancing, worship and ancestral rites. This sacred Bo (Fig) tree has a definite association with Buddhism as its spatial affinity to Bodh Gaya also testifies, however in the period of 7 days of ancestral rites, Hindu pilgrims visit this place on the 4th day. It is evident that this was an object of worship by the Hindus as early as the 7th century. However, in about 600 CE the Bengal king Shashank, a devoted adherent of Brahmanism, dug it up and burnt it with fire. It is also believed that in ca. 620 CE king Purnaverma again planted the sacred tree, and poured the milk of one thousand cows upon it, causing it to sprout again and grow 3 m in a single night.

Brahmayoni (Gayashirsha) and the Buddha

About 450 m west of the Akshayavata is Brahmayoni ('the female energy of Brahma'), or Gayashirsha (Gayasisa in Pali) hill. From its top a good view of the city is seen. To get to the summit (240 m), one has to climb up 470 high stone steps that were built by the patronage of Queen Ahilyabai Holkar in ca. 1785. There are two narrow caves (*yonis*, female organ) at the summit called *Brahmayoni* and *Matriyoni* caves. It is believed that if one passes through these caves he/she will not experience re-birth. There is a temple dedicated to *Astabhuja Devi* and to other folk goddesses at the top of the hill.

Gaya and Gayashirsha are described as well known sacred centres during the Buddhist period (e.g. *Mahavagga*, 1.21.1; and *Anguttara Nikaya*, IV.302). According to Buddhaghosha, the hill's original name was Gajashisha — Elephant's Head — because of its resemblance to a

114

crouching elephant, and the town took its name from the hill, Gaya being a variant of 'gaja'. Gayashisha was the headquarters of Devadatta, a cousin brother of Siddhartha who later became a follower monk of the Buddha. The Buddha paid a visit to this place several times. In one of his visits for a week 200 devotees of the master Gaya Kassapa were also ordained as monks, and they all became deeply devoted students of the Buddha.

One day after all the monks had returned from begging, the Buddha summoned them to gather on the slopes of the mountain in Gaya (Gayashisha). The 900 monks (*bhikkhus*) ate in silence with the Buddha and the three Kassapa brothers. When they had finished eating, they all turned their gaze to the Buddha. It was here that the Buddha delivered his celebrated Fire Sermon, the *Adittapariyaya Sutta*, to the thousand newly ordained monks (cf. *Vinaya* IV.34).

The ancient commentary says that the Buddha and his audience sat on a large flat rock while the discourse was delivered. No single rock this big can be seen today, but the shoulder beside the main summit has a large flat area of exposed rock on its top that could comfortably accommodate a thousand people. The faint traces of what was probably a *stupa* can be seen on the side of this area. To get there walk up the stairs and just after passing through the pavilion halfway up, take the rough path to the left. There is a fine view from here across the Phalgu and beyond to Pragbodhi.

Sitting serenely upon a large rock at Gayashisa (known as Brahmayoni hill), the Buddha began to speak,

"Dear Monks!, all Dhammas are on fire. What is on fire? The six sense organs — eyes, ears, nose, tongue, body and mind are all on fire. The six objects of the senses — form, sound, smell, taste, touch, and objects of mind are all on fire. The six consciousnesses — sight, hearing, smell, taste, feeling, and thought — are all on fire. They are burning from the flames of desire, hatred, and illusion. They are burning from the flames of birth, old age, sickness, and death, and from the flames of pain, anxiety, frustration, worry, fear, and despair.

"Monks! Every feeling is burning whether it is an unpleasant, pleasant, or neutral feeling. Feelings arise and are conditioned by the sense organs, objects of the sense organs, and the sense-consciousness. Feelings are burning from the flames of desire, hatred, and illusion. Feelings are burning from the flames of birth, old age, sickness, and death, and from the flames of pain, anxiety, frustration, worry, fear, and despair.

"Monks! Do not allow yourselves to be consumed by the flames of desire, hatred, and illusion. See the impermanent and interdependent nature of all *Dhammas* in order not to be enslaved by the cycle of birth and death created by the sense organs, objects of the senses, and the sense-consciousness."

In another interesting discourse, we are told that looking out from Gayashisha the Buddha could see people bathing in the river in the belief that they could wash away the evil they had done. He then uttered this verse:

"Not by water is one made pure,
Though many people may here bathe.
But one in whom there is truth and Dhamma,
He is pure, he is a brahmin."

(Uddan Sutta, 7)

The Buddha remained in Gayashisa for three months to teach the new monks, and the monks made great progress. The Kassapa brothers were talented assistants to the Buddha, and they helped him guide and teach the *sangha*. *(Samyutta Nikaya, 35.28)*

Towards the end of the Buddha's life, Devadatta split the community of monks and went off with his five hundred followers to stay at Gayashisha, where King Ajatashatru built them a monastery. The Buddha sent Maha Moggallana and Sariputta to reason with the schismatic monks and they eventually won them back.

When Hsüan-tsang visited Gaya there were only about a thousand families living in the town. By that time Gayashisha had been given an importance related to the ascension of kings. He says: "From olden days it has been the custom for the ruling sovereign when he comes to the throne, with a view to conciliate his subjects at a distance and to cause his renown to exceed previous generations to ascend the mountain and declare his succession with accompanying ceremonies." He also mentions a *stupa* on the top of the hill built by King Ashoka. Today Brahmayoni is considered sacred by Hindus. Brahmayoni is the last hill one passes when leaving Gaya on the old road that follows the river to Bodh Gaya and is easily recognized by the radio tower on its peak.

Suraj Kund

The Suraj Kund is the most popular water pool for Hindus for Sun worship. To get to Suraj Kund take the road leading to the Vishnupad Temple. About 100 m before the temple in its north, a small alley branches off to the left. Proceed down the alley and turn right. There are two small shrines along this water pool consisting of images of the Sun god and his disc. The most popular festival, called

Chatha ('worshipping the Sun god on 6th day') is celebrated twice a year in the light-half fortnights of *Chaitra* (March-April) and *Karttika* (October-November), when over about half a million Hindu devotees come to Suraj Kunda.

The tank is a rectangular body of water surrounded by a high wall made of huge blocks of well-dressed stones and with a *ghat* at one end. It was at this tank that the events described in the *Suchiloma Sutta* took place (*Sutta Nipata*, 270-273). At the side of the tank was a tower-like structure called Tankitamancha in which the *yaksha* Suchiloma (Spiky Hair) lived. It is interesting to note that this same tower is mentioned in the *Mahabharata* where it is called Brahmaripa. Suchiloma attempted, unsuccessfully, to frighten the Buddha and then asked him a question, threatening to throw him over the river if he could not answer. "From where," Suchiloma asked, "do passion and hatred spring? From where do like, dislike and fear arise? From where do evil thoughts arise and harass the mind as boys do a crow?" The Buddha answered in part:

"Passion and hatred spring from egoism,
As do like, dislike and fear.
Evil thoughts, too, spring from egoism,
And harass the mind as boys do a crow."

No traces of Tankitamancha can be seen today, but the tank's name is obviously derived from 'Suchiloma' and at the foot of the sacred tree, near the *ghat*, there are several ancient sculptures including some Buddhist *stupas*.

It is believed that after returning back from his first sermon at Sarnath, the Buddha paid a visit to Gaya accompanied by a newly-ordained thousand monks, and finally delivered several discourses here. It is doubtful that the Buddha ever returned to Gaya, probably because it was a centre for religious rituals with which he had little sympathy. In the *Vatthupama Sutta* he says:

"If you speak no lie nor harm any living being,
If you do not steal, are not mean and have faith,
What can you do by going to Gaya?
Gaya is no different from the well-water at home."
(*Majjhima Nikaya*, I.39)

117

Sacred Performance and Ritualscape

Textual and traditional Hinduism persuades devotees and pilgrims to perform ancestors-rites at Gaya in order to help the ancestors' spirits, who due to bad *karma* or untimely death may not yet be settled down, to finally get a seat in the prescribed abode of the manes. This is one of the ideals of Hindus, followed by the masses, especially in the countryside. By this the ancestral spirits get relief from the ghostly-life full of sufferings and proceed to get liberation from transmigration (*moksha*). There are two types of sacred performances most commonly related to ancestors: (a) *tarpana*, the offering of sacred water to please and purify the spirit, a type of preparatory or starting rites, and (b) *pindadana*, the offering of rice balls, a complex form of rituals performed under the guidance of specialist priests known as Gayavals, who follow several stages of rituals and performances. The *tarpana* is offered to four groups of ancestors, viz. the *devas* (divinities), the *rishis* (seven ancient holy sages), Yama (Lord of Death) and his accountant Chitragupta, and the *pitris* (immediate paternal ancestors — father, grandfather, great-grandfather and other progenitors). The 7 days ancestors-rituals are presented in Table 1.

Table 1. Gaya : Weekly Ancestors Rituals and the Spots / Vedis
Places visited and rituals performed

1st Day. Purificatory and ritual bath and water offering at the bank of the Punpun and the Phalgu rivers, and at Sita Kund; also water offering at Pretashila.

2nd Day. After a holy bath in the Phalgu river, visit Pretashila and offer water there and in the holy water pool at the foothill, Brahma Kund. Followed up by rituals at Ramashila, its foothill, Surya Kund, and Kakabali altar.

3rd Day. Visit to five sacred places, Panchatirthi : Uttarmanas, Udichi, Dakshina Manas, Kankhal, and Adi Gadadhar; visit also two images of the Sun god (Dakshinarka and Maunarka). After a holy bath in the Phalgu and initiation rites, the sacrificer may re-visit these places.

4th Day. Visit the SW part : Dharmaranya and Matangavapi; at the end perform rites at the Mahabodhi tree.

5th Day. Visit to Goprachar, Brahmayoni, Brahmasar, and special offerings of water to the mango groves near Goprachar.

6th Day. After a holy dip in the Phalgu, visit and rituals at Gayashirsh, Adi Gadadhara, Vishnupad, Gaya Kupa.

7th Day. Visit to Gadalola, Prapitamaheshvara, and the last rituals at Akshayavata. At the end return again back to Vishnupad where a donation has to be given to the priest, last ritual of thanksgiving at nearby Gayatri Ghat, and at the end worship Lord Vishnu.

The **Gaya Museum** (10.00-17.00 hrs, closed on Mondays), located near the tank from where the buses depart to Bodh Gaya, is the building next to the Dak Bungalow just near the Gaya Court. The museum is housed in a shabby, almost derelict building and has a small collection of Buddhist and Hindu sculptures, terracotta, paintings, arms and manuscripts found in and around Gaya. In fact, it is only open during the few times the curator comes.

Accommodation

There are many basic and cheap hotels, mostly concentrated near the railway station; of course these tend to be noisy. **Hotel Buddha** (Tel. 223428), down the lane opposite the railway st. on Laxman Sahay Lane is much quieter, organised around a small atrium. Several hundred meters to the right of the station, after passing Ajatashatru Hotel, the cheapest accommodation and spacious restaurant is available in **Station View Hotel** (Tel. 220512). Across the railway station on the left side, **Ajatashatru Hotel** (Tel. 221514, 223714) has a range of decent rooms with high fluctuation of charges, from Rs 300 single to Rs 600 suite. The **Hotel Siddhartha International** (Tel. 221254), 500 m to the right from the railway station, the best hotel in the city, caters to upmarket pilgrims and also has a good non-vegetarian restaurant. The room rent is Rs 1000/ 1500. Near the railway station the other reasonable choices are **Pal Rest House** (Tel; 2433139), **Madras Hotel** and **Shanti Rest House**. On Swarajpuri road, about 1 km from the railway st., **Hotel Surya** (Tel. 2224254) and nearby **Samrat Hotel** (Tel. 224004) are the other choices. Some other cheaper places are **Sri Kailash Guest House**, north of Azad Park, and **Shyam** (Tel. 222416) on Ramna Road.

Food. Most hotel restaurants on Station Rd are narrow, fly-infested holes. The exceptions are the ones attached to the good hotels. **Siddhartha** (Tel. 2436243, 2436252) in Siddhartha International and **Sujata** (Tel. 223714) in Ajatashatru are the best restaurants. The best of the budget hotel restaurants is in the **Station View Hotel**. **Punjab Hotel** on Station Rd is acceptable for Indian meals. Though restaurants are rare in other parts of the town, *dal*-and-rice *dhabas* abound en route to the Vishnupad temple. All the vegetarian eating-places in town are very basic.

Gaya is famous for a crispy sweet biscuit-like cookie, called *tilakuta*, made of sesame (*tila*) cooked in milk with a sugar coating; it can easily be preserved and used for ten days. A market lane is called as Tilakuta Bazaar. All over Bihar everywhere stalls are seen selling the popular puff-pastry sweet known as *khajja*, which originated in a village between Gaya and Rajgir. Catch them as they come out of the oil — flies are an essential part of it.

EXCURSION

Barabar Caves

The **Barabar Caves,** dating back to the 3rd century BCE, are 36 km north of Gaya. The 22 km track leading to the caves built into an impressive granite hill turns east off the main road to Patna (short route via Jahanabad) at **Belaganj** (½ hr from Gaya, 2 hr from Patna) where buses stop. From here allow 5 hr to walk up to the two groups of caves (45 km by 4 wheel-drive). Two of the caves contain Ashokan inscriptions. These are the 'Marabar' caves of E. M. Forster's classic, *A Passage to India*. These caves are the earliest examples of rock-cut sanctuaries in India. With the tolerance required by Buddhism, Ashoka permitted non-Buddhists to practice their religion. They created these rock-cut temples.

The whale-backed quartzite gneiss hill stands in a wild and rugged country. Inscriptions reveal that, on instruction from Ashoka, 4 chambers were excavated, cut and chiselled to a high polish by the stone masons. They constituted retreats for ascetics who belonged to a sect related to Jainism. Percy Brown pointed out that the extraordinary caves, particularly the *Lomasa Rishi* (Fig. 41) and the *Sudama* are exact copies of ordinary beehive shaped huts built with bamboo, wood and thatch. The barrel-vaulted chamber inside the *Sudama* is 10 m long, 6m wide and 3.5 m high, which through another inner doorway leads to a circular cell of 6m diameter. The most impressive craftsmanship is seen on the façade of the *Lomasa Rishi*, which replicates the horseshoe shaped gable end of a wooden structure with 2 lunettes that have very fine carvings of lattice-work and rows of elephants paying homage to Buddhist *stupas* (Fig. 42). These caves, dedicated to the mendicants of the Ajivika sect, dated to ca. 250 BCE, refer to Ashoka's twelfth year, the same year in which most of his edicts were built. These are the oldest architectural examples in India. Excavation is incomplete, as there was a possibility of the caves collapsing. There is also a Shiva temple on the **Siddhesvara Peak.**

About 1 km northeast from Barabar there are 3 further rock-cut sanctuaries on the **Nagarjuna Hill.** The **Gopi** ('milkmaid's') cave has the largest chamber measuring 13.5 m x 6 m in width and 3 m in height. Inscriptions date these two about 50 years after the excavations at Barabar and clearly indicate that they were cut when Ashoka's grandson Dasharath acceded to the Mauryan throne.

Fig. 41. Barabar Hills: Exterior of Lomasa Rishi cave (mid 3rd century BCE).

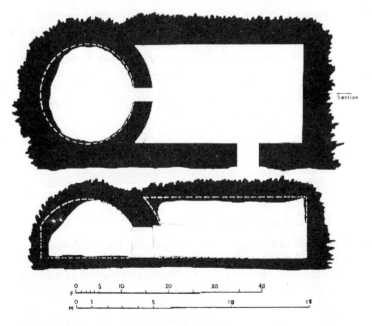

Fig. 42. Barabar Hills: Plan and elevation of Lomasa Rishi cave (mid 3rd century BCE)

5. Sarnath (Varanasi)
Where the Buddha turned 12 wheels of *Dhamma*

"Keep in mind this most beautiful wood, named by the great sages, where ninety-one thousand and over a billion of Buddhas formerly turned the Wheel. This place is matchless, perfectly calm, contemplating, always frequented by deer. In this most beautiful of parks, whose name was given by the sages, I will turn the holy Wheel."

Voice of the Buddha

Here at Sarnath, the Blessed One set the wheel of the most excellent law rolling, and he began to preach to the five bhikkhus, opening to them the gate of immortality, and showing them the bliss of Nirvana. The Buddha said: "The spokes of the wheel are the rules of pure conduct: Justice is the uniformity of their length; wisdom is the tyre; modesty and thoughtfulness are the hub in which the immovable axle of truth is fixed.

He who recognises the existence of suffering, its cause, its remedy, and its cessation has fathomed the four noble truths. He will walk in the right path. Right views will be the torch to light his way. Right aspirations will be his guide. Right speech will be his dwelling-place on the road. His gait will be straight, for it is right behaviour. His refreshments will be the right way of earning his livelihood. Right efforts will be his steps: right thoughts his breath; and right contemplation will give him the peace that follows in his footprints".

The Mahavagga, 1, 11~10, 47.

Population: 31,000 (Sarnath township).
Postal Code: 221008. STD Tel Code: 0542.

The Buddha and Kashi

The Pali text *Angutara Nikaya* mentions the 16 Mahajanapadas ('great kingdoms'), of which 'Kashi' was a powerful stronghold before the Buddha's times. However, during the period of the Buddha the kingdom went under the control of the Koshalas ruled by the king Prasenajit. The *Mahagovinda Sutta* refers that Dhritarashtra (*Pali*: Dhatarattha) was the earliest king of Kashi, and the city of Varanasi was settled by Mahagovinda, a minister of the ancient legendary king

122

Renu. The Buddhist literature *Jatakas* described Kashi (Varanasi) under different names like Surundhana (in *Udaya Jataka*), Sudarshana (*Sutasona*), Brahmavardhana (*Somananda*), Puphphavati/ Pushpavati (*Khandahala*), Rammanagar/ Ramyanagar (*Yuvanjna*), and Molini/ Mukulini (*Samrava Jataka*). Most of these names are of ephemeral nature, and some indicate its importance as a centre of philosophical discourses. In the *Cakkavati Sihanada Sutta* of the *Digha Nikaya* (3.3.3.29.2-3), it is mentioned that "in the time of Metteyya Buddho, Varanasi will be known as Ketumati ('intellect-bannered'), mighty and prosperous, full of people, crowded and well-fed". The *Guttila Jataka* eulogised Kashi as the famous city of Asia.

Even without being a capital city, Varanasi was a prosperous commercial township during the time of the Buddha. It was the main connecting centre for trade routes linking Taxila (in the west), Shravasti (in the north) and Rajagriha (in the east). By the river route, trade transactions were carried out from Varanasi to Kaushambi, Patna and Vaishali. The *Malindapajho* mentions the fine clothes made in Kashi, which were sold in the capital city of Sagala (Syalkot), ruled by the king Yavanaraj Milinda. The *Jatakas* also described Varanasi as a market place for sandalwood, crafts, fine clothes, jewellery, and training of horses and elephants.

The Pali texts narrate that after getting enlightenment at Bodh Gaya the Buddha came to know intuitively that his five old friends who had left him earlier, viz. Kondanna (Kondajja), Bhaddiya, Vappa, Mahanama and Assaji were leading an ascetic life at Isipattana Migadaya (*Sanskrit*: Rishipattana Mrigadaya, 'the deer park of Sarnath'). The Buddha reached Isipattana and soon transformed his five friends and accepted them as his first five disciples (*bhikkhu*) by preaching to them the noble rules, called Dhammacakka Pavattana (*Sanskrit*: Dharmacakra Parivartana). Soon afterwards the Buddha converted 55 noble men, including the merchant Yasha and his relatives, who became Buddhist monks and his disciples. Slowly the number of disciples reached to 60, who were sent in various directions to disseminate the message of the Buddha.

A tale from the *Nigrodhamiga Jataka* refers that the Buddha in his previous life was born as a Golden Deer at Sarnath, and saved the life of a pregnant deer. By this incidence the king of Kashi declared this territory as 'protected area', protected from hunting and preserved for mendicants and deers.

The Buddha passed his first stay during the rainy season at Sarnath, and there for the first time he challenged the fundamental, conservative and superstitious rules of Brahminism through his teaching called *Anattalakkhana Sutta*. The Pali texts have mentioned names of many great Brahmin priests in the middle Ganga valley, but no one from Kashi. This indicates that during the period of the Buddha Kashi was not a stronghold of religious-ritual institutions and was also not dominated by conservative groups.

When the retreat season ended, the Buddha returned south. He stopped by the Deer Park in Isipatana, the place where he had delivered his first *Dhamma* talk on the Four Noble Truths thirty-six years earlier.

Thirty-six years after his first teaching the Buddha visited Sarnath together with his main disciples, like Sariputta, Moggallana and Mahokotithata, and also gave religious discourses and teachings, mostly challenging the superstitious rituals, sacrifices and totemism performed under the Brahminic traditions. This second visit was later followed by several visits to Sarnath. However, after the death of the Buddha the cultural arena turned into different directions where Brahminism superseded over Buddhism.

At Sarnath, addressing his five old friends, the Buddha said,

"Listen! My friends, I have found the Great Way, and I will show it to you. You will be the first to hear my Teaching. This Dharma (Pali: *Dhamma*) is not the result of thinking. It is the fruit of direct experience. Listen serenely with all your awareness."

The Buddha's voice was filled with such spiritual authority that his five friends joined their palms and looked up at him. Kondanna spoke for them all,"Please, friend Gautama, show us compassion and teach us the Way."

The Buddha began serenely:

"My brothers, there are two extremes that a person on the path should avoid. One is to plunge oneself into sensual pleasures, and the other is to practice austerities that deprive the body of its needs. Both of these extremes lead to failure. The path I have discovered is the Middle Way, which avoids both extremes and has the capacity to lead one to understanding, liberation, and peace. It is the Noble Eight-fold Path of right understanding, right thought, right speech, right action, right livelihood, right effort, right mindfulness, and right concentration. I have followed this Noble Eightfold Path and have realised understanding, liberation, and peace.

"Brothers, why do I call this path the Right Path? I call it the Right Path because it does not avoid or deny suffering, but allows for a direct confrontation with suffering as the means to overcome it. The Noble Eightfold Path is the path of living in awareness. Mindfulness is the foundation. By practising mindfulness, you can develop concentration, which enables you to attain Understanding. Thanks to right concentration, you realise right awareness, thoughts, speech, action, livelihood, and effort. The Understanding that develops can liberate you from every shackle of suffering and give birth to true peace and joy.

"Brothers, there are four truths: the existence of suffering, the cause of suffering, the cessation of suffering, and the path which leads to the cessation of suffering. I call these the Four Noble Truths. The first is the existence of suffering. Birth, old age, sickness, and death are suffering. Sadness, anger, jealousy, worry, anxiety, fear, and despair are suffering. Separation from loved ones is suffering. Association with those you hate is suffering. Desire, attachment, and clinging to the five aggregates are suffering.

"Brothers, the second truth is the cause of suffering. Because of ignorance, people cannot see the truth about life, and they become caught in the flames of desire, anger, jealousy, grief, worry, fear, and despair.

"Brothers, the third truth is the cessation of suffering. Understanding the truth of life brings about the cessation of every grief and sorrow and gives rise to peace and joy.

"Brothers, the fourth truth is the path which leads to the cessation of suffering. It is the Noble Eightfold Path, which I have just explained. The Noble Eightfold Path is nourished by living mindfully. Mindfulness leads to concentration and understanding which liberates you from every pain and sorrow and leads to peace and joy. I will guide you along this path of realisation."

While Siddhartha was explaining the Four Noble Truths, Kondanna suddenly felt a great light shining within his own heart. He could taste the liberation he had sought for so long. His face beamed with joy. The Buddha pointed at him and said "Kondanna! You've got it! You've got it!"

(*Vinaya Mahavagga Khuddaka Nikaya* 1, and *Samyutta Nikaya*, LVI.11)

Approach and Background

Lying at a distance of about 10 km northeast of Varanasi City, Sarnath is a part of the Varanasi Municipal Corporation. Sarnath records regular connection with Varanasi by means of city buses, tourist buses, taxis, rickshaws and horse carts. The railway track linking Varanasi and Aurihar passes through Sarnath and has a *railway station* of the same name. The building of the railway station is made in a typical Buddhist architecture.

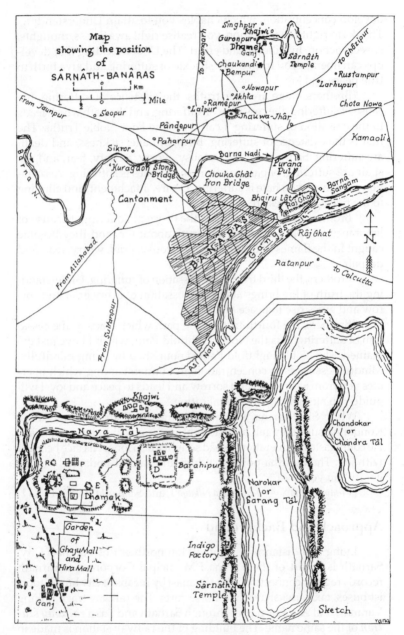

Fig. 43. Sarnath and Banaras (after A. Cunningham, ASI Report 1935-36)

Sarnath

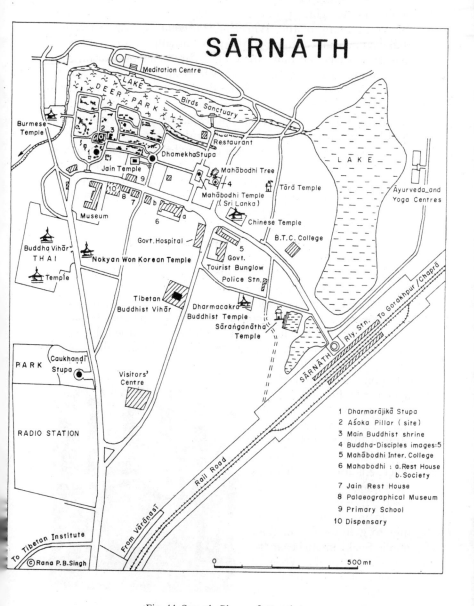

Fig. 44. Sarnath: Places of attraction

1 Dharmarājikā Stupa
2 Aśoka Pillar (site)
3 Main Buddhist shrine
4 Buddha-Disciples images:5
5 Mahābodhi Inter. College
6 Mahabodhi : a.Rest House
              b.Society
7 Jain Rest House
8 Palaeographical Museum
9 Primary School
10 Dispensary

127

All the 1,000 Buddhas of this aeon, after demonstrating the attainment of enlightenment at Vajrasana, proceed to Sarnath to give the first turning of the *'Wheel of Dhamma'*. In a like manner, Shakyamuni walked from Bodh Gaya to Sarnath in order to meet the five ascetics who left him earlier. He entered Banaras (Kashi) early one morning, made his alms round, bathed, ate his meal and, leaving by the east gate of the city, walked northwards to Isipattana Migadava, the Sage's Deer Park, i.e. present Sarnath (Figs. 43, 44). The name Deer Park derives from an occasion in one of Shakyamuni's former lives as Boddhisattva, when he was leading a herd of deer.

At this place the five ascetics resumed their austere practices. When they saw the Buddha approaching, thinking him still to be the Gautama who had forsaken their path, they decided not to welcome him. Yet, as he neared they found themselves involuntarily rising and paying respect. Proclaiming that he was Buddha, Shakyamuni assured them that the goal had been attained.

Hsüan-tsang saw a large, dome-shaped *stupa* on this spot, where a large mound, probably its remains, surrounded by an octagonal Muslim structure (now called **Chaukhandi Stupa**), stands at a short distance south from the park.

During the first watch of the night the Buddha was silent, during the second he made a little conversation and at the third began the teaching. At the site where all the Buddhas first turned the wheel, 1,000 thrones appeared. Shakyamuni circumambulated those of the three previous Buddhas and sat upon the fourth. Light radiated from his body, illuminating the 3,000 worlds, and the earth trembled. Brahma offered him a 1,000-spoked golden wheel, and Indra and other gods also made offerings, all imploring the Buddha to teach (Fig. 45).

In order to help living beings to gain control of their minds, Shakyamuni began the first turning of the Wheel of *Dhamma*. He taught the middle way that avoids the extremes of pleasure and austerity, the four noble truths, and the eight-

Fig. 45. The Buddha preaching at Sarnath
(an example of Gandhara art)

fold path. Among the five disciples Kondanna was the first to understand and realise the teaching; Assaji was the last. The rest were Vappa,
Bhaddiya and Mahanama. All eventually became *arhats*. The teaching
included in the collection known as the first turning of the wheel, which
began here, extended over a period of seven years. Other teachings,
such as those on the Vinaya and on the practice of close placement of
mindfulness, were given elsewhere, but the Wheel was turned twelve
times at Sarnath. From the time of the Buddha, monastic tradition flourished for over 1,500 years on the site of the Deer Park.

Amongst the many ruins, archaeologists have found traces dating from as early as ca. 260 BCE, and the existing inscription of
Ashoka's pillar, dating from that time, implies that a monastery was
already established during Ashoka's reign (273-232 BCE). Remains of
carved railing pillars ascribable to the Shunga period (2nd-1st century BCE) are also found here. With the advent of the Kushana (1st-
2nd century CE) parallel to the Mathura school of art Sarnath also
flourished as centre of art. The colossal image of Boddhisattva im-
ported from Mathura in the 3rd regnal year of Kanishka is now exhibited in the museum. By the Gupta period (4th-6th century CE) Sarnath
was established as a great seat of Buddhist art, producing exquisite
sandstone images of the Buddha. The Chinese pilgrim Fa-hsien (ca.
405 CE) narrated its scenic beauty and glory at the time of
Chandragupta II (CE 376-414) (cf. Fig. 46).

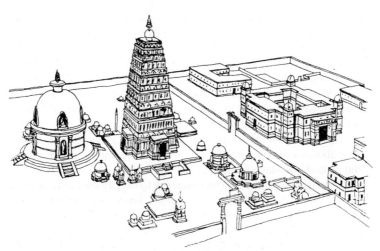

Fig. 46. Sarnath: Reconstructed plan of the township of Sarnath (after Brown, 1962)

Dhamekha Stupa

Formerly, two great *stupas* adorned the site. Only the **Dhamekha** remains, assigned by its inscription to the 6th century. The **Dharmarajika** *stupa* built by Ashoka, some say upon the very place of the teaching, was pulled down in the 18th century by Jagat Singh, who consigned the casket of relics contained within it to the Ganga River. Hsüan-tsang (ca. 635 CE) tells us that the Ashoka's pillar, which stood in front of the *stupa*, was so highly polished that it constantly reflected the *stupa*'s statue of the Buddha. Banaras, which was the second city to reappear following the last destruction of the world, was also a site of the previous Buddha's manifestations. Kashyapa, the third Buddha of this aeon, built a monastery near the Deer Park, where he ordained the Brahmin boy Jotipala, an earlier incarnation of Shakyamuni. Hsüan-tsang records *stupas* and an artificial platform at the places where several previous Buddhas walked and sat in meditation. The Deer Park was also the location of Shakyamuni's deeds as a Boddhisattva in former lives. Hsüan-tsang mentions a number of *stupas* commemorating these near the monastery. The first was where the Boddhisattva offered himself as a deer, the second, where, as a six-tusked elephant, he offered his tusks to a deceitful hunter; and a third where the Boddhisattva had been a bird, with Moggallana and Sariputta as a monkey and an elephant.

During the reign of Skandagupta (CE 455-467) Sarnath had flourished, but later was destroyed by Huna. Again since the 8th century the town was continuously expanding its glory until 1017 when Mahmud of Ghazni destroyed most of the monuments, destruction that was repeated again in 1033 by Ahmad Nialtgin. However, during the reign of then Gahadavala king Govindachandra (1114-1154), with the support of his Buddhist wife Kumaradevi, the town was rebuilt, repaired and monuments were preserved. Kumaradevi built a large monastery at Sarnath, which is probably the last of the impressive monuments raised here, after which the architectural and artistic activities came to a halt. Again in ca. 1193 the Turk king destroyed and abandoned the monuments at Sarnath.

In 1567 the Mughal emperor Akbar made a memorial octagonal tower above one of the ruined stupas in memory of his father, Humayun, who visited and stayed there in 1532. Afterwards only in 1793 Sarnath came into light with the destruction work to supply the building materials for making a market by Jagat Singh. Thereafter during the 19th century several excavations were done by Alexander Cunningham (1834-36), Markham Kittoe (1851-52), C.A. Horn (1865), and by A. Rivett-Carnac (1877). Followed up excavations were continued by F. O. Oertel (1904-05), John H. Marshall (1907), H. Hargreaves (1914-15) and Daya

Ram Sahni (1927-32). In February 1912 the first archaeological site museum was opened at Sarnath. In the period of 30th December 1990 to 1st January 1991 the 14th Kalachakra Puja (a Buddhist-Tantric ritual process) was held at Sarnath under the guidance of H.H. the 14th Dalai Lama, Tenzin Gyatso. The archaeological area is spread over an area of 16.73 ha, enshrining many monuments and *stupas;* the religious and historical monuments are spread over an area of 9.59 ha.

Chaukhandi Stupa. About 600 m before the museum along the main road, on the left side one encounters the first *stupa.* Through the recent renovation, landscape gardening and preservations the scenic beauty of the area becomes more attractive. Based on archaeological excavations it is believed that this *stupa,* or a terraced temple, appears to be constructed prior to the times of Gupta kings, i.e. 5th century. This site is assumed to be the actual spot where the Buddha after his enlightenment met five ascetics who earlier had left him in disgust at his alleged backsliding, and to whom he finally gave the First Sermon, "The Four Noble Truths". The Persian inscription over one of the doorways of the *stupa* reads, "As Humayun, king of the Seven Climes, now residing in paradise, deigned to come and sit here one day, thereby increasing the splendour of the sun, so Akbar, his son and humble servant, resolved to build on this spot a lofty tower reaching to the blue sky." By the order of Akbar, Govardhan, son of Raja Todarmal, the finance secretary in Akbar's court, built this octagonal tower on top of the *stupa* in 1588 (Fig. 47).

Fig. 47. Sarnath: Chaukhandi Stupa

Padma Samye Dharma Chakra Vihar (Tibetan Temple)

From the Sarnath-Ashapur crossing, at a distance of 350 m, close to the Chaukhandi Stupa, on the right a road leads to this temple (House: SA-10/9KA, Sarnath, Tel: 2586296). This temple was patronised by Khonzen-Palden-Sherab and Khenpo Tsenangun Gyal and opened in 1996. The entrance is at the east. The local management is under the control of Premaji Yaltjen. One of the main objectives behind its construction is to provide basic and religious-moral education to poor and orphan Tibetan children. The students receive training and education for 8-10 years and afterwards they will return to their native places and serve their society to make it more harmonious and educated.

The Thai Temple (*The Mrigadayavana Mahavihara Society*)

About 350 m north towards the Chaukhandi Stupa on the main road going to the Museum and archaeological site, one meets the Thai Temple on the left. Under the leadership of Ven. Phrakru Prakassmadhikun a group of Thai pilgrims visited Sarnath in 1969 to pay homage to Lord Buddha. This group visited all the sacred Buddhist sites in India. Though the leader of the group was pleased to find quite an appreciable number of Buddhists in India, he was quite justifiably concerned to see a negligible number of Buddhist temples and institutions. With this feeling, on 27th January 1969 a committee was constituted to develop a temple compound and an associated institution. The foundation stone was laid on 28 November 1974, and on 10 February 1976 this was opened for visitors. The recently built (1993) temple of the Hinayana sect in this compound contains the stone statue of the Buddha in the posture of *bhumisparshamudra*, "the earth-touching gesture", symbolising the Buddha's response by calling the earth-spirit to witness his enlightenment. The underground hall of this temple is used as meditation hall. A primary school (grades 1st to 5th) is also attached to the temple. The headquarters of the temple trust, *Mrigadayavana Mahavihara Foundation*, is in Bangkok (Thailand).

About 185 m north on the main road, you can get off the vehicle to see the museum and walk around the archaeological site, the religious monuments and the Deer Park.

The Archaeological Museum

Open everyday except Fridays, 10 am to 5 pm, Entry Fee Rs 5. At least 3 hrs time should be spared for a deeper understanding of the exhibits. The creation of the 'Site' Museum at Sarnath was initiated by Dr. J.H. Marshall, the then Director-General of Archaeology in India, who was personally involved in the excavations at Sarnath. The building and architectural plans were prepared by James Ransome, late consulting architect to the Government of India, and by early 1909 the building was completed. By December 1910 the work of arranging the sculptures had just been started and by February 1912 the work was completed and opened to visitors. The central hall, called Shakyasimha gallery (2.5 x 11 x 9 m) is attached to two galleries at the sides (Fig. 48). These two galleries are further attached to associated galleries. Altogether there are over 2700 objects.

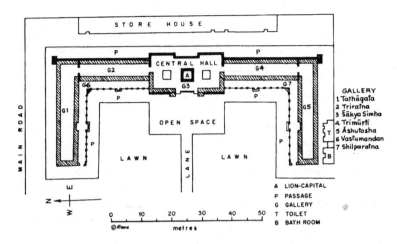

Fig. 48. Sarnath: Plan of the Archaeological Museum

The oldest and the finest piece of sculpture found at Sarnath is the **Ashokan Lion-Capital,** carved out of a single block of black-spotted buff-coloured sandstone from Chunar, which is placed in the Shakyasimha hall (central), and which is the 'National Emblem' of the Republic of India 'Bharat' (Fig. 49). It measures 2.31 m in height and is of the Persepolitan bell-shaped type, surmounted by four magnificent lions sitting back with a wheel between them, perhaps symbolising the Law of the Buddha. It consisted of four parts from bottom upwards, viz. (1) bell-shaped base covered with inverted lotus leaves, (2) a round abacus adorned with the figures of four animals, (3) four seated front faces of lions emerging from one block, and (4) a crowning *dharmachakra* with 32 spokes of which only four fragments were recovered. The four animal figures on the abacus are described in several ways. Some ascribe them to great events in the life of Buddha, i.e. a lion (symbol of the *Shakya* clan to which he belonged), a bull (zodiac *Taurus* in which he was born), the elephant (his mother

Fig. 49. Sarnath,
Lion Capital
(ca. mid 3rd century BCE)

Mayadevi's dream about the appearance of a divine creature) and a horse (on the back of which he left his home). Respectively, these animals also symbolise the natural order, farming, strength, and speed — the four basic aspects of the Buddhist theory of cosmic integration. In this way the **Capital** refers to the overall nature of Buddhism. According to a popular explanation these four animals denote the four directions as laid down in Buddhist literature in connection with the Anotatta Lake in which the Buddha used to bathe. The same animals have been depicted on a pillar at Anuradhapura (Sri Lanka).

The standing image made of red stone, 2.87 m high, showing an inscribed **colossal Bodhisattva** in the *abhayamudra* ('posture of imparting security') in the central hall is a representative of the Mathura school of Art. Monk Bala dedicated it in the 3rd regnal year of the Kushana ruler Kanishka. The octagonal shaft now set up behind the statue once carried a beautifully carved **monolithic parasol** exhibited at the northern side of the hall. This stone-umbrella is 3.05 m in diameter, and is adorned with concentric circular bands of decoration. The pierced projecting portion in the centre assumes the shape of a bloomed lotus flower bearing auspicious signs. On the outside of the rim of the umbrella are small narrow holes cut at distances of 0.48 m from one another, from which probably streamers, flower garlands or other similar objects were suspended by the Buddhist votaries in past days. The **images of Buddha** in different postures like *varadamudra* (gift bestowing attitude), *dhyanamudra* (attitude of contemplation), *abhayamudra* (attitude of granting security), lying in the central hall, are known for their elegance, simplicity of forms and sublimity; they are representative of the Sarnath school of Art.

In the left side central gallery (Triratna), a **standing Tara**, holding in a hand a pomegranate which has burst upon to reveal a row of seeds, is a fine example of the sculptural art of the 5th century. The weight of the body is thrown gently on the right leg. The jewellery is rich, yet delicate and consists of a multi-stranded girdle, festooned armlets, and a series of 3 necklaces. Large circular earrings adorn the ears. Although the face is damaged, the gentle meditative expression remains. A **Leograph**, a mythical animal, a seated **Bodhisattva Padmapani** with a stem of full-bloomed lotus, a stele depicting the miracle of Shravasti when the Buddha multiplied himself in many forms in order to defeat heretical teachers, a pot-bellied **Jambhala**, the god of wealth and prosperity along with his female consort Vasudhara, the **Ramagrama Stupa** being protected by *nagas*, and the **inscription of Kumaradevi**, the Buddhist queen of the Gahadavala king Govindachandra which refers to the construction of the

Dharmachakra Jinavihara by the queen, are some of the important antiquities displayed in the Triratna gallery. The stele depicting *ashtamahasthana* (eight great places), four of them associated with the main life events of the Buddha (cf. Figs. 5 and 9) and four with his great miracles is another important piece in this gallery.

The northeast gallery (Tathagata) displays images of the Buddha, **Vajrasattva, Bodhisattva Padmapani** with a stem of full-bloomed lotus in his hand, **Nilakantha Lokeshvara** with a cup of poison, and **Maitreya** standing and holding a nectar vase in his left hand and a rosary in his right hand with a stupa in the head-dress.

The most notable and the best sculpture of the Sarnath School of Art is the image of **Buddha in *dharmacakramudra*** (the pose showing 'Turning the Wheel of Law'), which is made of Chunar sandstone and retains traces of red colouring (Fig. 50). This image (1.6 m high up to the top of the halo, 0.79 m width at base), preaching the first sermon at Sarnath seated cross-legged on a thick cushion supported on a seat with moulded legs, is lying at a corner in the Tathagata gallery. This image is a remarkable example of the Buddha's personality as the Compassionate One, glowing with spirituality and inner-bliss. The calm, relaxed and introspective face is adorned with the gentlest smile playing on the sensuous lips, drooping eyes, aquiline nose, gently curved eyebrows joined with each other, ears with distended lobes, and rows of curls covering the head sacred cranial protuberance (*Ushnisha*). The fingers connected to each other by a thin webbing of stone and the transparent drapery make this image remarkable and impressive. The halo is carved with a pair of celestial figures and conventionalised floral scrollwork. The *dharmachakra* occupies the central position of the pedestal, on both sides of which has been placed the figure of a deer, denoting the place as Mrigadava (deer park). On the lower part of the image the figures of the five disciples to whom the Buddha preached the first sermon are depicted along with a lady and child, probably representing the donor of the sculpture.

The Trimurti gallery, lying on the southern side, exhibits mostly Brahmanical deities, including the **Trimurti** (Brahma, Vishnu and Shiva), Surya, Sarasvati, and Mahishasuramardini (Durga). Some secular objects like figures of birds, animals, male and female heads ranging from the 3rd century BCE to the 12th century CE are displayed in different showcases. Benevolent and malevolent figures of **Kirtimukha** (face of victory) are utilised as doorkeepers for the Ashutosh (Shiva) gallery in the southern part.

The Ashutosh gallery exhibits *Brahmanical deities* like Shiva, Vishnu, Ganesha, Karttikeya, Agni, Parvati, Navagrahas (the Nine

Fig. 50. Buddha in the preaching pose

planets) with Ganesha, Lakshmi and Sarasvati. A panel depicting the **Navagrahas** with Brahma, Vishnu and Shiva is also remarkable. Shiva as Bhairava (an aggressive form of Shiva) is one of the finest Brahmanical images found at Sarnath. A colossal **Andhakasuravadha** (killing of the demon Andhaka) image of a ten-armed **Shiva** in his terrific form is an unfinished sculpture, dated ca. the 12th century. Spearing his adversary, Andhaka or Tripura, Shiva holds his head on his trident with two of his hands, right and left. A second right hand holds a sword; a third holds two arrows; a fourth his *damaru* (drum) and the fifth grasps an uncertain object that is broken at the upper end. The second left hand holds the mace, adorned with a skull (*khatvanga*); the third grasps a shield, the handle of which is visible; the fourth supports the bowl for catching the blood of the demon Andhaka; and the fifth holds a bow of double flexure (*pinaka*). Made in medieval style, dated ca. the 12th century CE, a **Nataraja Shiva** image shows him engaged in wild dance (*tandava*). His head and feet are broken off, so is also the right hand, which was thrown up. He bears a long garland of human skulls (*munda-mala*) and holds a tri-dent (*trishula*) in the left hand.

Two verandas, in the south and north, named *Vastumandan* and *Shilparatna*, exhibit mostly architectural remnants. A large lintel de-picting the story of **Shantivadina Jataka** is a beautiful piece of art.

The Archaeological & Excavation Area

At the left of the gate purchase an entry ticket: US $ 5 (equivalent in rupees, i.e. Rs 240 at present) for foreigners, and Rs 5 for Indians and Nepalese.

Monastery V and **VII**. Near the starting point from the entrance to the archaeological area, one finds two monasteries on the right and left of the path. Mj. Markhan Kittoe excavated the right one, **Monas-tery V**, in 1851-52. It contains an open courtyard, 15.25 sq.m, a series of cells, 2.6 m by 2.65 m, and a well in the centre of the court. This is a structure named *Catuhsalasangharama*. In front of the cells inside the courtyard was a veranda supported on pillars. The central room on the inner side was the reception, or entrance-chamber (*pratyupa-sthanshala*). This plan gives a clear idea of the most common monas-tery in the Gupta and later periods (Fig. 51).

The left one, **Monastery VII**, belongs to the medieval period. It was built on the ruins of an older structure consisting of an open court-yard, 9.15 sq.m in area, and is surrounded by a running veranda and ranges of cells on all sides. It is believed that the monasteries V and VII were destroyed by fire.

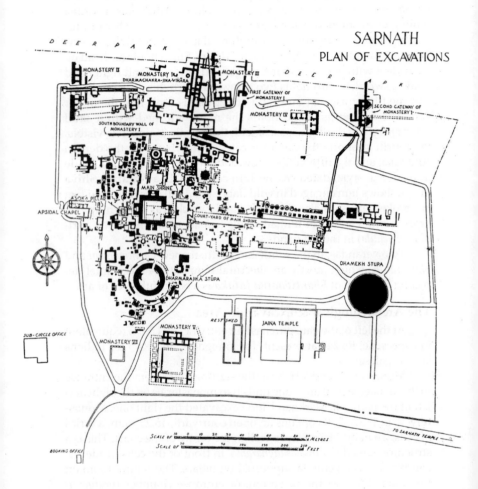

Fig. 51. Sarnath: Archaeological area

Dharmarajika Stupa. This *stupa,*
built by Ashoka in the 3rd century BCE,
represents one of the light 'Divine Towers', all of them making reference to certain leading events in the life of the Buddha. In 1794, Jagat Singh, Dewan of the
Maharaja of Banaras, pulled it down,
and a green marble casket containing
human bones and pearls was found.
From the successive excavations at
Sarnath, it has been revealed that the
Dharmarajika Stupa was enlarged six
times in succession (Fig. 52). The first
enlargement was done in the Kushana
period with brick measuring 38.1 x 26.2
x 7 cm. The second was made during

Fig. 52. Sarnath: Reconstructed
plan of Dharmarajika
(after Brown, 1962)

the 5th-6th centuries CE with the addition of circumambulation path
(*pradakshinapatha*), nearly 4.88 m wide, comprising a stone fencing of
1.35 m height and having four directional gates. The third was ef-
fected in the 7th century, during the period of Harsha, when the
pradakshinapatha was filled up and access to the *stupa* was provided by
placing four monolithic staircases. The fourth and fifth enlargements
were attributed to the 9th and 11th centuries. The sixth, the last enlargement, was done when the Dharmachakra Jina Vihar monastery
of Kumaradevi was built in the 12th century. The best known statue
of the Buddha in the gesture of *dharmachakra* was found at this site.

Main Shrine. This ruined shrine (3rd century BCE and 5th century CE) is a rectangular building of 29 x 27 m with doubly recessed
corners and 5.5 m high. The building, marking the place of the Buddha's meditation, is attributed to Ashoka and the later Guptas. The
concrete path and interior brick walls were added later to reinforce
the building. To the rear is the 5 m lower portion of a polished sandstone Ashokan Column (3rd century BCE). The original was about 15
m high with a lion capital that is now in the archaeological museum.

Ashokan Lion-pillar. The Lion-Pillar at Sarnath is the finest and
the most famous of all the examples of Mauryan art. Discovered in
1905, this consists of a shaft made of a single piece of block of black
spotted buff-coloured sandstone that supports a capital made of another single piece of stone. The inscribed stump of the Ashokan column, presently of a height of only 2.03 m, was originally 15.25 m high,
and it was surmounted by the famous Lion-capital with a crowning
dharmachakra fitted above the heads of the four lions, on a contrivance

139

into a groove in the centre. The portion of the pillar embedded in the ground in rough rests on a large flat stone, 20.3 x 15.2 x 45.7 cm. The pillar bears *three inscriptions*. The first, an edict of Ashoka in Brahmi characters refers to the emperor giving a warning to the monks and nuns against creating schism. The second is of the Kushana period and refers to the 40th year of Ashvaghosha. The third inscription, an early Gupta script, mentions the teacher of the Sammitiya sect and the Vastiputraka School.

Mulagandhakuti Vihara (ancient). This monument, square on plan, measuring 18.29 m along each side, represents the main shrine where the Buddha used to sit in meditation for three months during the rainy season. According to Hsüan-tsang it was 61 m high. The style of decoration and moulding indicate that the monument was raised in the Gupta period. The concern pavement round the monument was added later when the brick walls were also added inside the main chamber to give support to the roof (Fig. 53).

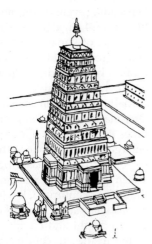

Fig. 53. Sarnath: Reconstructed plan of Mulagandha Kutivihara (after Brown, 1962)

Dhamekha Stupa (Sanskrit: *Dharmachakra*). This spot is believed to be exactly the place where the Buddha delivered his Second Sermon on *Anattalakkhana Sutta* to his five disciples. This monument is considered to be the most important and sacred among the structures at Sarnath. This solid cylindrical tower, 28.5 m in diameter at the base and 33.5 m in height, or 42.1 m including the foundations, consists of a circular drum to a height of 11.2 m, resting on the ground without the usual rectangular basement (Fig. 54). It shows 8 faces at a height of 6 m, each with an arched recess for an image. Below the arched recess is a band of design. The upper band of ornamentation is generally a scroll of the lotus plant with leaves and buds only; while the lower

Fig. 54. Sarnath, Dhamekha Stupa (perspectives of the ancient and the present)

band also having a lotus scroll contains full-blown flowers and buds. The upper portion of the *stupa* is built of large bricks. The outer facing of this portion has now vanished and it is very difficult to say whether this part was also cased in stone like the lower portion or only plastered over. Cunningham opines that this portion might have been simply plastered over. The central portion is elaborately decorated with Gupta designs, e.g. luxuriant foliation, geometric patterns, birds and flowers — the most intricate scroll-pattern (Fig. 55). The well known figures of the Boddhisattva standing and the Buddha teaching were found around this monument.

Dharmachakra Jina Vihar

Referred as *Monastery I*, lying 232 m from east to west and occupied by a central block of buildings, this monument was the gift of Kumaradevi, the Buddhist queen of the great Gahadavala king Govindachandra of Kashi (CE 1114-1154). All the halls and apartments of the monks have disappeared. This monastery had two gateways towards the east, there being a distance of 88.45 m between the two. At the westernmost edge of the site a distinct covered passage leads to a small medieval shrine.

Burmese Monastery

The Maha Wijitawi Sima or the Burmese (Myanmar) Temple is built on the low land west of the excavation area. It was built in CE 1934 by Daw Ryu with her daughter Ma Than Nyun, and Daw Goom with her son Maung Hla Khaing of Rangoon (Burma). There lies a Buddhist image made of white marble with two other images of the Lord's disciples. U. Shwe Hlwa Myomathugyi, Dawtlla and Sons, Bassein, Daw Pyu, Daw Goon and Sons of Rangoon donated the Buddha image. In front of the temple there is a library building, *Saddhammaransi Library*, built by the donation of U. Shwe Win and his wife. In the open courtyard a Buddha image was installed under an umbrella in 1994.

Vajra Vidya Sansthan

Located about 450 m north from the Mahabodhi Temple in the village Khajuri, the 'Vajra Vidya Institute & Monastery' is the latest addition in the sacred territory of Sarnath. Following the road behind the Sale Counter of the museum, one meets the Burmese Monastery, and continuing along the same road about 1 km through Srinagar Bazar one reaches the monastery. Spread over one hectare of land this monastery was constructed by the patronage of Thrangu

Photographed og D. Tresham, Esq.

Photographed by D. Tresham, Esq.

Fig. 55. Sarnath, Dhamekha Stupa, details of carving (after Sherring 1868: pp. 240-241)

Tulku Rinpoche, a Buddhist Bhikshu (monk) of Sikkim. This is a unique example of the integration of ancient and modern Tibetan architecture. Its construction started on 18 December 1993 and was completed on 29 October 1999; it costs IN Rs 20 million. It consists of a 4.6 m tall image of Shakyamuni Buddha; this image made of brass with a thick layer of golden polish is unique and unparalleled in Sarnath. The ceremony of 'putting life into the image' (*prana-pratistha*) was performed during 29-31 October 1999. Officially His Highness The 14th Dalai Lama Tenzin Gyatso inaugurated it on 15 December 1999, i.e. the 7th day of the 11th month of the Female Iron Rabbit year, and opened it for the public. Together with the main image of Shakyamuni there are 30 more images, each 1 m high, of the Buddha in different gestures, and 1000 images of the Buddha each 20 cm high. There are also images of Tara inside the main hall. In the inner court-yard there are images of Mahakala, Brahma, Indra and several other Hindu gods. The basic plan and architectural design of this temple are based on the Great 'Samyasha' Buddhist Vihara, which is itself a replica of the Buddhist Vihara at Odantapuri in Bihar. This Institute also runs master degree courses of five years on Buddhist philosophy, religion and meditation.

Jain Temple

Standing in the immediate vicinity of the Dhamekha Stupa, this temple was erected in 1824 to commemorate the penance and birth of the 11th Jain Tirthankara *Shreyamsanatha*, whose imposing image is enshrined there. The interior of the temple is decorated with attractive frescos depicting the life of Lord Mahavira. The present site of the temple is believed to have formed a part of the village Simhapur in the ancient past; this may be compared to a village of the same name existing at a distance of about 1.5 km from this place.

Mulagandhakuti Vihara (Sri Lankan Mahabodhi Temple)

Some way east of the ruins, through the gardens, is the Mulagandhakuti Vihara, built in 1931 by the great Anagarika Dharmapala (1864-1933), the founder of the Mahabodhi Society. In many ways, the temple represents the universality of the Buddha's teachings. Most of the funds for the temple were provided by Mrs Mary Foster, Anagarika Dharmapala's American patron. A British nobleman, Sir Harcourt Butler, laid the foundation of this temple in November 1922 (Fig. 56). Raja Shiva Prasad, Raja Moti Chand and Rajarshi Udai Pratap Singh gave the major share of donations of land and money.

Fig. 56. Sarnath, Mahabodhi Sri Lankan Temple

Made of Chunar red sandstone with simple carvings of conventional bell designs, this *vihara* was opened to the public by its inauguration on 11 November 1931, which was attended by representatives from almost every Buddhist country. The chief feature of this temple is a series of interior *frescos* drawn by a Japanese artist, **Kosetsu Nosu**. Nosu was inspired by the *Buddhacharita* (*The Acts of the Buddha*) and worked almost single-handed taking a period of four years (1932-36) in order to put his composition of frescos together piece by piece. The motifs of the frescos comprise episodes and scenes from the life of the Buddha, from his birth to *parinirvana*, the great end of his mortal frame. During that period Rs 10,000 were spent on these frescos; an English Buddhist B.L. Browton donated this entire amount. The Mahabodhi Society of Japan presented the **huge bell** in the corridor leading to the temple, which is supposed to emit its echo up to a distance of 8 km. The temple also possesses a pot containing certain relics of the Buddha.

The **21 Wall Paintings** on the walls of the Mulagandhakuti Vihara contain the following scenes:

South wall:
1. The Bodhisattva in the Tushita Heaven awaiting to be reborn;
2. Mahadevi's auspicious dream at the Bodhisattva's conception;
3. The Bodhisattva's birth in Lumbini Park;
4. Prince Siddhartha spontaneously attaining *jnana* while watching his father perform the annual ploughing festival;
5. The Four Sights that prompted Prince Siddhartha to renounce the world in quest of truth;
6. The prince taking his last look at his wife and new-born child before leaving the palace.

West wall:
7. Accompanied by Channa and mounted upon his steed Kanthaka, the Bodhisattva riding into the night;
8. Taking instruction from his teachers;
9. Weakened by years of austerities, the Bodhisattva accepts food from Sujata while his five companions look on with disapproval;
10. Mara and his army attacking;
11. The Buddha being greeted by the five companions who had formerly abandoned him as he arrives in Sarnath to teach them the *Dhamma*;
12. Preaching to King Bimbisara;
13. Anathapindika's purchase of the Jetavana.

East wall:
14. The Buddha and Ananda nursing a sick monk who has been neglected by his fellow monks;
15. The Buddha reconciling the Shakyans and the Koliyans who are about to go to war over the water in the Rohini River;
16. The Buddha returning to Kapilavastu;
17. The Buddha attaining final Nirvana while Anuruddha exhorts the monks not to cry. On the right is the wandering ascetic Subhadda who became the Buddha's last disciple;
18. The Buddha teaching the Abhidhamma to his mother in the Tavatimsa Heaven;
19. The conversion of Angulimala;
20. Devadatta and Ajatasattu scheming to kill the Buddha and King Bimbisara;
21. Ananda asking a girl to give him some water. She hesitates, saying that she is an out-caste. Emphasising the Buddhist rejection of the Hindu caste system, Ananda says to the girl: "I did not ask you what your caste was. I asked you for water." The story is from the *Divyavadana*.

The main shrine in the Mulagandhakuti Vihara contains relics believed to be those of the Buddha, found in a *stupa* at Taxila, and another one at Nagarjunakonda and presented to the Mahabodhi Society by the Viceroy of India, Lord Irwin. Behind the shrine is the small *stupa* containing the ashes of Anagarika Dharmapala. Directly behind the temple itself is a park for deer, and right behind that is a monument marking the site where Dharmapala's body was cremated. To the right of the main path leading to the entrance of the temple is a statue of Anagarika Dharmapala, arms folded in front of him, looking down sternly.

Right hand side to the Mulagandhakuti Vihara, across the lane, is the **Bodhi Tree**, a sampling of the Bodhi Tree at Anuradhapura, Sri Lanka, that was bought and planted by Ven. Anagarika Dharmapala in 1931. Attached to it is a small platform with a pavilion built in 1989 by the Burmese Buddhist Society, consisting of statues of the Buddha preaching to his first five disciples, viz. Kondanna, Vappa, Bhaddiya, Mahanama and Assaji. A beautifully carved gate was also built in 1999, and all around the Bodhi tree Bodhisattva images are arranged in glass chambers. After a 100 m straight walk you can reach to the Deer Park and a small **Zoo** consisting of crocodiles, alligators, and migratory birds like herons.

Deer Park

As already mentioned, in Buddhist literature Sarnath was known as *Mrigadava* (the resort of deers) and the description tells us that hundreds of deer lived there in the time of Buddha. The present Deer Park has been set up as a memorial of that ancient Mrigadava. A number of deer are still preserved in the park by the State Government of Uttar Pradesh. This park came into being on the occasion of the 2500th *Mahaparinirvana* Day of Buddha, which was gloriously observed at Sarnath and all over India. The park area covers a little over 4 ha, running along a lake. Over Rs 4 million had been spent by the Govt. of Uttar Pradesh in beautifying the site of Sarnath. Coming out of the temple compound one finds the office of the **Mahabodhi Society**. This is the biggest and oldest of all the Buddhist institutions in Sarnath. It forms a branch of the Mahabodhi Society, which was shifted from Colombo (Sri Lanka) to Kolkata in 1891.

Korean Temple

This temple is about 350 m north from the main crossing, near Mahabodhi Inter College. John Kinz built it, and it is run under the supervision of Bisuddha Bhante. It was inaugurated on 1st February

1996, and covers an area of 0.61 ha. The main entrance to the temple faces the south. The inner sanctum consists of a Buddha image made of marble.

Chinese Temple

By walking about 200 m east towards the Railway Station, on the left stands the Chinese Temple that was founded in 1939 by Ven.Te-Yu, a disciple of His Holiness Tao-Kai, Abbot of Beijing, and Fa-Yuan-Tsu, the President of the Eastern Asian Buddhist association. A banker of Singapore, named Lee Choong Seng, gave the main fund. The gate and the compound wall of the temple were erected in 1952 by Rev. Pau-Chao and Rev. Cheu-Tsau, High Priests and successors of the late Ven. Te-Yu, out of donations from the overseas Chinese in India. There is a main hall, square in shape, having a beautiful marble image of the Buddha at the centre. The image was sculpted in Burma, and gives a fine and lively impression of Burmese art and craft.

Saranganatha (Shiva) Temple

Following the road that goes straight from the Chinese temple to the Railway Station, 150 m before the station turn right and visit the solitary temple on a high mound, dedicated to Shiva in his form of 'Lord of the Deer', known as the Saranganatha. In the same cascade there is another *linga* called Shobhanatha. On the eastern side of the temple is a big tank, sometimes full of lotus flowers. It is believed that this temple is built on the site of an ancient shrine of the Shaivite cult developed in the historical past. During the month of *Shravana* (July-August) the whole neighbourhood converges into a festive environment, which attracts people everyday to enjoy a religious picnic by offering flowers and sweets to Saranganatha and cooking special food on open fires in the gardens. About 150 m west on the lane, there is a Japanese temple.

Nichigatsuzan Horinji (Japanese) Temple

About 100 m west of the Saranganatha Temple, the Dharmachakra Indo-Japanese Society has built a temple, covering an area of 2500 sq.m, which is known as **Indo-Japanese Temple** (*Na Mu Myo Ho Ren Ge Kyo*). Its land purification ceremony was performed on the 30th September 1986. Made in the Japanese pagoda style, the tiles and other important objects were brought from Japan; its cost was above IN Rs 10 million. The Mitsusui Construction Co. supervised the construction, and it was finally opened to the public on 21st November 1992. In the inner sanctum there is an image of the Buddha in the meditation posture along with several Bodhisattvas. Going further west on the lane one comes to the main road. About 100 m south on the main road you will find the Tibetan Buddhist Vihara.

Tibetan Buddhist Vihara (Temple)

In 1955, under the leadership of the monk Goshelama, the refugees of the Sino-Tibetan War have built this monastery and temple. The largest image of the Buddha in Sarnath is in this temple. There are 9 other images also, 2 of them are of the Buddha, 2 of his disciples, one of Tara, one of Maiteya, one of Rev. Tsong Khapa of Tibet and 2 of his followers. Rev. Tsong Khapa belonged to the Gelupa sect of Tibetan Buddhism; the other 3 notable sects in Tibet are Nyingapa, Shakya, and Kagyudpa. Hundred of Tibetans, irrespective of their sect, come every year in order to worship in this temple. Inside the temple are preserved 150 rare Buddhist scriptures that were translated into the Tibetan language during CE 7th-9th century. Another astonishing item of the temple is a number of frescos made on cloth wall hanging; they are several hundred years old but their colours are still bright and fresh. Following the road further down at the junction to the main road, you find Rangoli Restaurant, an excellent place to have food. Going further about 300 m turn right, and following the road you will reach the Tibetan Institute.

Singhpuri Tirtha

In 1800 Acharya Kushalachandra Suri built a Jain temple in the village Hiramanpur as was evident by an inscription at the gate — now disappeared. Hiramanpur lies at 1.5 km southeast from Sarnath, across the rail track. The image of Shreyamsanatha in the form of Mulanayaka-Ji is installed here. At the four corners of the inner hall the symbolic signs of the four stages of the Lord are inscribed. There is a rest house for pilgrims. Greenery, flowers, shrubs and gardens surround the temple.

Central Institute of Higher Tibetan Studies (CIHTS)

During the 1950s the Sino-Tibetan discord finally decimated the political freedom, religious institutions and culture of Tibet. The Tibetan people since then have been gripped with the anxiety that if the legacy of their past and their heritage disappear they will completely lose their identity. Taking this view, by the initiatives of Pt. Jawaharlal Nehru, the then Prime Minister of India and H.H. the 14th Dalai Lama Tensing Gyatso, Tibetan Institutes were opened in 1967 at four places. They are at Gangtok (Sikkim), Leh (Laddakh), Delhi and Sarnath. The basic objectives of these institutes have been to provide alternative opportunities to get a Tibetan education out of Tibet, to reconstruct the lost literature of Sanskrit texts preserved in the Tibetan language, to experiment the traditional monastery education together with modern education, and to preserve and promote Tibetan culture and traditions. The institutes are also engaged in the restoration of Indian science and literature (which are lost in their original forms) and in imparting higher education in Buddhist studies to broader area students who formerly availed such opportunities of acquisition of ancient monastic educational system. The CIHTS was formerly opened as part of Varanaseya Sanskrit University, and became independent in 1988 when it was granted a status of Deemed University by the UGCA. The architectural plan and design of buildings are based on the old Tibetan monasteries. The Institute has developed excellent archival facilities for preserving the old and rare Buddhist literary works and is also engaged in teaching, research, and publication programmes. Under the five faculties of teaching, i.e. Languages, Logic, Art and Craft, Philosophy and Religion, and Health and Healing, the courses are run to provide education from 9th grade to graduate and research levels. There is also an arrangement of research for doctoral degree and also non-degree long-term research studentship. In the year 2000, there were 300 male students (in *Padmasambhava Hostel*), and 62 girl students (in *Prajapati Hostel*), and about ninety teachers. Students are also enrolled from countries like Nepal, Bhutan, Mongolia, China, Korea and Russia. The CIHTS has a good library with a collection of rare texts, manuscripts and 85,000 titles in microfilm and microfiche. Since its independent status, the director of the institute had been Prof. **Samdong Rinpoche**, who in fact was the craftsman and the spirit behind all the developments.

Accommodation

Most visitors don't spend the night at Sarnath, but it is possible to stay in some of the monasteries for a small donation. The UP Tourism runs a tourist bungalow, called **Mrigadaya Hotel** (Tel.: 2586965, Fax 2587508), which has double rooms, each with bath, air-cooling, and soft mattress at reasonable prices (between Rs 300 for Deluxe, Rs 550 for AC, and Rs 400 for Family suits). The other places of stay are: **The Golden Buddha Hotel** (Tel: 2587933), tariff Rs 350/ 450; **Chitra Vihar** (Tel: 2586280); **Jain Paying Guest House** (Tel: 2595621, contact: Dr. A.K. Jain, jpgh@rediffmail.com), 14/37A Baraipur; and **Mahabodhi Guest House** (Tel: 2585595). There are three big *Dharmashalas* (pilgrims' rest houses), named **Birla**, **Burmese** and **Jain**. Besides there are two other rest houses: **Officers' Rest House** maintained by the Department of Archaeology, and **Forest Department Rest House** (Tel.: 25866-35 and 36).

Food. About 1 km south from the Mrigadaya Hotel, close to the road crossing is **Rangoli Garden Restaurant** (Tel.: 2585025, 2587125), the only worth mentioning. During the tourist season a friendly **Bhutanese** family, near the Tibetan monastery, prepares great Chinese food. In the main township there are some average Indian style restaurants; one acceptable is **Anand**. Near Ashapur road crossing there are two restaurants, named **Hotel Highway Inn** and **Open Restaurant**.

Other Facilities. The only bank in Sarnath is the Central Bank of India, however about 1.5 km south at Ashapur there are branches of the State Bank of India and the Canara Bank. Their services are very poor and they do not deal with money exchange. There is a Post & Telegraphic Office (Tel.: 2585013), and also a Government Hospital.

LINK STATION: VARANASI

Population 1.5 million, STD: 0542, Postal Code: 221001.

The city of Varanasi is situated on the west bank of the Ganga at a point where it sweeps in a great bend north before resuming its southeast course to the sea. India's most sacred city, it was probably already an important town by the 7th century BCE when Babylon and Nineveh were at the peak of their power. It was mentioned in both the *Mahabharata* and the *Ramayana*. The Buddha came to it in ca. 528 BCE. It derives its name from two streams, the Varana on the north side of the city and the Asi, a small trickle on the south (Fig. 57). **Banaras** is a colloquial and popular name of Varanasi. It is also called *Kashi*, 'The City of Light', by Hindus who as a mark of respect add the suffix *-ji* to it. About 8 km from the city centre is **Sarnath**, a suburb, where the Buddha gave his first sermon. According to recent statistics the number of visitors every year to this city include around a million pilgrims, about half a million Indian tourists, and around 150,000 foreign tourists.

Varanasi is said to combine all the virtues of all other places of pilgrimage. It is believed that anyone dying within the area marked by the Panchakroshi road is transported straight to heaven. Hence some devout Hindus move to Varanasi to end their days and have their ashes scattered in the holy Ganga.

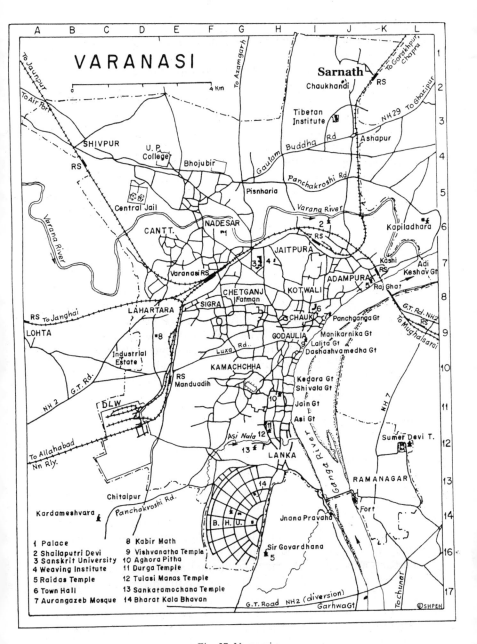

Fig. 57. Varanasi

Early settlement

The earliest inhabitants of Varanasi (ca. 1000 BCE) were the Aryans who made it a centre of culture, education, commerce and craftsmanship. Since the Mauryan period (3rd-4th century BCE) to the Gupta period (5th-6th century CE), the city of Varanasi had recorded a glorious history. Its growth and prosperity reached to its height in the Gahadavala period (11th-12th century). It was raided by Mahmud of Ghazni's army in 1033. In 1194 Qutb-ud-din Aibak defeated the local Raja's army and Ala-ud-din Khalji, the King of Delhi (1294-1316) destroyed temples and built mosques on their sites. By the order of the Mughal emperor Aurangzeb (1658-1707) all the major temples were destroyed and on their foundations mosques were constructed with the debris. Despite early foundation, hardly any building in the city dates before the 17th century and few are more than 200 years old.

A centre of learning

Varanasi stands as the chief centre of Sanskrit learning in north India. Sanskrit, the oldest of the known Indo-European languages, is the language of learning and religious ritual and has been sustained here long after it ceased to be a living language elsewhere. The **Sanskrit University,** for example, has over 150,000 rare manuscripts (Sanskrit Vidya Bhavan). Hindu devotional movements flourished here, especially in the 15th century under Ramananda, and Kabir, one of India's greatest poet-saints, lived in the city. Tulasi Das rewrote the *Ramayana* from Sanskrit into Hindi.

Places of interest

Varanasi is famous for the crescent shaped bank of the holy river Ganga where there exist 84 ghats (stairways to the river), five of which are most important for sacred bathing and Hindu rituals. Watching sunrise in the morning along the ghats is a spectacular and memorable scene. The other important places include the golden temple of Vishvanatha and its nearby sanctuaries, the temples of Kala Bhairava, Durga, Tulsi Manas, Bharat Mata Temple (temple of the mother India, represented by a marble made map on the ground), Ramnagar Fort and museum across the river, Bharat Kala Bhavan (a museum in the Banaras Hindu University), Banaras Hindu University, Asia's biggest residential university, the cosmic circuit of the Panchakroshi pilgrimage route with its associated shrines, the Kardameshvara temple (a temple existing and maintaining its ritual traditions since the 7th century), and several other sites.

The issue of the Ganga pollution

All along the Ganga, the major problem of waste disposal (of human effluent and industrial toxins) has defied the best efforts of the Ganga Action Plan (GAP) set up in 1986 to solve it. The diversion and treatment of raw sewage in 7 main cities is planned at Kanpur, Allahabad, Mirzapur, Varanasi, Patna, Bhagalpur and Kolkata. In Varanasi however, the 17th-century sewers, the inadequate capacity of the sewage works, the increased waterflow during the monsoons and the erratic electricity supply (essential for pumping) have all remained problems. In addition, although most Hindus are cremated, an estimated 25,000 uncremated or partially cremated bodies are put in the Ganga each year. A breed of scavenger turtles which dispose of rotting flesh was introduced down river but the turtles disappeared.

The Uttar Pradesh Water Board (Jal Nigam) has put forward a Ganga Action Plan II, but critics of the first failed scheme are proposing an alternative. That is how the work is not in operation. It remains to be a question of implementation under such a threatening controversy, and it is doubtful that in the near future Varanasi will manage to purify the tide of filth that enters it everyday.

The clean-up campaign of the Ganga has failed miserably in almost all respects. There is a lack of public participation and a lack of awareness of the river's problems. At the same time there has also been a failure to revive the old religious ethics of harmony with nature and the spirit of sustainability.

Although the Ganga may be one of the world's most polluted rivers, like many tropical rivers it can cleanse itself quickly. Scientists had discovered the river's exceptional property in the last century. The cholera microbe did not survive three hours in Ganga water whereas in distilled water it survived 24 hours!

ACCOMODATION

Hotels

Varanasi has an enormous range of hotels, from a few top class hotels to very cheap lodges, guesthouses and rest houses for pilgrims (*dharmashalas*). Considering the facilities available and the prices, the hotels in Varanasi City may be classified into 5 categories.

Web: www.visitvaranasi.com/hotel/

(**A,******) Usually international class hotel, having central a/c, having all the expected facilities, including exchange and sports; tariff, Rs 3000/ 5000.

153

Clarks Varanasi (140 rooms), The Mall (Cantt.), Email: clarkvns@satyam.net.in, Tel: 23485-01 to 10; Fax: 2348186 — best known for services in the city; **Hindustan International** (68 rooms), Maldahiya, Tel: 23514-84 to 90, Fax: 2350931 — new construction and a good restaurant; **Taj Ganges** (130 rooms), Nadesar Palace Ground, Web: www.tajhotels.com, Tel: 23451-00 to 17, Fax: 0542-2348067 — the most opulent place with excellent facilities; **Varanasi Ashok** (84 rooms), The Mall (Cantt.), Tel: 23460-20 to 30; Fax: 2348089 — a quiet location, one of the better Ashok Hotels at very good value; **Radisson** Hotel (120 rooms), The Mall, Cantt., Email: radvar@sify.com, Web: www.radisson.com, Tel: 091-542-2501515, Fax: 091-542-2501516 — the world class famous chain of Radisson.

(**B,***) Having central a/c and offering most of the facilities of A class but without the luxury; tariff, Rs 1500/ 3000.

Best Western Ideal (40 rooms), The Mall (Cantt.), Tel: 2348091; **Hotel de Paris** (50 rooms), 15 The Mall (Cantt.), near Tourist Office, Tel: 23466-01 to 08, Fax: 2348520; **Hotel India** (80 rooms), 59 Patel Nagar, Cantt., Tel: 2343309, 23429-12 and 13, Fax: 2348327; **M.M. Continental**, The Mall (Cantt.), Tel: 23452-72 & 73, Fax: 2342839; **Hotel Palace on Ganges** (22 rooms), Assi Ghat — an expensive choice with a little value; **Hotel Pallavi International** (55 rooms), Hathwa Place, Chetganj, Tel: 23569-39 to 42; Fax: 2322943.

(**C,***) Often the best hotels available, but always the best value; tariff, Rs 1000/ 1500.

Barahdari (16 rooms), Maidagin, Tel: 2330-040 and 581; **Diamond** (55 rooms), Bhelupura, Tel: 2310-696 to 700; **Hotel Ganga View** (14 rooms), Assi Ghat, Tel: 2313218; **Jai Ganges** (18 rooms, all a/c), Maldahiya, Tel: 23459-51 to 54 & 343777; **Malti** (80 rooms), Vidyapith Road, Tel: 2356844 & 2351395, Fax: 2322161; **Padmini International** (30 rooms), D 59/150 K Shivpurva, Sigra-Mahmoorganj Road, Tel: 2220972 & 2222274; **Hotel Pradeep** (45 rooms), C 27/153 Jagatganj, Lahurabir, Tel: 2344963 & 2344594; Fax: 2344898; **Surya** (35 rooms), Varana Bridge Road, Cantt.,Tel: 2348330 & 2343014.

(**D**) Air-cooled rooms with bath attached and sometimes TV, restaurant and room service; tariff, Rs 500/ 1000.

Ajay (19 rooms), Lahurabir, Tel: 2344763; **Dak Bungalow** ITDC, Caravan Park, the Mall, Cantt., Tel; 2342182; **Gautam**, C 26/35 Ramkatora (37 air-cooled rooms), between Rly Stn and Chowk, Tel: 2346239; **New International**, Lahurabir, Station Rd (36 rooms), Tel: 350805; **Shahi River View Hotel** (12 rooms), B 1/158 A2 Assi Ghat, Tel: 2366730; **Siddhartha** (26 rooms), Sigra, Tel: 2358161 & 2351852;

Temple on Ganges (20 rooms), Assi Ghat, Tel: 2312340; **Tourist Bungalow** (UPSTDC; 39 rooms), off Pared Kothi, GT Road, opp. Rly Stn, Tel: 2341162 — some a/c rooms with bath, 'deluxe suites' and dorm in modern 2-storey building, **Vaibhav** (15 rooms), Patel Nagar, Cantt., Tel: 2346-477 and 588.

(E) Simple room with fan (occasionally a/c), shower or bucket 'bath'. May have shared toilet facilities. Limited room service may include meals brought in when no restaurant is available; tariff, Rs 400/ 600.

Ashok, Sigra, Tel: 2350058; **Buddha**, M/ S C 26/35 Ramkatora, Tel: 2343686; **Chandra**, Sonia, Sigra, Tel: 2356318; **Empire**, Godaulia, Tel: 2392129; **Garden View**, Sigra, Tel: 2360851 & 2361093; **JK International** (20 rooms), D 46/19/1 Luxa Road, Tel: 2392141 & 2358917; **Hotel Jyoti**, Luxa Road, Tel: 2320333, & 2393050, Fax: 0542-2328333; **Lara India**, Dashashvamedh Road, Tel: 2320323 & 2320327; **Shalimar**, Varana Pul, Tel: 2346227, 2342133; **Seema**, Godaulia, Tel: 2352686, 2352785.

Guesthouses; tariff, Rs 100/ 200.

Amrit Guest House, Bhojubir, Tel: 2313264; **Beriwala Atithi Bhavan**, Ramapura, Tel: 2357117; **Chitragupta Atithi Bhavan**, Pared Kothi, 2345071; **Dashashvamedh Boarding House**, Dashashvamedha, Tel: 2321701; **Ganga Guest House**, Pandey Ghat, Tel: 2321137; **Jaipuriya Atithi Bhavan**, Godaulia, Tel: 2352709 and 2352674; **Kapoor Guest House**, Pared Kothi, Tel: 2343802; **Keshari Vishram Bhavan**, D 47/184 Luxa Road, Tel: 2320262; **Sri Atithi Bhavan**, A 7/3 C Mukimganj, Tel: 2331595 (PP); **Sri Kishan Beriwala Atithi Bhavan**, Luxa Road, Tel; 2321550; **Sri Lodge**, B 20/41 Bhelupur, near Police Stn, Tel: 2392894; **Sri Marwari Yuvak Sangh**, Luxa Road, Tel: 2358612; **Yogi Guest House**, Kamachha, Tel: 2320806.

Pilgrims' Resthouses (*Dharmashalas*)

Annapurna Telwala, D 53/98 Chhoti Gaibi, Tel: 2350025; **Bagla**, D 38/139-40 Haujkatora, Tel.: 2329219; **Brindavan**, CK 9/167 Gomath; **Buddha Burmese**, S 17/330 Cantt.; **Divan Tara Chand**, C K 15/97 Sudiya; **Dudhvewala (Baijnath)**, K 62/86 Bulanala, Tel: 2354670; **Har Sundari**, D 40/8/8A Godaulia; **Kamala**, D 15/69 Dashashvamedh, Tel: 2321499; **Kanpur**, K 61/96 Bulanala; **Kashi Mumuksha Bhavan**, B 1/87 Assi, Tel: 2311187; **Parshvanath Digambar Jain**, B 20/46 Bhelupur, Tel.: 2312892; **Sindhi**, D 38/20 Misir Pokhra, Godaulia, Tel: 2358441; **Tanpure Mahraj Maharastrian**, D 17/91 Dashashvamedha; **Tulasiram**, D 40/2 Lakshmanpura.

RESTAURANTS

The city restaurants are not allowed to serve alcohol. Hotels observe 'Dry Days' on the 1st and the 7th day of each month, and on certain Public holidays. Varied menus are served in top hotels. Some of the notable restaurants are given below.

Amrapali Restaurant, in Hotel Relex, Pared Kothi, Cantt., Tel: 2343503; **Anamika Coffe & Kulfi House**, Shastri Nagar, Sigra; **Bread of Life Bakery**, B 3/322 Shivala, Tel: 2318912 — the only place in the city with 'European breads and American cookies'; **Canton's**, in Hotel Surya, Varana Bridge Road — good for Chinese dishes; **Chahat Restaurant**, Natraj Cinema, Sigra, Tel: 2363900; **El Parador**, Maldahiya Road, behind City Bus Stand — great variety, good quality; Hotel Gopal, E 4/4 Chetganj, Tel: 2358348; **Kerala Café** (South Indian), Bhelupur Crossing, Tel: 2312105 — worth for South Indian food; **Hotel Labela Restaurant** (Chinese), B 31/26 B.H.U. Rd, Lanka, Tel: 2366970; **Marwari Bhojanalaya**, K 15/1 Bulanala, Tel: 2333550; **Pizzeria Vaatika**, Assi Ghat, Tel: 2313208 — famous for Gopal's scrumptious pizza or pasta, muesli and yogurt; **Pragati Café**, Ganesh Katra, CK 28/15Chowk; *Restaurant* at Hotel Barahdari, Maidagin — serving good Jain vegetarian food; **Shahi Restaurant**, Gurubagh, Rathyatra Road, Tel: 2351069; **Shanti Guest House Rooftop Restaurant**, near Manikarnika Ghat; **Sindhi Restaurant**, near Lalita Cinema, Bhelupur — good Indian *thali* and Veg. food; **The Coffe House**, B 20/45 Bhelupur, Tel: 2393890; **The Kesari Restaurant**, D 14/9 Dashashvamedh Road, Tel: 2321472 — popular among upper-middle-class Indians, serving Veg. and South Indian dishes, including *thali* with variety of dishes for Rs 75 that feeds 2 easily; **Yelchiko Bar & Restaurant**, near Sigra Crossing, close to Natraj Cinema. The restaurants in **Diamond Hotel** and **Hotel Pradeep** (see Hotels, C) are known for their good food and reasonable price.

TRAVEL AGENCIES

Air People (AP), Sridas Fd, The Mall, Varuna Bridge, Tel: 2340562, Fax: 2340562 & 2346416; **Asia Travel & Tours**, Maldahiya, Tel: 2351484, 2357873; **Cosmic Travels & Movers**, Varuna Bridge, Tel: 2346726 & 2340246; **India Travels Services**, CK 21/31,Thatheri Bazar, Tel: 2320628, 2329426; **ITDC Transport Unit**, Hotel Varanasi Ashok, Tel: 2346032; **Kushinagar Travels & Tours**, D 64/135, Sigra, Tel: 2224026, 2331612; **Mercury Travel**, Tel: 2343296; **M.N. Travels**, Harishchandra Rd, Sonarpura, Tel: 2355650; **New Shashi Travel & Travels**, Mint House, Tel: 2344542; **Oasis International Tour & Travels**, 52 Maharaja Palace, Patel Nagar, Tel: 2345595; **Overseas Travels Pvt.Ltd.**,

Ranavir Market, Dashashvamedh Rd, Tel: 321465, 393840; **Radiant Services**, D 48/139-A, Misir Pokhra, Godaulia, Tel: 2351218, 2358852; **Raj Travels**, Maidagin Chauraha, Tel: 2391595, 2391596; **Siddharth Tours & Travels**, Hotel Siddharth, Sigra, Tel: 2352301; **Sita World Travels (I.) Ltd.**, Bungalow No. 53, The Mall, Tel: 2342447, 2344692, 2348485; **Sri Subh Travels**, Shop No. 4, Ananta Gate, Nadesar, Tel: 2344844 & 2344944; **Sunny Travels**, Hotel Jai Ganges Bldg, Maldahiya, Tel: 2344435; **Surabhi Travel & Tours**, Cooperative Bldg, Nadesar, Tel & Fax: 2348632; **Tiwari Tour's & Travel's**, B1/160, Radha Swami Dham, Assi Ghat, Tel: 2366727, (Res) 2367079; **Tour Aids**, Hotel India, Nadesar, Tel: 2346881 & 2345627; **Travel Bureau**, The Mall, Tel: 2346621 & 2345530; **Travel Corporation of India**, Sri Das Foundation, The Mall, Tel: 2345281, 23462-09 & 10; **Travel King**, CK 16/33-A Sudiya, Tel: 333-920 & 620; **Vandana Travels**, Hotel Bhaibhav, Patel Nagar, Tel: 23464- 66 and 77; **Varuna Travels**, Pandey Haveli, Sonarpura, Tel: Tel: 23933-70 & 71; **World View Travels & Tours**, 3 Mint House, Nadesar, Tel: 2346357 & 2345530.

BOOKSHOPS

Chaukhambha Vidya Bhavan, CK 29/9 Chowk, Tel: 2320404; **Harmony**, The Book Shop, B 1/160 Assi Ghat, Tel. & Fax: 2310218, rakeshsingh42@rediffmail.com; **Indica Books**, D 40/18 Godaulia crossing, Tel. 2357401, 2452258, indicabooks@satyam.net.in; **Motilal Banarasidass**, Raja Katra, Chowk, Tel: 2352331; **Nagari Pracharini Sabha**, Vishveshvarganj, Tel: 2331488; **National Book Agency**, CK15/ 63 Sudiya, Bulanala, Tel: 2331958; **Pilgrims Book House**, B 27/98-A-8 Nababganj, Durgakund, Tel: 23124-56 & 96, Fax: 2314059, pilgrims@satyam.net.in; **Sharda Sanskrit Sansthan**, C-27/59 Jagatganj, Tel: 2324477; **Students' Friends** & Co., Lanka, B.H.U. Rd, Tel: 2310785.

REF. BOOKS

Singh, Rana P.B. 1993. Ed. **Banaras (Varanasi). Cosmic Order, Sacred City, Hindu traditions**. Tara Book Agency, Varanasi: "Sarnath": pp. 235-256.

Singh, Rana P.B. and Rana, Pravin S. 2002. **Banaras Region: A Spiritual and Cultural Guide**. Indica Books, Varanasi.

6. SHRAVASTI

Where the Buddha performed great miracles

After defeating the six philosophers and converting them to his teaching, the Enlightened One performed the Great Miracle of the Pairs ... Standing in the air at the height of a palm tree, flames engulfed the lower part of his body, and five hundred jets of water streamed from the upper part. Then flames leapt from the upper part of his body, and five hundred jets of water streamed from the lower part. Then by his magic power, the Blessed one transformed himself into a bull with a quivering hump. Appearing in the east, the bull vanished and reappeared in the west. Vanishing in the west, it reappeared in the north. Vanishing in the north, it reappeared in the south. ... Several thousand millions of beings, seeing this great miracle, became glad, joyful, and pleased.

Mahavastu

At Jetavana vihara (Savatthi), after receiving the honour and welcome by Anathapindika, the Blessed One said:
"The teachings of all religions should centre here, for without wisdom there is no reason. This truth is not for the hermit alone; it concerns every human being, priest and layman alike. There is no distinction between the monk who has taken the vows, and the man of the world living with his family. There are hermits who fall into perdition, and there are humble householders who mount to the rank of rishis.
Hankering after pleasure is a danger common to all; it carries away the world. He who is involved in its eddies finds no escape. But wisdom is the handy boat, reflection is the rudder. The slogan of religion calls you to overcome the assaults of Mara, the enemy.
Since it is impossible to escape the result of our deeds, let us practise good works.
Let us guard our thoughts that we do no evil, for as we sow so shall we reap."

Ashvaghosha, *A Life of Buddha*, v. 1522-1533.

Approach & Cultural Background

Situated 134 km northeast from Lucknow, 47 km east from Bahraich and 18 km west from Balrampur, Shravasti (Pali: *Savatthi*) identified with the ruins of Saheth-Maheth (spread in Shravasti and Gonda districts, U.P.) was the capital of the ancient kingdom of Koshala.

It is situated on the banks of the Rapti (old name *Achiravati*) river, a tributary of the Ganga river. The *Mahabharata* makes a reference to the legendary king Shravasta who gave his name to it. According to the *Vishnu Purana* (II.4) it was founded by Shravasta, a king of the Solar race. Belonging to the same lineage, Rama, the king of Ayodhya, made his son Lava the ruler of Shravasti. According to archaeological evidences its antiquity goes back to ca. 600 BCE. The ancient Jain sources refer to this place as Champakapuri and Chandrikapuri, and eulogised it as the birthplace of two Tirthankaras, viz. Sambhavanatha and Chandraprabha. Shravasti had the honour of sheltering the Buddha for 25 rainy seasons in the Jetavana gardens (Fig. 58).

At Shravasti, in accordance with the practice of previous Buddhas, Gautama Buddha performed one of the **Greatest Miracles**. It was here that the Buddha had to take part in a contest of miraculous feats with the Tirthikas in front of King Prasenajit of Koshala and the assembled audience. The Buddha levitated on a thousand petalled lotus, causing fire and water to leap out of his body, and created multiple representations of himself which went up to the highest heaven. The heretical teachers, discomfited at this miraculous event, dared not show their own feats and were finally confounded by a violent thunderstorm and obliged to run away. The supreme position of the Buddha was thus vindicated, and he preached the Law before a huge assemblage of people that had come to witness the miracle. The Shravasti episode has been a favourite theme in Buddhist art from very early times.

While answering the question raised by King Prasenajit, the Buddha concluded:

"Compassion is the fruit of understanding. Practising the Way of Awareness is to realise the true face of life. That true face is impermanence. Everything is impermanent and without a separate self. Everything must one day pass away. One day your own body will pass away. When a person sees into the impermanent nature of all things, his way of looking becomes calm and serene. The presence of impermanence does not disturb his heart and mind. And thus the feelings of pain that result from compassion do not carry the bitter and heavy nature that other kinds of suffering do. On the contrary, compassion gives a person greater strength. Great King! Today you have heard some of the basic tenets of the Way of Liberation. On another day, I would like to share more of the teachings with you."

King Pasenadi's heart was filled with gratitude. He stood up and bowed to the Buddha. He knew that one day soon he would ask to be accepted as a lay disciple of the Buddha. (*Majjhima Nikaya*, 87)

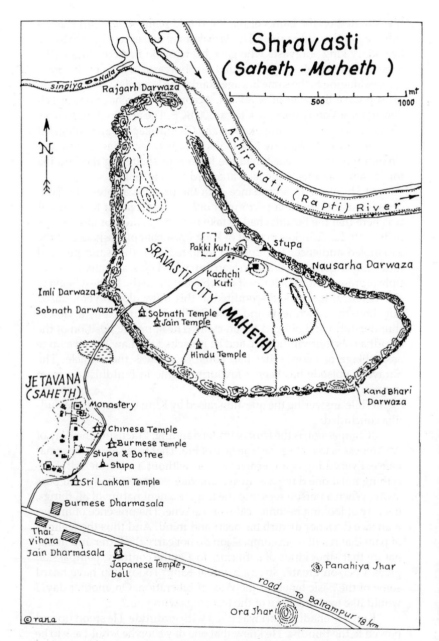

Fig. 58. Shravasti (Saheth Maheth)

It was here that the Buddha accepted Sunita, an untouchable, as an ordained monk into his *sangha*. This resulted in a strong opposition, which was resolved later on by royal support. Answering to this accusation, the Buddha said, "Accepting untouchables into the *sangha* was simply a question of time. Our way is a way of equality. We do not recognise caste. Though we may encounter difficulties over Sunita's ordination now, we will have opened a door for the first time in history that future generations will thank us for. We must have courage." (*Tripitaka*, 190)

At his 13th retreat during the rains at Shravasti, the Buddha recited a *gatha* (poetic tale) to summarise his teaching:

"Do not pursue the past.
Do not lose yourself in the future.
The past no longer is. The future has not yet come.
Looking deeply at life as it is
in the very here and now,
the practitioner dwells
in stability and freedom.
We must be diligent today.
To wait until tomorrow is too late.
Death comes unexpectedly.
How can we bargain with it?
The sage calls a person who knows
how to dwell in mindfulness
night and day
one who knows
the better way to live alone."
Samyutta Nikaya XXX.10; and *Sutta-nipatta* I.8

Shravasti is best remembered as the place where Shakyamuni defeated the holders of the other doctrines. Some accounts say that this was accomplished by debate, others that by miracles; perhaps there were both. The leaders of India's six main philosophical schools challenged the Buddha to a contest of miraculous powers many times as he wandered through the surrounding kingdoms. Finally, in his 57th year he accepted the challenge at Shravasti. King Prasenajit built a hall especially for the event; in it seven thrones were erected (Fig. 59). On the first day of spring, the six other teachers took their seats and Shakyamuni came to his flying through the air. He sent forth fire and water from his body and the hall was destroyed, then reformed as a transparent palace. Planting his toothpick in the ground, he caused a great tree to spring up, fragrant and fully laden with flowers and

Fig. 59. The broken pillar of King Prasenajit,
showing the Bodhi Tree, a Stupa and Dhamma Cakra
(from Bharhut, ca. 100-80 BCE)

ripe fruit. He multiplied his body infinitely, filling all space with Buddhas expounding the *Dhamma*. These and many other miracles he performed and in eight days utterly defeated his opponents, whose followers later adopted the Buddhist doctrines. For a further seven days he continued to show miracles and give teachings to the great assembly. Both Chinese pilgrims describe a tall temple containing a statue of the Buddha, which stood outside Jetavana Grove in commemoration of these events. Nearby is the place where Devadatta, failing in his attempt to scratch the Buddha with poisoned nails, finally went down to hell.

One of the most stirring episodes in the ministry of the Buddha at Shravasti was the conversion of a robber named *Angulimala*, an oft-told story. Fa-hsien and Hsüan-tsang locate the actual spot of conversion. Angulimala, whose name literally means 'finger-garland', was a wicked man who harried the city and the country killing people and cutting a finger off each person killed in order to make a garland for himself. One day in a fit of brutal rage he tried to kill his own mother. It was at this moment that the Lord met Angulimala.

Angulimala raised his quest and asked the Lord, "Human beings do not love each other. Why should I love other people? Humans are cruel and deceptive, I will not rest until I have killed them all."

162

The Buddha replied gently, "O pity Angulimala! I know you have suffered deeply at the hands of other humans. Sometimes humans can be most cruel. Such cruelty is the result of ignorance, hatred, desire, and jealousy. But humans can also be understanding and compassionate. Have you ever met a monk before? Monks vow to protect the lives of all other beings. They vow to overcome desire, hatred, and ignorance. There are many people, not just monks, whose lives are based on understanding and love. Angulimala, there may be cruel people in this world, but there are also many kind people. Do not be blinded. My path can transform cruelty into kindness. Hatred is the path you are on now. You should stop. Choose the path of forgiveness, understanding, and love instead."

Angulimala was moved by the Buddha's words. He could see that the Buddha spoke from love. There was no hatred in the Buddha, no aversion. The Buddha grasped Angulimala's hand and said, "Angulimala, I will protect you if you vow to abandon your mind of hatred and devote yourself to the study and practice of the Way." Shakyamuni's enlightening words had a calming effect on his stone heart. Angulimala decided to give up his evil ways and follow the path of the Lord. (*Satipatthana Sutta*, M.10)

The erstwhile robber was admitted into the order and even attained *arhat*-ship. But his earlier record made him a victim of ridicule and stones were thrown at him wherever he went for begging, so that Buddha often showed him up as an instance of the inevitableness of collecting the fruits of evil-doing.

During the time of Shakyamuni, Sudatta, a rich and pious merchant, lived in Shravasti. While on a visit to Rajgir, he heard the Buddha's sermon and decided to become the Lord's disciple. But he was caught in a dilemma and asked the Lord whether he could become a follower without forsaking worldly life. To his query, the Master replied that it was enough that he followed his vocation in a righteous manner.

> "Not by a shaven head does an undisciplined man
> Who utters lies, become an ascetic.
> How will one be an ascetic who is full of desire and greed?
> He who wholly subdues evil — both small and great —
> is called an ascetic, because he has overcome all evil."
>
> *Dhammapada* 264, 265

Sudatta invited the Lord to Shravasti and began to look for a suitable place to build a *vihara*. A beautiful park at the southern edge of the town attracted his attention. The park belonged to Jeta, son of

the king of Shravasti, Prasenajit.
Jeta demanded that Sudatta cover
the entire park with gold coins.
Sudatta painstakingly paved
every inch of the land with gold.
Then Jeta said that since the trees
were left uncovered they belonged to him. But finally, he had
a change of heart and donated
valuable wood to build the vihara.
The park came to be known as
Jetavana Vihara (Fig. 60) after
Prince Jeta's donation to the
Sangha. This magnificent, seven-
storied *vihara* was duly presented
to the Buddha, who resided in the
Gandhakuti of the *vihara*.

The Buddha so much liked
Jetavana that he spent there 24
rainy seasons, preaching to
monks, laymen and women.
Sudatta came to be known as
Anathapindika (the incompara-
ble alms giver). The grandeur of this *vihara* was commented upon by
Chinese travellers several centuries later. Jetavana continues to attract
pilgrims from all over the world who come here to pray and meditate
in its serene atmosphere. One of the most beautiful spots in Jetavana
is under the Anandabodhi tree. An eternal witness to the vicissitudes
of history, this sacred tree was brought as a cutting from the Bodhi
tree in Anuradhapura in Sri Lanka, which itself grew from a sapling
of the original Bodhi tree in Bodh Gaya. The ruins of Anandakuti and
Gandhakuti exude an aura of sacredness because it was here that the
Lord stayed during his many visits to Jetavana Vihara.

Fig. 60. Shravasti: Round-shaped
Vedika showing the purchase
of Jetavana
(ca. 100-80 BCE; from Bharhut)

The Buddha accepted the challenge from adherents of Jain and
Ajivika faiths to prove his miraculous powers, and caused a mango-
tree to sprout up in a day. Under it he created a huge array of representations of himself, seated and standing on lotuses and causing fire
and water to emanate from his body. This incidence is also an important subject in Buddhist art.

The Buddha told several *suttas* and 416 of *Jataka* stories while
residing here. In Shravasti, the Master expounded a major part of the
Tripitakas. Devadatta, the cousin brother of the Buddha, made several

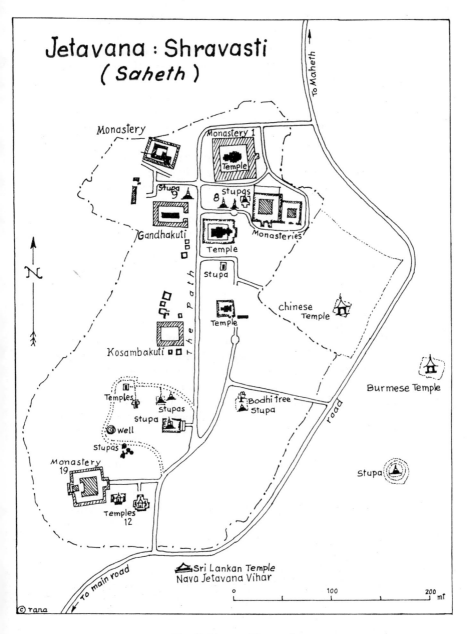

Jetavana : Shravasti
(Saheth)

Monastery

Monastery 1

Temple

Stupa 9

Stupas 8

Gandhakuti

Temple

Monasteries

The Path

Stupa

N

Temple

chinese Temple

Kosambakuti

Temple

Burmese Temple

Temples

Stupas

stupa

Bodhi tree Stupa

well

road

Stupas

Monastery 19

Stupa

Temples 12

To main road

Sri Lankan Temple
Nava Jetavana Vihar

To Maheth

0   100   200 mr

© rana

Fig. 61. Jetavana (Shravasti)

attempts on the Buddha's life during his stay at Shravasti. But Devadatta failed in his attempts and eventually died here. After the death of the Lord, his disciples continued the mission in Shravasti and other places in Koshala. By the time of Ashoka, Jetavana had become famous for its sanctity (Fig. 61).

During the Kushana period, Shravasti was a growing town, an important centre of trade famous for its merchants, and a centre of Buddhist teaching under royal support. During the reign of the Buddhist king Kanishka many new *stupas* and shrines were erected and images of the Buddha installed. After the Kushana period began the decline of Shravasti. The Chinese pilgrim Fa-hsien visited this place in the early 5th century CE and found that there were only 200 families living there. However, he mentions the active role of *Jetavana-vihara* and some of the *stupas* amidst luxuriant groves and colourful flowers. He further mentions the great fire which destroyed the 7-storied building of Jetavana. By the turn of the 7th century, Hsüan-tsang describes this city as a deserted township, except *Jetavana-vihara* that was still active. He states that Ashoka erected two pillars, each 21 m high, on the left and right sides of the eastern gate of *Jetavana-vihara*. He also mentions the existence of 100 Hindu temples with a large number of followers.

The glory of Jetavana continued till the 12th century CE under the royal patronage of the Gahadavala kings of Kanauj. One of the latest patrons of the establishment was Kumaradevi, the queen of Govinda-chandra, the Gahadavala king, who donated some land for the maintenance of the *Jetavana-vihara* in CE 1128-29. It appears that afterwards the Buddhist monks left Jetavana due to adverse political circumstances and constant threat under the Muslim rulers. Jetavana then became totally deserted. During 1863-1875 Alexander Cunningham excavated the ruins and identified some of the monuments, including 16 *stupas*. Again during 1875-76 and 1884-85 William Hoey continued the excavations and brought to the light the remains of 34 ancient buildings.

The twin name of Saheth-Maheth is applied to two distinct **groups of remains**. **Saheth**, covering an area of 13 ha, lies about 250 m north from the Balrampur-Bahraich road. This is the site of the ancient monastery known as *Jetavana-vihara*, which lay outside the limits of the ancient city. The ruins consist mainly of plinths and foundations of Buddhist monasteries and *stupas*. There are remains of 8 temples, 4 monasteries (*viharas*) and 14 *stupas* (Fig. 62). In the recent excavation (1999-2000) in the nearby village Kolga the whole monastery city of Shravasti was found, which consists of several monasteries, dormitories for monks and a huge water pool for sacred bathing for female

Fig. 62. Jetavana: Temple and Monastery

monks. One can start from the south and after having a view of the remains leave the mound at the north, from where the road takes you back to the other side of the old city. The most conspicuous conical mound is a *stupa*, consisting of a square structure of solid brick basement, 7.5 m on each side. Votive offerings of clay seals inscribed with the Buddhist creed were found deposited at the foot of the closed entrance. It would appear that originally there was a *stupa* here; on this was erected a shrine, which again was converted into a *stupa*. A number of Buddha images were recovered here. Among them, the most notable are the Buddha seated in *dharmachakra-mudra* (gesture of preaching) and *bhumisparsha-mudra* (gesture of touching the Earth). In those images miniature forms of Avalokiteshvara and Maitreya are sculpted. Proceeding a few paces east of the *stupa* one can see the **bodhi-tree** (fig-tree, *Ficus religiosa*), the base of which is enclosed in a modern platform. The tree is believed to mark the spot where Anathapindaka planted a *bodhi*-sapling. The Sinhalese chronicle *Pujavaliya* relates the story of this pious act.

Maheth, situated about 500 m northeast of Saheth, denotes the Shravasti city proper and is a much larger site, situated south of the river Rapti (*Achiravati*) which flows about 300 m north. All that remains at Mahet, once a heavily fortified city, are two *stupas* known locally as Pakki Kuti and Kachchi Kuti; the latter is identified as Sudatta's Stupa. The outline of the city is distinctly marked by a high earthen rampart with a brick wall at the top running along a circuit of 5.2 km and pierced by several gates distinguished by high bastions. Four of these openings (*darwaza*), viz. Imli, Rajgarh, Nausahra and Kandabhari, situated respectively at the southwest, northwest, northeast and southeast corners of the city-wall, may possibly represent real gates of the ancient city; their present names being due to local usage. The remains within the city-area

Fig. 63. Shravasti: Temple of Sobhanatha

include Buddhist, Brahmanical and Jain structures and a few medieval tombs. The **Sobhanatha Temple** (Fig. 63) is believed to be the birthplace of Sambhavanatha, the 3rd Jain *Tirthankara*. There is a large enclosure consisting of the remains of two rectangular rooms on the northwest and southeast corners of the enclosures, which are also paved with concrete as the courtyard. The northwestern room yielded an image of Rishabhadeva, the first Jain *Tirthankara*.

From the Sobhanatha temple the road leads to **Pakki Kuti**, at a distance of 500 m northeast; this is one of the two largest mounds inside the city-area. Cunningham identified it with the remains of the *stupa* of **Angulimala** as seen by the Chinese pilgrims. Angulimala (literally, necklace of fingers) was a dreaded dacoit who wore a necklace of fingers that were chopped from his victims. According to another interpretation this is the ruins of the 'Hall of the Law' that king Prasenajit is stated to have built for the Buddha. But the overall structure, the architectural designs, the layouts and provision of doors and windows, all support to justify it as a *stupa*.

About 60 m east of Pakki Kuti is **Kachchi Kuti**, an example of a most imposing monument. It owes its modern name to a renovation in *kachcha* (silt-mud) brick made to the topmost shrine by an ascetic who lived there. The ruins present structural remains of different periods, of which the earliest is dated to the Kushana period and the latest to about the 12th century. A large collection of plaques belonging to the Gupta period was unearthed here, and some of them show in high relief scenes from the *Ramayana*. They confirm the supposition that the edifice of the Gupta period that stood here was a Hindu temple. According to the *Vishnu Purana* (II.4) Shravasti was the capital of the ancient state of Koshala.

A new park has been created around these ruins with flowers and trees shading the lawns. In this case restoration has regained some of the qualities that made the place attractive of old; peace and tranquillity pervade it. Three new Buddhist temples have been built alongside the park, one of which was founded by two Burmese ladies and another by a Sri Lankan monk. Both offer accommodation to pilgrims. A fine Tibetan *stupa* has recently been completed in the courtyard of this latter building. The third temple has a sad story. It was built during many years through the efforts of a solitary Chinese monk, who, unfortunately, died before its completion. Now the Chinese temple and a seven-storied pagoda with a number of out-buildings are empty and locked, pending a legal decision of possession and responsibility. Apart from the intrinsic value of these constructions, it would be a fitting tribute to Fa-hsien and Hsüan-tsang if they were to be restored and opened.

Nava Jetavana Mahavihara

Just across the road from the main entrance of the archaeological park is the Nava Jetavana Mahavihara, a modern temple built by the well-known Sri Lankan monk Ven. Metivala Sangharatna. The temple shrine contains some of the best contemporary Buddhist paintings to be found in India. The majority of the paintings represent incidents in the Buddha's life that took place at Shravasti, though the four main events in the Buddha's as well as other important events in Buddhist history are also represented. The paintings are in numbered panels, in total 31. One of them show a group of half a million untouchable Hindus accepting Buddhism under the leadership of Bhimrao Ambedkar on 14 October 1955. Another one depicts a ceremony of the Nava Jetavana Mahavihara, showing Ven. Sangharatna in front of a simple hut, while another one shows the opening of the temple on 31 December 1988 by Dr Shankar Dayal Sharma, the Vice-President of India.

Temple 12

Entering the Jetavana by the main gate, proceeding along the path and turning left, one will meet a small temple. It consists of a main shrine with a circumambulatory passage around it and two smaller shrines on both sides. It is likely that the main shrine contained a statue of the Buddha, while the two smaller ones contained statues of Avalokiteshvara and Maitreya. During the excavation of this temple, a human skull and other bones were found on the floor.

Monastery 19

At the end of the path is a monastery consisting of a courtyard with a well surrounded by 21 cells. On the eastern side is a shrine with a circumambulatory passage around it. This monastery was first built in the 6th century and then rebuilt again on the same plan in either the 11th or 12th century. Among the many antiquities found in this monastery is a statue of Avalokiteshvara from the 8th-9th century, a terracotta tablet containing a representation of the Buddha from the 5th or 6th century, a statue of the god Kubera made of red Mathura sandstone, and fragmentary sculptures made of the black stone found around Gaya. One cell was found to contain a bed made of brick, with one end slightly raised to form a pillow. Another cell had a large earthen jar half buried in the floor, probably used to store grain, and beside it was a bronze cup and an iron ladle.

But the most interesting object found in this monastery was a copper-plate inscription of King Govindachandra, the husband of Queen Kumaradevi (12th century), who built the Dharmachakrajina Monastery at Sarnath. The inscription was found carefully packed in a clay case buried under the floor of a cell and was issued on a date equivalent to the 23rd June 1130 CE. It records the gift of 6 villages together with their revenue to the monks residing at the Jetavana, of whom a monk named Buddhabhattaraka was the chief. To make sure the grant was known to all, it was announced before the whole court: "Kings, queens, heirs-apparent, ministers, priests, door-keepers, generals, treasurers, record keepers, physicians, astrologers, chamberlains, messengers and officers charged with the care of elephants, horses, towns and mines." It is interesting to note that some of the villages mentioned in the inscription still exist and are still known by their ancient names.

The Eight Stupas

A short distance to the north of Monastery 19 is a cluster of 8 brick *stupas*. These *stupas* were probably built to enshrine the ashes of particularly revered monks who resided in the Jetavana throughout the centuries. One *stupa* was found to contain a sealing dating from the 5th century with the name Buddhadeva on it.

The Bodhi Tree

Further along the main path are the foundations of several structures with a tree growing out of them, often identified with the Ananda Bodhi Tree. According to the commentary on the *Jatakas*, when people came to Jetavana to pay their respects to the Buddha and found him absent, they would leave their flowers and garland offerings at the door of the Gandhakuti. When Anathapindika heard about this, he asked the Buddha how people could pay their respects to him when he was absent, and the Buddha suggested that it could be done by placing the offerings at a Bodhi Tree. Accordingly, a seed was brought from the Bodhi Tree at Bodh Gaya which was planted at the Jetavana with great ceremony. Because the seed was planted by Ananda, the tree came to be known as the Ananda Bodhi Tree (cf. *Jatakas*, IV. 228). However, as the Jetavana was abandoned to the jungle for nearly a thousand years, and as there is no archaeological evidence indicating where the Anandabodhi Tree actually stood, the identification of this tree with the original is highly doubtful. The commentary to the *Jataka* says the tree was planted near the main gate of the Jetavana, which is thought to have been somewhere near the present Burmese Temple.

Kosambakuti

A little to the north of the Bodhi Tree and to the left of the path are the ruins of the Kosambakuti, one of the two favourite resorts of the Buddha at Jetavana. The original structure was probably a small wood and thatch hut in which the Buddha would sleep, meditate and converse with visitors. A relief from the Bharhut Stupa depicting the purchase of the Jetavana shows both the Kosambakuti and the Gandhakuli, giving some idea of what the two structures may have looked like (Fig. 60). The Kosambakuti appears to be a small gabled roofed structure, square in plan with a clay pinnacle on the roof. It was not built of durable material and was later replaced by a brick structure. This replacement, the foundation of which the pilgrim sees today, was 5.75 x 5.45 m, and enclosed a shrine.

Cunningham found a large statue carved out of pink sandstone when he excavated at the Kosambakuti. The inscription on the statue, much damaged, tells us that it was erected at the Kosambakuti by the monk Bala. The statue is now in the Indian Museum in Calcutta. When Hsüan-tsang came here (CE 639), he saw this statue and the Kosambakuti, which was the only structure in the Jetavana not in ruins. Just in front of the Kosambakuti is a long plinth made of brick marking the place where the Buddha would walk up and down in the evenings to take exercise.

The Gandhakuti

Further along the path are the foundations of what was the most celebrated building in the ancient Buddhist world, the Gandhakuti, the Fragrant Hut. The Bharhut relief indicates that the original

171

Gandhakuti was similar to the Kosambakuti, only larger, and built on a cross plan. The ruins the visitor sees today date from the Gupta period and consist of a rectangular terrace with stairs and entrance towards the east, a pavilion and a smaller shrine 2.85 sq.m, with walls about 1.8 meters thick. This small shrine is no doubt a later Gandhakuti built over the original one, while the pavilion must have been added at a later date. Cunningham found a well-constructed road leading from the Gandhakuti to what was thought to be the front gate of the Jetavana, indicating its central position in the complex.

Stupa 9

Just a little to the north of the Gandhakuti and to the left of the path are the ruins of a small *stupa* dating to the late Gupta period, in which a Buddha statue was found. The statue is small, only 50 cm high, and shows the Buddha sitting with his hand in the gesture of granting fearlessness. The circular halo behind his head, of which only parts remain, is ornamented with the design of a full-blown lotus. On either end of the pedestal are two lions with protruding tongues, and between them a relief representing a seated Bodhisattva flanked on both sides by two attendants bearing garlands. Along the bottom of the pedestal is an inscription written in late Kushana characters that read: "The pious gift of Sihadeva, a Pravarika from Saketa."

Stupa 8

On the other side of the path from Stupa 9 is another larger *stupa*. This *stupa* was originally round, but at a later date, between the 9th and 10th centuries, was rebuilt on a square plan. The second phase of this *stupa* was found to contain the lower part of a statue: crossed legs sitting on a pedestal. The inscription on the pedestal, written in characters from the early Kushana period, reads: "A Bodhisattva (has been set up) in the Jetavana at Shravasti (and is) a gift of ... and Sivadhara, Kshatriyas, brothers from Vilishta and sons of Dharmananda of Mathura. Versed in the scriptures and (knowing) the unreality of pleasures and the instability of life (they) give (this statue) in honour of all the Buddhas, for the welfare of all beings, with special regard to their mother and father and to accumulate merit both in this world and the next. This Bodhisattva was made by Sivamitra, a sculptor from Mathura." Below this, the Epitome of the *Dhamma* is inscribed in characters from the 8 or 9th century CE. The statue seems to have been already broken when it was enshrined in the *stupa*, and was probably placed there because, whereas it was too badly damaged to be worshipped, it was also considered too sacred to be simply thrown away.

Monastery 1

At the northern end of the ruins, this structure is the largest so far discovered at the Jetavana and seems to have been built during the 10th century. The entrance faces the east and leads to a hall with four pillars. The courtyard is surrounded by 35 cells and has a temple in the middle. Like most of the monasteries at the Jetavana, this one contained evidence of having been destroyed by fire.

Pond

Leaving the ruins of the Jetavana by the back gate and proceeding northwest along the road, the visitor will soon cross a bridge over a pond. According to the *Udana* (st. 51), the Buddha was once going on his alms-round when he came upon a group of boys tormenting fish. He stopped and in a gentle and skilful way asked the boys if they liked pain. They answered that they did not and the Buddha then suggested that they should act towards others the way they would like to be treated themselves. The Udana tells us that this encounter took place between Shravasti and Jetavana, and as this is the only body of water between the two places, it must have occurred near this pond.

Close to Jetavana are the Sri Lankan, Chinese, Myanmarese (Burmese) and Thai monasteries and temples. Also worth seeing is the park with a large bell donated by Japanese pilgrims.

Less than a kilometre away are the ruins of a medieval Jain temple, revered by the Jains as the birthplace of the third Jain Tirthankara, Swayambunatha. For Jain pilgrims there is an organisation at Shravasti called **Sri Shravasti Jain Svetambara Tirtha Committee** (Dt. Shravasti, UP 271813), which also promotes pilgrimages and research.

Accommodation

Inspection Bungalow of PWD, Burmese Temple Resthouse, Chinese Temple Resthouse, Burmese Temple Resthouse, Jain Dharmashala, Tourist Bungalow at Katra, in **Shravasti**; and Maya, a TCI hotel, and a Tourist Bungalow, both in **Balrampur**. The only high class hotel is **Lotus Nikko Hotel** (a unit of Lotus Trans Travel Pvt Ltd, New Delhi) at Balrampur-Bahraich Highway, Tel: 091-5252-265291 and 265292, Fax: 091-5252-265293; at Delhi head office, E-mail: lotus.del@rmt.sprintrpg.ems.vsnl.net.in

173

EXCURSION

About 28 km northeast towards the Nepalese border lies a famous *Shaktipitha* (seat of the Goddess), known as **Devi Patan** ('splitting of the goddess'). According to myths and legends this is the spot where Devi's right hand or shoulder (*skandha*) fell, and also where Sita disappeared into the earth while proving her innocence (as told in the *Ramayana*). This place is associated with one of the great warriors of the *Mahabharata*, Karna, who had received mystical knowledge from his guru Parashurama at this place. Another legend tells us that the mythological king Vikramaditya built this temple, which was demolished by the Mughal emperor Aurangzeb in the late 17th century. It attracts pilgrims from the whole of north India. The main temple is dedicated to **Pateshvari Devi** (goddess) and the monastery belongs to the sect of Kanphata Yogis (Gorakhnath Sampradaya). The place was famous for goat sacrifice as offering to the goddess; however in 1967 Shantinath, the then chief of the monastery, stopped this practice. There are some smaller shrines close to the compound. There is only one *dharmashala* where pilgrims get shelter during the main festive days.

174

7. KAUSHAMBI

Where the Buddha gave sermons in the 6th & 9th years

While the Blessed One dwelt at Kosambi, a certain bhikkhu was accused of having committed an offence, and, as he refused to acknowledge it, the brotherhood pronounced against him the sentence of expulsion.

[...]

Then the Blessed One rose and went to the brethren who sided with the expelled brother and said to them:

"Do not think, O bhikkhus, that if you have given offence you need not atone for it, thinking: 'We are without offence'. When a bhikkhu has committed an offence, which he considers no offence while the brotherhood consider him guilty, he should think: 'These brethren know the *Dhamma* and the rules of the order; they are learned, wise, intelligent, modest, conscientious, and ready to submit themselves to discipline; it is impossible that they should on my account act with selfishness or in malice or in delusion or in fear.' Let him stand in awe of causing divisions, and rather acknowledge his offence on the authority of his brethren."

The Mahavagga, x, 1, 2 ≈1 - 2≈20.

Approach & Cultural History

On the way to Chitrakut, at a distance of 55 km from Allahabad (132 km from Varanasi linked by the G.T. Road, NH 2) is Kaushambi, an ancient Buddhist site. Take the NH 2 west out of Allahabad to Bamauli (10 km), then the left turn that leads past the airport to Kaushambi (35 km) on the Chitrakut Road. Buses depart irregularly from Leader Road bus stand, Allahabad. Those not planning to visit Chitrakut can return in the evening back to Allahabad and pass the night there.

It is said that the Kuru king Nikakshu, contemporary of Janaka, transferred his capital from Hastinapur to Kaushambi. Nikakshu was a descendant of Janmejaya and was instrumental in bringing the Bharata dynasty to this place. King Satanika Paranatapa belonged to this dynasty. His son was king Udena (Udaya), who was a contemporary of the Buddha. Udena's son Bodhiraja Kumara was more faithful to the Buddha than his father. He invited the Buddha to inaugurate his new palace, Kokanada, built at Sumsumaragiri in the Bhagga country. The Buddha, after taking meals in his palace, delivered to the prince a discourse in which he explained that austerities did not always lead to happiness. He himself practised them and found this to be so. He then explained to him that as a person needed faith, energy, straightforwardness and good health for learning any worldly act or craft, so also a monk needed them to attain perfection in knowledge.

Kaushambi is traditionally associated with the *Mahabharata*; however the early Buddhist texts also mention the pilgrimage route starting from Kaushambi, then an industrial township. This town was one among the six big towns of the great kingdoms of north India during the time of the Buddha; the others were Champa, Rajagriha, Saketa, Varanasi and Shravasti. At that time three great monasteries (*viharas*) are said to have been constructed here: Ghositarama, Kukkutarama and Pavarika Ambavana. Of these only remain the ruins of Ghositarama Monastery. A headless image of the Buddha dated to the second year of Kanishka's reign (i.e. CE 80) was found here. Several inscriptions of the Gupta period of the 2nd-3rd centuries CE, and coins, beads and minor antiquities which were found here support the above history. The Buddhist texts mention the ethical norms to be followed by monks at Kaushambi: prohibition of digging the earth, cutting trees and prevaricating in statements. Instructions were also given about roofing a hermitage at Kaushambi. One of the early Vedic texts (i.e. *Shatapatha Brahmana,*12.2.2.13) refers to a teacher who was native of Kaushambi, a contemporary of the famous Upanishadic figure Uddalaka Aruni.

In his first visit to Kaushambi, before the Buddha left the three monks Nandiya, Kimbila, and Anuruddha, he spoke to them,

"Monks, the very nature of a *sangha* is harmony. I believe harmony can be realised by following these principles:

1. Sharing a common space such as a forest or home.
2. Sharing the essentials of daily life together.
3. Observing the precepts together.
4.Using only words that contribute to harmony, avoiding all words that can cause the community to break.
5. Sharing insights and understanding together.
6. Respecting others' viewpoints and not forcing another to follow your own viewpoint.

A *sangha* that follows these principles will have happiness and harmony. Monks, let us always observe these six principles."

The monks were happy to receive this teaching from the Buddha. The Buddha bid them farewell and walked until he reached Rakkhita Forest, near Parileyyaka. After sitting in meditation beneath a lush sal tree, he decided to spend the approaching rainy season alone in the forest. (*Kosambiya Sutta*, M. 48)

The enormous ruins are spread through several villages. Two — **Kosam-Inam** and **Kosam-Khiraj** — have names suggesting their links with the ruins of the city of Kausam (Kaushambi). It was the capital of the Vatsa King Udena, a contemporary of the Buddha, and the Enlightened One is said to have preached several sermons here in his 6th and 9th years after enlightenment.

Ashoka's Pillar

The road passes through the ramparts of the ancient city, and following it for some distance you will find on the left of the road the remains of an Ashoka's pillar in the fields surrounded by the walls of a **fortress**. The pillar has no inscription, but there is a large amount of graffiti from later ages, and also some unusual circular designs on it. The pillar stood in a residential area of the city, probably at a main crossroads, or in a square. The remains of houses and other buildings are scattered around the pillar. According to the Chinese pilgrim Hsüan-tsang (639 CE) the Buddha preached here (see Fig. 64) and two *viharas* (monasteries) were built to commemorate the event. The

Fig. 64. The Buddha preaching (a scene from Thailand, ca. 7th-8th century).

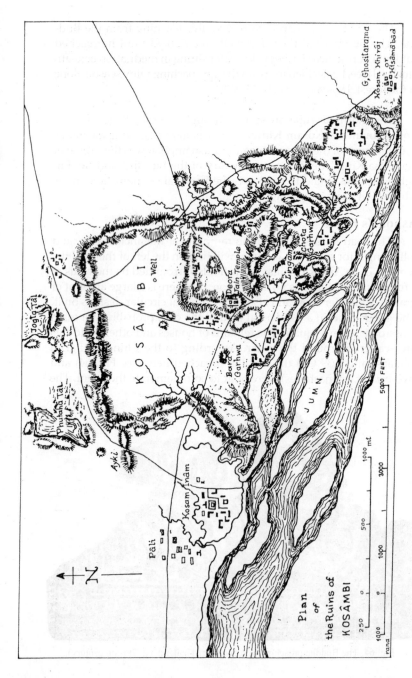

Fig. 65. Kaushambi: the ancient mounds and ruins (after A. Cunningham, 1875)

town was inhabited continuously from about the 8th century BCE to the 6th century CE. In the southwest corner are what is possibly the remains of a palace. Today one can see the ruins of an **Ashokan Pillar**, an old fort and the **Ghositarama Monastery** (Fig. 65).

Another of Ashoka's pillars, having an inscription referring to religious officials at Kaushambi, presently stands in the Allahabad fort. This pillar may have originally stood at the Ghositarama, though neither of the Chinese pilgrims, Fa-hien nor Hsüan-tsang, mention seeing any pillars at Kaushambi.

Ghositarama

About 500 m southeast of Ashoka's pillar, in the fields, are the ruins of the Ghositarama, the most famous of the several places where the Buddha used to pass the nights while in Kaushambi. The Ghositarama is situated right against the inside of the walls of Kaushambi, just near the east gate, and is unique in that it is the only one of the monasteries established during the Buddha's time that is situated inside, rather than outside, a city (Fig. 66).

The Buddha delivered the *Upakkilesa Sutta*, the *Kosambiya Sutta*, the *Jaliya Sutta* and several other discourses here (cf. *Majjhima Nikaya*, III: 152, and I: 320; *Digha Nikaya*, I; 159). Ananda too must have frequented the Ghositarama often, as narrated in many of the discourses he delivered at this monastery (cf. *Samyutta Nikaya*, IV: 113).

It is known from inscriptions found on the site that in the 1st century CE, a monk named Phagol donated a stone slab to be used "for the worship of all the Buddhas by the monks residing in the Ghositarama monastery, the abode of the Buddha."

In the 3rd year of Kanishka's reign, the nun Buddhamitra donated three statues of the Bodhisattva to this monastery. This generous and devout woman is also described as a disciple of the monk Bala in the inscription on the famous statue of the Bodhisattva in Sarnath. When Fa-hien visited Kaushambi (early 5th century) he found monks residing in the Ghositarama 'as of old', but by the time of Hsüan-tsang's (CE 639) it had become a deserted ruin. The Ghositarama was identified during excavations which began at Kaushambi in 1951. Inhabited as it was from the fifth century BCE to the fifth century CE, the various layers exposed during the excavation make the outlines of the individual structures difficult to detect, though several of the main ones are fairly clear.

The oldest structure on the site is a large *stupa* of 25 x 25 m size, first built during the Mauryan period (3rd century BCE?). This is certainly the 61 m high *stupa* that Hsüan-tsang saw in the Ghositarama,

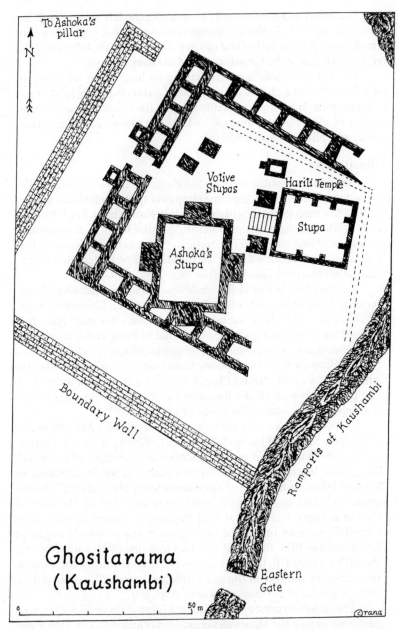

To Ashoka's pillar

N

Votive Stupas

Hariti Temple

Stupa

Ashoka's Stupa

Boundary Wall

Ramparts of Kaushambi

Ghositarama
(Kaushambi)

Eastern Gate

0   50 m

©rana

Fig. 66. Kaushambi: Ghositarama Monastery

and which he credited to Emperor Ashoka. The base of the *stupa* was originally square, but during later expansions some recesses were added, making it polygonal in shape. The *stupa* was provided with an elaborate system of drainage. A little to the east of the main *stupa* is the base of a smaller one, rectangular in shape, with a flight of stairs leading up to it. On either side of the stairs are two smaller *stupas* with shrines attached to them. There is also the damaged shaft of a sandstone column, probably erected during the rule of the Mauryan Emperor Ashoka. The Mughals removed this column and brought it to the Allahabad Fort. The Allahabad Ashokan pillar was formerly set up at Kaushambi, and one of its edicts was addressed to the officials of Kaushambi.

Next to the *stupa* is a small well-built shrine in which was found a seated statue of Hariti, a demi-god *yakshini*, who used to eat children until she was converted by the Buddha; after which she came to be considered as a sort of patron saint of children. The Chinese pilgrims often mention seeing shrines to Hariti in the Buddhist monasteries all over India.

All of these structures are in a courtyard of the main monastery, and are surrounded by the monks' cells, of which about 23 can still be traced. The main entrance to the monastery is on the northwest. In turn, the monastery is surrounded by a large wall nearly 4 m thick at some places.

Prabhosa Hill

The Buddha spent his sixth rainy season near Kaushambi at a place called Mankula Hill about which neither the *suttas* nor the commentaries give any information, except that it was in the vicinity of Kaushambi. As the only high ground for many kilometers around the city is a rocky outcrop called Prabhosa, one can easily identify it with Mankula Hill. To get to Prabhosa, return to where the road cuts through the main ramparts, turn left, and proceed towards the southwest for about 4 km. The road is unpaved but in acceptable condition. Prabhosa rises suddenly from the surrounding countryside and overlooks the Yamuna River. The cave now called Sita's Window is most likely where the Buddha stayed when he came here. When Hsüan-tsang visited Mankula he reported seeing this cave and two *stupas* near it, one built by Ashoka and another believed to enshrine the Buddha's hair and nail clippings, though no traces of these monuments can be seen today. A barely visible inscription on the wall of the cave mentions gifts made to "the *arahats* of the Kasyapiya sect."

The archaeological evidences suggest that the earliest examples of Kaushambi's art expression in the form of **Polished Grey Ware** (PGW) paintings (1000-800 BCE) belong to the proto-historic period. The PGW seems to be elementary in design and mainly comprise horizontal bands on the rim or the body of the vessels, and marks the first cultural period of earliest settlement. The **Northern Black Polished Ware**, NBPW (600-200 BCE) refers to the second period that included the first brick building. The **post-NBPW** phases (175 BCE to CE 325) correspond to the 3rd cultural period. The coins found in the third period testify to a succession of rulers: the Mitras, followed by the Kushana kings and then by the Maghas. Svastika, Chakra, Nandipada, tree-in-railing, mountain/hill with or without crescent, elephant, bull and Gajalakshmi are some of the important symbols and forms depicted on the coins of Kaushambi. The road evidently continued in use up to about CE 300 and the site itself was occupied until about CE 400. The existing enormous defensive structures are its testimony.

The terracotta of Kaushambi has a special place in the history of Indian clay art. With reference to manufacturing techniques they can be classified into 3 groups. The 1st consists of early handmade grey and dull-red pieces, sometimes with applied decorations. The 2nd consists of moulded ones, dated to the 2nd-1st century BCE, representing conceptual rather than realistic portrayal of figures and reflecting the traits of contemporary art in dress, ornamentation, etc. And the 3rd is made of partly-modelled and partly moulded clay and recalls the features of contemporary Kushana art, particularly in facial features. Important are those with elaborate decorations, mother goddesses, reclining women, dancers and drummers with peaked caps indicating Shaka-Parthian influence. Many of the coins and terracotta discovered here are now on display in the Allahabad City Museum and Kaushambi Museum at the University of Allahabad.

MAIN LINK STATION: ALLAHABAD (PRAYAGA)

Population: 1,016,500. Postal Code: 211001. STD code: 0532
Connected by two National Highways, 2 and 27, Allahabad lies
at a distance of 127 km west of Varanasi. Some of the road distances
are: Agra 433 km, Chitrakut 134 km, Delhi 643 km, Khajuraho 294 km,
and Lucknow 204 km. Allahabad is well connected by trains with all
the major cities of India. The nearest big airports are at Varanasi (148
km) and Lucknow (215 km). On the way to Chitrakut at a distance of
55 km from Allahabad is **Kaushambi**. Take the NH 2 west out of
Allahabad to Bamauli (10 km), on the Chitrakut Road, then the left
turn that leads to the Bamauli airport goes to Kaushambi (35 km).
Buses depart irregularly from Leader Road bus stand, Allahabad.

Allahabad, culturally known as Prayaga, is eulogised in Puranic
mythologies as the '*Tirtharaja*', the king of all sacred places. Situated
picturesquely at the confluence of the rivers Ganga, Yamuna and the
invisible Sarasvati, it is one of the three holy cities symbolising the
pillars of the Bridge to Heaven; the other two are Varanasi and Gaya.
People from different parts of India come to Allahabad (Prayaga) especially during the month of *Magha* (January-February) to bathe in
the sacred waters of the confluence (*Sangam*) and every twelve years
they come by the millions to the world's greatest religious bath-fair,
the **Kumbha Mela**. The greatness of Prayaga is eulogised in *Vedic*
literature, in the *Puranic* mythologies, in treatises, epigraphic records,
Buddhist and Jain literature and foreign accounts. The land between
the rivers Ganga and Yamuna is said to be the *mons veneris* of the
Earth Goddess, and Prayaga is regarded as its generative organ (cf.
Mahabharata, III.87.71; *Matsya Purana*, 105.19). This is a cosmogonic
allusion to the place, suggesting that Prayaga is the symbolic centre
(*axis mundi*) of the creation of the universe.

About 6 km to the east of the Allahabad Railway Station and
close to the confluence area is the lofty **Allahabad Fort**. Built in four
stages by the Mughal emperor Akbar in 1583 on the Yamuna River,
this was the largest of the forts built by him; it spreads over an area of
2273 x 1418 m. Much of the fort remains occupied by the military,
and thus public access is restricted to the corner around the Patalapuri
temple and the Akshayavata. At the main gate of the fort stands the
restored polished-stone **Ashokan Pillar**, dating back to 232 BCE,
which was moved to the fort from Kaushambi under Akbar's orders.
The 10.6 m high pillar has several edicts recorded on it along with a

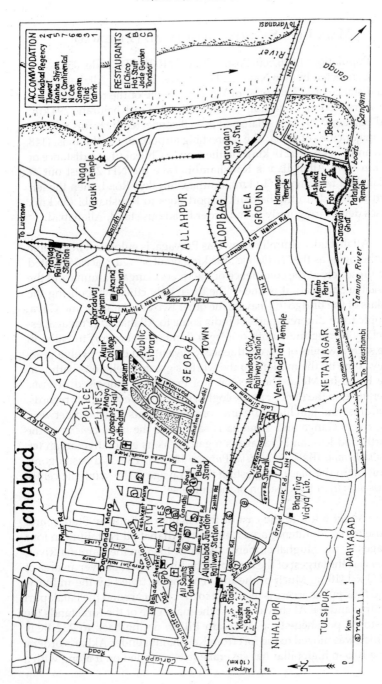

Fig. 67. Allahabad

Persian inscription by the Mughal emperor Jahangir (1603-1627), on the occasion of his accession to the throne.

The **Patalapuri Temple**, accessible through a small doorway in the wall of the fort, is famous for miracles and the special merit of giving relief from transmigration. This underground temple stands on 100 pillars and spreads over an area of 25.5 m x 149.1 m. Inside are housed 43 weird toy-boxes of gods and goddesses illuminated through gates in the ceiling. Inside the fort is the **Akshayavata** ('imperishable banyan', *Ficus indica*), the most popular site of worship. The Chinese pilgrim Hsüan-tsang (ca. 644 CE) has described this tree. Although at present there is no trace of the ancient tree, however it appears in the form of a bifurcated log in one corner of the Patalapuri Temple (cf. Fig. 67).

In the shadow of the fort's outer wall facing the *Sangam* side is a unique and largest reclining image of Hanuman, the Monkey-god. This is known as **Hanuman Temple**, though of course the temple itself is only a shed. Nearby on the high ground overlooking the trees is the **Shankar Viman Mandapam**, a 39.6 m high four-storied modern temple. The *murtis* (sculptures) of Kumarila Bhatta, Jagat Guru Shankaracharya, Kamakshi Devi, Tirupati Balaji (with 108 Vishnus), and Yogashastra Sahastrayoga Linga (having 108 Shiva *lingas*) adorn the interior.

Along the Ganga river, in the locality of Daraganj, a ghat named **Dashasvamedhika** is believed to be the site where the Bhara Shiva Nagas, an imperial dynasty of the 3rd-4th centuries CE, took their ceremonial bath and performed the ritual of 'ten-horses-sacrifice' (*Dash-ashva-medhika*). Presently there is a small temple that houses fragments of images in its outer platform.

About 3 km north of the Fort, connected by the Bandh (dam) Road, and close to the bank of the Ganga is the **Naga Vasuki Temple**, representing an ancient site of the Naga Hrida ('snake's water pool'). The beautifully carved and architecturally designed snake image in black marble is the main image and deity. The building of the temple is dated to the 18th century, when Raja Sridhar Bhonsle of Nagpur rebuilt it. The setting and surrounding of the temple is serene and soothing with an aura of peace and beatitude.

Near the Ganga River, on the way to the Sangam from downtown is a **Rupa Gaudiya Math** temple, on South Mallaca Street, in the Madhavapir area. Shrila Prabhupada, the founder of ISKCON (International Society for Krishna Consciousness), took initiation here from Shrila Bhaktisiddhanta Sarasvati. Shrila Prabhupada came to Allahabad in 1971 for the Ardha Kumbha Mela and also in 1977 to attend the Maha Kumbha Mela.

About 3 km west of the Naga Vasuki Temple, in the neighbourhood of Colonelganj there are many places worth visiting, such as Bhardvaja Ashram, Anand Bhavan, the Planetarium, and the nearby museum. This is the main downtown in the city. The **Bhardvaja Ashram** is eulogised in the *Ramayana* (II.58.8). The excavations close to this site (1977-79) suggest the antiquity of this place. The typical pottery and terracotta seals and sealings and brick structures found there prove its antiquity back to the Gupta period (4th-6th centuries CE). It is believed that Lord Rama visited this place during his exile. An image of Bhairava in the *Saptarishi temple* in this compound is dated to the Gupta period. The Allahabad University now occupies the archaeological site. Nearby there is a sacred compound on a raised platform consisting of many temples and shrines in honour of and associated with the sage Bhardvaja.

Across the main road is **Anand Bhavan** (Tel: 2600476), the erstwhile ancestral home of the Nehru family, built by Motilal Nehru (1861-1931). This is the former home of three Prime Ministers of India, i.e. Jawaharlal Nehru (1889-1964), Indira Gandhi (1917-1984) and Rajiv Gandhi (1944-1991).

About 600 m south of the Allahabad Ralway Station, in Khuldabad, approached by Leader Road from the north and G.T. Road (NH 2) from the south, is the walled garden called **Khusru Bagh**, covering an area of 2.75 hectares. Prince Khusru, the eldest son of Jahangir, was murdered in 1615 by his own brother, later the emperor Shah Jahan (r 1627-1658). After staging an unsuccessful rebellion against his father Jahangir (r 1605-1627) in 1607, Khusru spent the next year in chains. When freed later on, he encouraged a plot to assassinate his father but was discovered. He was blinded, though he did regain partial sight, and spent the rest of his life as a captive and ultimately died there through intentional negligence and malnutrition. The typical Mughal garden enclosure is entered through an 18 m high archway. The burial chamber is underground with decorative plasterwork. The tomb to the west is thought to be of Khusru's sister. Further west is the 2-storey tomb of his mother, Shah Begum.

Canning Town (now called Civil Lines), opposite to the Allahabad Ralway Station, was laid out on a grid in the 1860s. Within it are the Old High Court and Public Offices, and classical style buildings from the late 19th century including the Gothic style **All Saint's Cathedral**, set in the middle of the traffic circle here as if it were on a coaster. Described as the finest Anglican cathedral in Asia, following the 13th century Gothic style, this Cathedral is a remarkable example of colonial architecture in India. [Services: Sunday, 8 am].

The high **mounds of Jhusi** on the eastern bank of the Ganga overlooking the confluence, called **Pratishthanapuri**, represent the ruins of the ancient township. However, a large portion of the site appears to have been eroded by the Ganga during the course of the centuries. On its southern side is the Samudrakupa, believed to have been built by Samudragupta. Due to encroachments on all its sides, the place has lost its sanctity and scenic beauty.

Located at the edge of C.S. Azad Park, on Kamla Nehru Road, the **Allahabad Museum** (Tel: 2600834) has an excellent collection of sculptures and artefacts. The Museum has 18 galleries containing a wide range of stone sculptures (2nd century BCE from Bharhut and Koshambi, 1st century CE Kushana from Mathura, 4th-6th century Gupta and 11th century carvings from Khajuraho). It has also a fine collection of Rajasthani miniatures, terracotta figures, coins, and paintings by Nicholas Roerich; Open: 10.00-17.00, Closed on Mondays, Ticket: Rs 5. Inside the C.S. Azad Park is found the oldest library of the city, **Allahabad Public Library** (Tel: 2600581). Founded in 1864, the building is a fine piece of architecture and houses about 10,000 rare books, old Government Publications, Parliamentary Papers and the Blue Books of the 19th century. The once-renowned **Allahabad University**, north of the museum, was one of the firsts opened by the British in India. Its buildings are in full 19th century Gothic style. The **University Archaeological Museum** (Tel: 2608083) in the campus keeps various artefacts from Kaushambi, including pottery, terracotta figurines, coins, beads and bangles.

The Kumbha Mela and the Sangam

The Maha (Great) Kumbha Mela is the largest gathering of humanity on planet earth. The last at Allahabad in 2001 (9 January-21 February) set the world record for the largest human gathering. About 90 million people were estimated to have come for this auspicious Hindu festival at the holiest time to bathe in the **Sangam**, the confluence place of the three rivers, viz. the Ganga, the Yamuna and the invisible Sarasvati. Every 12 years, at one precisely calculated moment based on astronomical conjunctions, all the pilgrims splash into the water, an act that is believed to undo lifetimes of sins. This moment is determined by the alignment of the planetary movements that generally happens in an eleven or twelve year cycle, at the entering of the planet Jupiter into Aries or Taurus, or the entering of the Sun and Moon into Capricorn. The Chinese pilgrim Hsüan-tsang, who attended the 6th quinquennial assembly organised by the king Harshavardhana at Prayaga in the month of *Magha* in CE 644, supplies the first historical reference to the Kumbha Mela (Ardha). In the 9th century CE Shankaracharya started an organised form of celebrating the Kumbha Mela, and transformed it into a pan-Indian meeting of ascetics, devout pilgrims and Hindus of various sects.

The story behind the **Kumbha Mela** concerns a *kumbha* (pitcher) that contained immortality-bestowing nectar (*amrita*). The demons battled with the gods for this pot in a struggle that lasted 12 days, during the period of which 4 drops of nectar were spilled at four places, viz. Allahabad, Haridvar (U.P.), Nasik (Maharashtra), and Ujjain (M.P.). It is believed that one drop of the nectar fell at the confluence of the three rivers, i.e. Ganga, Yamuna and the mythical Sarasvati, referred to as *Triveni*, and popularly called **Sangam**. The mythical 12-day fight is translated to 12-human years, the length of the festival's rotation cicle. Every 3 years approximately a Kumbha Mela is held in one of the four cities. In 2003 it will be at Nasik, in 2004 at Ujjain, and in 2010 at Haridvar.

General Information & Facilities. Area 63.07 sq. km. Altitude: 98 m. Local Transport: Taxis, buses, and cycle-rickshaws. PO & TO: at S. N. Marg (Tel: 2622766), Sub PO near Johnstonganj (Tel: 254341, 254929).

Tourist Information Office: Govt. of U.P. Regional Tourist Office, Tourist Bungalow, 35 M. G. Marg, Civil Lines (Tel: 2601873 & 2611374).

Travel Agencies: Krishna Travel Agency, 936 Dara Ganj (Tel: 2602832), Pratap Travel Agency, 50 Zero Rd (Tel: 2402540, 2607680), Varuna Travel Agency, Maya Bazar, Civil Lines (Tel: 2624323, 2623076).

Hospitals: Dufferin Hospital, Chowk (Tel: 2651822), Kamla Nehru Hospital, Tagore Town (Tel: 2600469), Motilal Nehru Hospital, Colvin (Tel: 2652141), Tej Bahadur Sapru Hospital, Stainley Rd (Tel: 2642687), Swaroop Rani Nehru Hospital, M. G. Road (Tel: 2603782).

Banks: State Bank of India, main branch (Tel: 2609196), Allahabad Bank, main branch (Tel: 2622288), Bank of Baroda, 61 M. G. Marg, Civil Lines (Tel: 2601-412 & 229), Canara Bank near Indian Coffee House, Civil Lines (Tel: 2624524), Bank of India, 10 Sardar Patel Marg, Civil Lines (Tel: 2624834, 2602165), Union Bank of India, 49 M. G. Marg, Civil Lines (Tel: 2623658, 2603152).

Accommodation/ Hotels

Allahabad Regency, 16 Tashkent Road (Tel: 2601519, 2601735), **Kanha Shyam**, Civil Lines (Tel: 2420281, Fax: 2622164; e-mail: info@kanhashyam.com), **Presidency**, 19-D Sarojini Naidu Road (Tel:

2623308, 2623309), **Yatrik**, 33 S.P. Road, Civil Lines (Tel: 2601713-14, 2601509, 2601799), **Hotel Samrat**, 49 A/25A Mahatma Gandhi Rd (Tel: 2604869, 2604879), **YMCA**, 13 Sarojini Naidu Road (Tel: 2624028), **Finaro**, 8 Hasting Rd, opposite High Court, Tel: 2622452, fax: 2622218, email: imtindia@sancharnet.in, U.P. **Tourist Bungalow**, 35 Mahatma Gandhi Road (Tel: 2601144, 2601104), **Santosh Palace**, 51/104 Katju Rd, **Royal**, Smith Rd (Tel: 2623285), and **Railway Retiring Rooms** and dormitories at Allahabad Junction.

Restaurants/ Bars

The city's various restaurants serve a variety of cuisine — Continental, Chinese, Indian and of course the traditional Mughlai. Notables are: Bar & Restaurants, Tourist Bungalow; Hasty Tasty, South Road, Civil Lines; Rajdoot Bar & Restaurant, Vivekananda Marg, Jade Garden; Hotel Tepso, Civil Lines; Tandoor Restaurant, Civil Lines; El Chicko Restaurant, 24 Mahatma Gandhi Road, Civil Lines, and nearby Kwality; Mangalam, J. L. Nehru Road; and Jade Garden, Tepso Hotel.

FURTHER EXCURSIONS

About 36 km northwest of Allahabad, the high mound of Singraur has preserved the story of **Shringaverapura** of the *Ramayana*. The site is situated about 3 km from the Allahabad-Unnao Road approachable through the village of Bhagawatipur, near Mansurabad. This site was visited by Cunningham in 1876-77; he described a modern shrine dedicated to sage Shringi, who was said to have performed a special fire-ritual (*puttreshti yajna*) for king Dasharatha of Ayodhya to have sons. Inside the shrine are an image of Hara-Gauri and a small figure of the Sun-god Surya seated on a chariot driven by seven horses. About 1 km to the north of the main site is a small mound, usually called **Surya Bhita**, suggesting the existence of a temple of the Sun at this spot in previous times.˙The excavations yielded different types of pottery, terracotta figurines, coins, seals, sealings, and other minor objects from different periods. The opening of a massive burnt brick tank of the Kushana period was the most outstanding discovery. This is held to be the largest tank ever revealed through an excavation in the country.

From Kaushambi/Allahabad you can plan to visit some more ancient Buddhist sites. The *Jataka tales* tell us that when the Buddha completed his 9th rainy season at Kaushambi, conflicts developed among the monks and he failed to solve the issue. With an aim to relax, he moved towards Shravasti in the north in search of an isolated serene place. While en-route to Shravasti he had stopped and stayed some time at the village of **Balakalonakara** (now known as *Balakmau*). The village Balakmau is at a distance of 45 km west of Allahabad, 18 km north of Kaushambi, and 5 km southwest of Bharwai railway station. This site was also associated with Jainism as one Jain monk, Upali Gahapati, was a resident of this village. In Jain literature this village is mentioned as '**Mau Grama**'. The images of the Jain Thirthankaras Kunthunatha, Ajitanatha and Mahavira found here and dated to the 9th century support this conclusion. At this site the Buddha gave his preaching about inner search in isolation. Here were found many Brahmanical and Buddhist images scattered in and around the village. The sculptures and images of this site are preserved in the museums in Allahabad and in the University of Allahabad. According to some recent interpretations, the Buddha had crossed the Ganga (Ganges) river near the village of Kada and stayed in a deer forest, called *Pachina Vamsa(miga)daya*, presently identified with village **Bihar**. From here the Lord turned further west following the bank of the Ganga river and halted at Parileyyaka, presently known as **Pariawan**, that lies 70 km west of Allahabad. According to the journey of the Chinese pilgrim Hsüan-tsang (ca. 7th century), he had passed through Ayomukha, presently known as **Unchdih**, that lies 38 km north of Allahabad on the bank of a small stream, Baklani Nadi. At this site one can see images and remains of the 9th-10th centuries scattered on and around the great mound.

Ref. Books

Dubey, D. P. 2000, **Prayaga: the Site of the Kumbha Mela**. Aryan International Publs., New Delhi, illustrated.

Dubey, D. P. eds. 2001, **Kumbha Mela**. Society of Pilgrimage Studies, Allahabad; 5 essays.

Singh, Rana P.B. and Rana, P.S. 2002. **Banaras Region. A Spiritual and Cultural Guide**. Indica Books, Varanasi. "Allahabad", pp. 287-299.

8. RAJGIR (RAJAGRIHA)

Where the Buddha converted Sariputta & Moggallana

King Ajatashatru possessed a very ferocious elephant. Devadatta, hearing that the Buddha was coming to Rajgir, arranged to have the elephant escape. As the Buddha came toward the city, Devadatta went to the palace terrace to see the Buddha killed, but when the elephant came rushing at the Buddha, the Enlightened One tamed the elephant with a few words, and the ferocious beast knelt at his feet.

Mulasarvastivadin Vinaya

At Rajagriha, the Buddha breathed forth this solemn utterance:
"Surrender the grasping disposition of selfishness,
and you will attain to that calm state of mind
which conveys perfect peace, goodness, and wisdom".
  [...]
"Do not deceive, do not despise
Each other, anywhere.
Do not be angry, nor should ye
Secret resentment bear;
For as a mother risks her life
And watches o'er her child,
So boundless be your love to all,
So tender, kind and mild."
"Yea, cherish good-will right and left,
All round, early and late,
And without hindrance, without stint,
From envy free and hate,
While standing, walking, sitting down,
Whate'er you have in mind,
The rule of life that's always best
Is to be loving-kind."

The Sutta Nipata, v. 148, cf. Rhys Davids, *Buddhism* (1890), p. 109.

Approach & Background

Population: 27,800. Postal Code: 803116. STD Tel. Code: 06119.
Rajgir (old name, *Rajagriha*, i.e. 'the Royal Palace'), situated at

92 km northeast of Bodh Gaya, and 105 km southeast of Patna, in the district of Nalanda, is well connected by roads. From Varanasi to Rajgir the distance is 333 km. Of course, Rajgir is connected by a branch rail track, but the buses are faster and frequently available from/ for Gaya, Patna and Pawapuri. The physical conditions of the area comprising the city, viz., the hills encircling it on all sides, have given it the name Girivraja, the 'enclosure of hills'.

According to a legend in the *Ramayana*, Vasu, the fourth son of Brahma the creator, founded Girivraja. During the period of the *Mahabharata* this place was the seat of the king Brihadrath of the Barhadratha dynasty; the most famous king of this dynasty was Jarasandha, the maternal uncle of Krishna, who founded the Magadhan Empire. When the Buddha was teaching his Law, a new dynasty with Bimbisara as the king (ca. 543-491 BCE) began ruling over Magadha. Gautama, the ascetic, first visited Rajgir on his way to Bodh Gaya and was met by King Bimbisara. The king was so impressed by the Bodhisattva that he tried every means to persuade him to stay. Failing in this, he received a promise from Gautama that he would return to Rajgir after his enlightenment. Accordingly, after teaching in Sarnath, the Buddha travelled to Rajgir followed by over a thousand monks of the new order. King Bimbisara welcomed them all and offered them the Veluvana Bamboo Grove. This was to be the first property of the Order and one of the Buddha's favourite residences.

The Buddha is believed to have converted the Magadhan king Bimbisara on the Gridhrakuta hill. In his old age Bimbisara is said to have been imprisoned and killed by his son Ajatashatru (ca. 491-459 BCE); however Ajatashatru later submitted himself to the Buddha as his follower. Rajgir was the capital of the Magadhan Empire and a known business township until Ajatashatru's successor Udayin (ca. 459-443 BCE) moved his capital to Pataliputra (Patna). Rajgir is known as the first recorded capital in Indian history. At this place the Buddha spent many years of his life. It was the place where Devadatta, a wicked cousin of the Buddha, made several attempts on his life, including using a mad elephant to kill the Master. But the Buddha tamed the elephant with a few words, and the ferocious beast knelt at his feet. Perhaps the most important event of the Buddha's first visit to Rajgir was the conversion of Sariputta and Moggallana.

On his first visit to Rajgir the Buddha stayed there for about three weeks. Throughout the following weeks, many seekers came to him and asked to be ordained as monks. Many of them were highly educated young men from wealthy families. The Buddha's senior students performed the ordination ceremonies and gave the new monks basic instruction in the practice. Other young people, women as well as men, came to Palm Forest and took the Three Refuges.

One day Kondanna gave the Three Refuges to a gathering of nearly 900 young people. After the ceremony, he spoke to them about the three precious gems — the Buddha, the *Dhamma*, and the *Sangha*, together known as '*triratna*'.

Said Kondanna, "The Buddha is the Awakened One. An awakened person sees the nature of life and the cosmos. Because of that, illusion, fear, anger, or desire do not bind an awakened person. An awakened person is a free person, filled with peace and joy, love and understanding. Master Gautama, the Buddha, is a completely awakened person. The Buddha is the first precious gem."

"The *Dhamma* is the path which leads to Awakening. It is the path that the Buddha teaches that helps us to transcend the prisons of ignorance, anger, fear, and desire. This path leads to freedom, peace, and joy. Understanding and love are the two most beautiful fruits of the Path of Awakening. The *Dhamma* is the second precious gem."

"The *Sangha* is the community of persons practising the Way of Awakening, those who travel this path together. If you want to practice the way of liberation, it is important to have a community to practice with. It is important to take refuge in the *Sangha*, whether you are an ordained *bhikkhu* or a lay person. The *Sangha* is the third precious gem."

Finally, Kondanna said, "O Young people! Today you have taken refuge in the Buddha, the *Dhamma*, and the *Sangha*. With the support of these refuges, you will not wander aimlessly but will be able to make real progress on the Path of Enlightenment. It has been two years since I took refuge in the three gems myself. Today you have vowed to travel the same path. Together we will practice the way of liberation to allow these three gems to shine from within us."

King Bimbisara, accompanied by 6,000 attendants and guests, came out to welcome the Buddha in the palace. The king led the Buddha and the monks to the royal courtyard where spacious tents had been set up to shade the guests from the hot sun. The Buddha was given the place of honour at the centre of the courtyard. All the places for the monks had been prepared with utmost care. Once the Buddha was seated, King Bimbisara invited everyone else to be seated. The king and Uruvela Kassapa (Kashyapa) sat on either side of the Buddha. The special feast started. King Bimbisara and his royal guests maintained perfect silence throughout the meal. All six thousand guests were impressed by the calm and joyous countenance of the Buddha and his monks.

When the Buddha and all of the 1,250 monks had finished eating, their bowls were taken and washed and then returned. King Bimbisara turned towards the Buddha and paid salutation with folded hands. Understanding the king's wishes, the Buddha began to teach the *Dhamma*. He spoke about the **five precepts** as the way to create peace and happiness for one's family and the entire kingdom. The Buddha said:

"The first precept is do not kill. Observing this precept nourishes compassion.

The second precept is do not steal. No one has the right to take away the belongings that another has earned by his/ her labour.

The third precept is to avoid sexual misconduct. Sexual relations should only take place with your spouse.

The fourth precept is do not lie. Do not speak words that can create division and hatred.

The fifth precept is do not drink alcohol or use other intoxicants. Alcohol and intoxicants rob the mind of clarity."

The ceremonial feast came to an end by the ritual of offering the Bamboo Forest (Venuvana) by King Bimbisara to the Buddha. And, thereafter the Buddha and his 1,250 disciple monks departed from the palace. (cf. *Khuddaka Nikaya* 1.23, 1 ff; *Tripitaka* 186)

Two important decisions were made during the last *Dhamma* meeting that took place in Visakha's Hall at Vulture Peak in Rajgir. The first was that Ananda should be the Buddha's permanent assistant. The second one was that the Buddha would return every year to Shravasti for the rainy retreat season. The monks concluded their meeting by agreeing to hold every rainy retreat in Shravasti, and they went directly to the Buddha's hut to present their ideas. The Buddha happily accepted both proposals. (cf. *Vinaya Mahavagga*, 8)

After the death of the Buddha (*parinirvana*), Ajatashatru brought his share of the corporal relics of the Master to Rajagriha and enshrined them inside a *stupa*. A few months later, when it was decided to hold the **First Buddhist Council** (*Sangiti*) in the Sattapanni (Saptaparni) cave of the Vaibhara hill, Ajatashatru built a large hall in front of the Sattapanni cave. On this occasion for the first time Buddha's teachings were written down under the guidance of his disciple Kassapa (Kashyapa) of Uruvela. After several discourses, the two codes of conducts (*suttas*) were shaped with common consensus; they are known as *Vinaya Sutta* ('code of compassion'), and *Dhammasutta* ('code of moral acts'). Ananda, Buddha's cousin, friend, and favourite disciple — and a man of prodigious memory! — recited Buddha's lessons

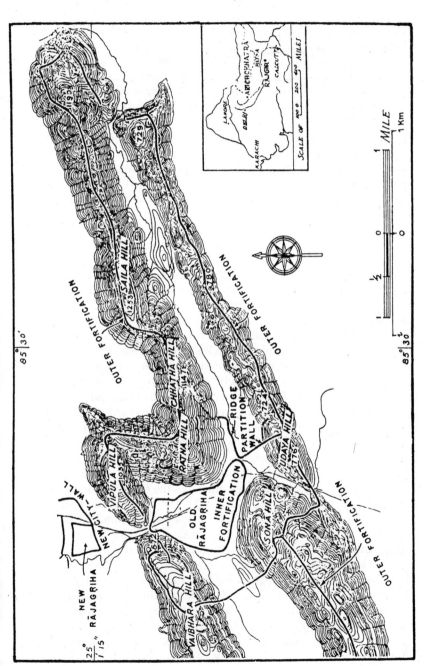

Fig. 68. Rajgir: Fortifications (based on ASI Report 1905-06)

(*suttas*). This great happening and its proceedings are described in detail in the Pali text *Chullavagga*. As 500 monks attended this congress, the proceedings were called *Panchashatika*.

Fa-hsien (Faxian), the Chinese pilgrim who visited India in the early 5th century CE, after ascending the Gridhrakuta Mountain offered his flowers and incense and lit his lamps for the night; he recited the *Surangama Sutta* in front of the cave and remained there all night. He found the valley desolate. Outside the hills there was a band of monks inhabiting the monastery of Karanda-venuvana. Hsüan-tsang, the famous Chinese pilgrim, visited Rajgir in the second quarter of the 7th century and found the city in a deserted condition. Of the ancient monasteries and *stupas* he found only the foundation-walls and ruins standing (Figs. 68, 69 and 70).

The most sacred places around Rajgir are the Venuvana and Gridhrakuta. **Venuvana**, meaning 'the Bamboo grove', was a park gifted to the Buddha in order to make it easier for his devotees to visit him. Bimbisara built a royal residence here for the Buddha. It is believed that the Lord had spent some time here. Excavations have revealed a room, some *stupas,* and the Karanda Tank where he bathed, now a Deer Park with a small zoo. There are springs at the foot of the Vaibhara hill, the largest of which is known as the Satadhara. About 150 m north of the modern temples and mosques near the hot springs is located a large tank immediately to the right of the footpath; it is identified as **Karanda Tank**, which is mentioned in Pali and Sanskrit Buddhist texts. A short distance from the southern bank of this tank is a large mound overgrown with shrubs and surmounted by a number of Muslim tombs. This mound is believed to mark the site of the *stupas* and *vihara* of Venuvana. On the other side of the stream are the remains of a stone wall crossing the stream, possibly an ancient causeway repaired in later times. To the south of Venuvana there are Jain and Hindu temples. To the east of Venuvana Hsüan-tsang saw a *stupa* built by Ajatashatru. The 4 km cyclorama dry stone wall that encircled the ancient city is in ruins as is the 5th century **Ajatashatru Fort**. The outer wall was built with blocks of stone, 1 m to 1.5 m long, with smaller stones. At the eastern edge of the Vaibhara Hill half a dozen hot springs, called **Satadhara**, are known for their healing powers. They are named Markandeya Kunda, Vyasa Kunda, Ganga-Yamuna Kunda, Ananta Kunda, Saptarshidhara, and Kashidhara. Later on these springs have been incorporated into the design of a pink building, a Hindu temple known as **Lakshmi Narayan**.

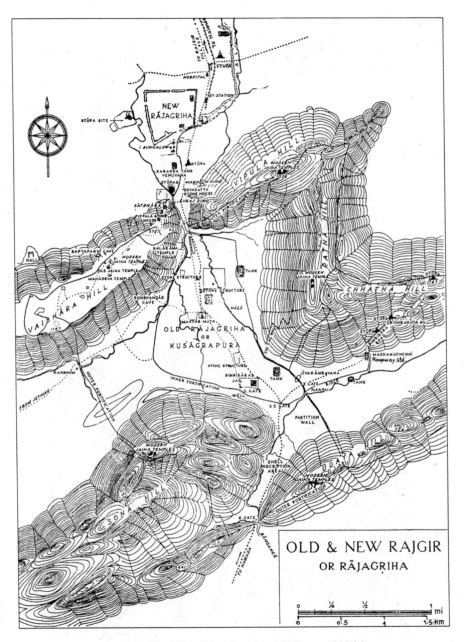

Fig. 69. Rajgir: Old and New (based on ASI Report 1905-06)

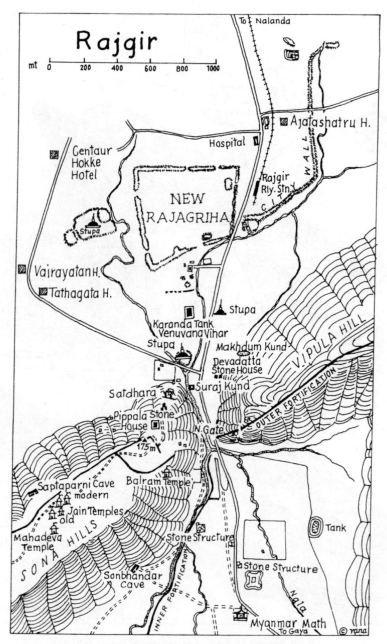

Fig. 70. Rajgir: The main township

A little above Satadhara, to the right of the pathway is a ruined temple of **Mahadeva** (Shiva), which is locally called *machan* ('watchtower') or **Jarasandha-ki-baithak**, a natural rectangular structure, assumed to be the residence of Pippala mentioned in Buddhist texts and in the accounts of the Chinese pilgrims (Fig. 71). Some of the

Fig. 71. Rajgir: Pippala Stone house

Pali texts describe the **Pippala cave**, hewn into the stone platform, popularly known as Jarasandh ki Baithak after the mythical Hindu king Jarasandha, as the residence of Mahakashyapa, the organiser of the First Council. Following a narrow rocky footpath descending to the northern scarp, a long artificial terrace leads to a group of six (originally there might have been seven) caves, identified as the original **Saptaparni Cave**. At this place the **First Buddhist Council** was held about six months after the Buddha's death to codify the teachings of the Great Master, when 500 monks gathered to compile in written form the Buddha's teachings.

Rajgir is also sacred to the followers of the Jain religion. Vardhaman Mahavira, the 24th Tirthankara (the last one), spent 14 rainy seasons at Rajagriha and its suburb of Nalanda. He had many rich supporters at Rajagriha. According to Jaina mythology, Bimbisara and Ajatashatru were votaries of their faith; they were known in the texts respectively as Shrenika and Kunika. This city was also regarded as the birthplace of Muni Suvrata, the 20th Tirthankara. A singular Jaina monument, known as Maniyar Matha, may be recognised in the cylindrical brick shrine, almost at the centre of the old city. According to local tradition the site was dedicated to the worship of Mani-naga, the guardian deity of the city of Rajagriha. Many of the hilltops are crowned with Jain temples, attracting a big mass of pilgrims and followers. On the summit of the hill is a large modern Jain **temple of Adinatha**. In the nearby area there are several **Jain temples** dedicated to the Tirthankaras, among whom the most popular are Rishabhadeva, Parshvanatha, Mahavira, Sambhavanatha, Adi Jina and Neminatha. A short drive from Venuvana Vihara leads to Virayatna, a Jain *ashram*, with a residential area and a museum. The cylindrical Jain shrine of the Maniyar Math is decorated with stucco figures.

Travelling about 200 m southeast of Satadhara one meets the **North Gate** of the outer fortifications of Old Rajagriha near the narrow gap between the Vaibhava and Vipula hills. About 1 km further south one meets the **Maniyar Math**, a stone compound-wall containing a cylindrical brick structure, about 6 m high, decorated with stucco figures all around it, and protected by a conical shelter of corrugated iron sheets and some other subsidiary structures. It consists of a small Jain shrine built on the top of a brick mound. The prevalence of Hindu images found here suggests that this was once a Hindu monastery, supposedly the monastery of Maninaga, the worshippers of Nagas ('snake-gods'). The archaeological remains support the view that during the period of the Buddha and Bimbisara this was an active place for rituals and councils. In course of time the Buddhists and Jains occupied this sacred place and left their marks. By a road running to the northwest of Maniyar Math there is a group of two caves in the southern scarp of the Vaibhava hill, known as **Sonbhandar**, built by the Jain saint Vairadeva. Inside the eastern cave, on the southern wall, are six small images of Jain Tirthankaras carved in relief that represent Padmaprabha, Parshvanatha and Mahavira. In the western cave is now placed a *shikhara*-shaped sculpture of black stone (known as *chaumukhi*) depicting a Jain Tirthankara on each of its four faces.

Proceeding southwards along the main road, at a distance of about 1 km from Maniyar Math there is a stone enclosure of about 60 sq m consisting of a 2 m thick wall with circular bastions at the corners, called **Bimbisara Jail**. The rock-cut steps lead to the 2 *stupas* related to Bimbisara. This is identified with the remains of the prison in which Ajatashatru confined his father Bimbisara, and finally killed him. It is said that from his prison Bimbisara was able to see the Buddha as he meditated on the Gridhrakuta. Ajatashatru, along with Devadatta, had conspired to take the life of the Lord by letting loose a mad elephant. But the Lord tamed the wild elephant, which stood still, overcome by the Lord's serene visage. After killing his father, Ajatashatru was filled with remorse and later embraced the Buddhist faith. From the foot to the top of the hill there is a stony stairway and road, believed to have been built by Bimbisara, which was used by the Chinese pilgrim Hsüan-tsang in the 7th century and still provides the best access.

Jivakamravana Monastery

Along the road to the new town built by Ajatashatru are the ruins of Jivakamravana Vihara. The main road continues towards the south and eventually divides into two. The left road leads to a clearing in the jungle containing the ruins of the Jivakam-ravana, Jivaka's mango grove that was the Buddha's favourite retreat within the valley. Jivaka was King Bimbisara's personal physician who later became a devoted follower of the Buddha. He also served the Buddha when he was injured by Devadatta. According to the commentaries, one day Jivaka thought to himself: "I have to wait upon the Buddha two or three times a day. Both the Gijjhakuta and the Veluvana are too far away. My mango grove is closer. Why don't I build a holy resort there for the Lord?" Thus, he built "night quarters and day quarters, cells, huts, pa-

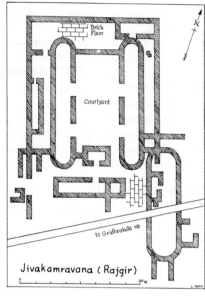

Fig. 72. Rajgir:
Jivakamravana Monastery

vilions, a Fragrant Hut suitable for the Lord, and surrounded the mango grove with a copper coloured wall eighteen cubits high". All ancient sources agree that the Jivakamravana was outside the east gate of Rajgir, and the visitors will notice that before arriving at the Jivakamravana, the road cuts through a long mound and then crosses a bridge. These represent the east wall and the moat of ancient Rajgir. The ruins of **Jivakamravana Monastery** (4th-3rd century BCE; cf. Fig. 72) with large elliptical walls and subsidiary rooms have been found with the remains of 4 halls and several rooms at the eastern end of the Old Rajagriha (Kushagrapura).

The Jivakamravana was the site of one of the most important of the Buddha's discourses, the *Samannaphala Sutta* (cf. *Digha Nikaya*, I: 47). One beautiful moonlit night, King Ajatashatru came to visit the Buddha at Jivakamravana and was deeply impressed by the silence and serenity of the large assembly. Ajatashatru had only recently had his father killed and was now starting to feel decidedly uneasy, due to guilt and perhaps also to the thought that his own son, Prince Udayibhadda, might one day have him killed, which in fact did eventually happen. Discovering that the fruits of worldly ambitions could at times be bitter, he came to ask the Buddha what the fruits of the

201

spiritual quest were and the Buddha replied with a long discourse describing the complete training of a Buddhist monk. The Buddha also delivered two other important discourses here, both of them to Jivaka. In the first, the *Jivaka Sutta*, he gives the conditions under which monks can eat meat, and in the second he defines a lay disciple as one who has taken the Three Refuges and observes the Five Precepts. The Jivakamravana was discovered and excavated in 1954. Although only the foundations remain, the complex is interesting in that it includes three long elliptical halls. The complex dates from before the time when monastery plans had become standard and very likely represents the structure built by Jivaka.

Gridhrakuta Hill

Following the road running parallel to the inner fortification in the east, one reaches Maddakuchchhi at the foot of Gridhrakuta Hill ('the Hill of Vultures'). Here the Enlightened One delivered the Lotus Sutra, which promises salvation for all beings. At the heart of this *sutra* is the compassion of the Buddha whose concern is with earthly suffering — each of us may attain Enlightenment, whoever may have folded their hands or uttered *namo* ('respectful salutations') to the Buddha. The Buddha also delivered the *Prajnaparamita* or Perfection of Wisdom Sutra at Gridhrakuta:

"Therefore, the mantra of the perfection of wisdom is
a mantra of great knowledge;
it is an unsurpassable mantra;
it is a mantra that totally pacifies all sufferings.
It will not deceive you, therefore know it to be true!
I proclaim the mantra of the perfection of wisdom."

The easy climb down from Gridhrakuta Hill crosses the site of Mardakukshi Vihara. It was here that Bimbisara's queen tried to get rid of her unborn child when it was prophesised that her son would one day kill his father. The Enlightened One was first brought here when he was wounded by a rock hurled by his envious cousin Devadatta. On the top of Gridhrakuta Hill the Buddha is believed to have converted the Magadhan King Bimbisara.

After crossing the deep gorge cut by a rocky stream one comes near the remains of Gridhrakuta. The strange rock protrusion resembling a vulture's beak probably gave the hill its name. The Buddha spent many rainy seasons in the rock-cut caves of this hill, meditating and preaching. There are two natural caves, representing 'stone houses', in which were found terracotta plaques with the Seven Past

Fig. 73. Rajgir: Antiquities from the Gridhrakuta

Buddhas and Maitreya, the Future Buddha, now in the Nalanda Museum (Fig. 73). Outside the caves we notice large stone walls of structures that once existed at this place. The whole area is studded with Buddhist monuments, which shows that Buddhists even down to later ages considered this place holy. This is quite natural, as Gridhrakuta was the favourite resort of the Buddha and the scene of many of his important sermons.

Visiting Rajgir in the 13th century, Dharmasvamin mentioned that the Gridhrakuta was "the abode for numerous carnivorous animals such as tiger, black bear and brown bear." In order to frighten away the animals, pilgrims visiting the Gridhrakuta would beat drums, blow conches and carry tubes of green bamboo that would emit sparks. A Buddha statue, dating from the 6th century CE, found on the Gridhrakuta, is now housed in the Archaeological Museum at Nalanda. After seeing the Gridhrakuta, the visitor can proceed down the path that leads back to the chair lift. This path is part of the original road built by King Bimbisara, though much renovated. The foundations of two *stupas* will be seen along the path. According to Hsüan-

tsang, one of these is called 'Dismounting from the Chariot' and marks
the place where King Bimbisara got out of his chariot during his first
ceremonial visit to the Buddha. The second *stupa* was called 'Turning
back the Crowd' and marks the place where the king, wishing to proceed alone, turned back the throng.

The Walls of Old Rajagriha

Proceeding about another kilometre along the road, one arrives
at the narrow pass between Sona and Udaya Hills, which formed the
southern gate of Old Rajgir and through which the Buddha must have
passed many times. The massive walls climb up both hills and run for
over 40 km, although in many places they are barely visible presently.
Climbing along the walls one can get a fine view of the fields of
Magadha. Once, when the Buddha was staying at Dakkhinagiri, the
Southern Mountains, very close to Rajgir and probably somewhere
near where the devotees now stands, he looked across the fields of
Magadha (*Magadhakhetta*) "laid out in strips, in lines, in embankments
and in squares", and suggested to Ananda that Buddhist monks' robes
should be cut to a similar pattern (cf. *Vinaya*, IV: 287). At that time the
fields were obviously square or rectangular and surrounded by narrow strips that separated one field from another. It is notable that although the shape of Magadha's fields has changed, the robes of
Theravada Buddhist monks have, to this day, retained their ancient
pattern.

The Shanti Stupa

Leaving the Jivakamravana and backtracking a bit from
Gridhrakuta, towards the east a path leads up to the new white mar-
ble and well-maintained monastery *stupa* with a 50 m high golden
stupa built by the famous Japanese Buddhist monk Ven. Nichidatsu
Fuji of the Nipponzan Myohoji sect in 1969. Located on the top of the
Chhatha Hill, a colossal sandstone dome on the Ratnagiri hill, the
Vishva Shanti Stupa is dedicated to world peace (Fig. 74). At this
point, the hill is very high, and looking north, the visitor has a magnificent view across the countryside. Opposite the *stupa* stands the
Saddharma Buddha Vihara. Around the dome are four golden images of the Buddha, representing his birth, enlightenment, teaching,
and death. A cable car (600 m) to the **Nipponzan Myohoji** (when
working: usually 10.00-17.00 h daily; Rs 20 two ways) takes you to the
hilltop where the *stupa* is alive with the chanting of *na-mu-kyo-ren-ge-
kyo* ('the only refuge one gets in you') amidst the beating of big drums.
Opposite the *stupa* stands the **Saddharma Buddha Vihara**.

Fig. 74. Rajgir: Shanti Stupa

Rajgir Festival: This festival-carnival is held every third year for a month during the intercalary month (*Malamasa*) (cf. for the dates from 2001 to 2044 in Appendix 2). Since the ancient past there is a tradition of holding the religious fair on a grand scale. Rajgir is the only place where festive and religious activities take place in this month. This is vividly narrated and eulogised in the *Puranic* literature that prescribe a variety of rituals and performances, including fasting and living a simple life with austerity in Rajgir. Since Independence the government authorities are involved in organising the fair and festival. With the increasing pace of tourism and religious consciousness, around a million tourists and devout Hindus and Buddhists alike gather during this month to have the direct experience of the spirit of place. Temporarily for a month a hospital and health care units, a police station, pilgrims' rest houses, water supply and an electricity board, a transport and communication centre, a security network, audio-visual aids and other infrastructural units of facilities and utilities are opened for the visitors. Programmes of music, dances, performances, exhibitions, and various means of recreations are organised. This requires a grant of around Rs 5 million from government sources. But in spite of this, the general perceptions of the visitors are not satisfactory; in fact, they blame the government for the mismanagement and misuse of the grant. Remember, above all, Bihar is well known for irregularities and corruption!

205

Accommodation

Near the bus stand, **Hotel Anand** (Tel. 06119-225030), and **Ajatashatru** (Tel. 225273) near the hot springs are the cheapest places with gloomy rooms at a cost of Rs 100/ 200. The **Burmese Buddhist Temple** (Tel. 225024), on the old road just before it reunites with the bypass, feeds, houses and entertains Buddhists from Myanmar. The **Bengali Buddhist Society Temple**, next to the Burmese temple, also has many rooms in exchange for a donation and provides clean and comfortable surroundings. **Hotel Siddharth** (Tel. 225216), in Kund Market, set within a pleasant courtyard in the south of the town, provides rooms with attached bathroom for Rs 300/ 600. The Government Bungalow, known as **Hotel Tathagata Vihar** (Tel. 225273), and **Hotel Gautam Bihar** (Tel. 225273), lying between the bus station and the railway station, on the road to Centaur Hokke, have large and high-ceilinged rooms at a moderate price between Rs 300 and Rs 600. **Hotel Rajgir** (Tel. 225266) has a garden, and the rooms with attached bathroom are acceptable; tariff Rs 100/ 200. Among the pilgrims' rest houses (*dharmashalas*) the most notable are **Digambar Jain**, **Svetambar Jain**, **Anandabai**, and **Sundar Shah** Dharmashalas. Many pilgrims get shelter in the houses of the *pandas* (pilgrims' priests).

The **Centaur Hokke Hotel** (Tel. 06119-255245, Fax: 255231; Email: centaur@sanchar.net.in), with an ugly concrete exterior, primarily for Japanese pilgrims, 3 km west from the hot springs and 4 km from the bus stop, has impressive buildings and is considered to be Rajgir's top expensive hotel; the room charges are US $ 90/ 125 per day (Rs 4500/ 6500). Japanese interest in Rajgir is not only evident in the huge Peace Pagoda, but also in the altogether more curious Centaur Hokke hotel. Designed by a Japanese architect, its strange shape and corridors act like a giant air-conditioning unit, with circulating air-keeping temperatures down. The hotel also has its own shrine room — cylindrical, roofless and 18 m high. There are 26 rooms in all, twenty Japanese-style and six Western-style, but it's the restaurant that takes the biscuit. The *Lotus* without doubt provides the finest Japanese food in Rajgir, and possibly in the whole of India. Guests are greeted with iced cologne-soaked flannels in the summer and steaming flannels in the cool season. Fresh fish and prawns are flown in daily from Kolkata, special Japanese rice is grown near Kathmandu by select farmers, vegetables are also brought in from Nepal, and to sample state-of-the-art Japanese haute cuisine in the middle of India's countryside costs from just $ 2.

Food

Restaurants are highly seasonal. Most visitors to Rajgir come on high-volume package tours and eat where they live. *Dhabas* and basic hotel restaurants around the bus stand feed locals. **Green Hotel Restaurant** (Tel: 225352), at the other end of the shopping strip containing the tourist office, has a wide selection of cheap Continental, Chinese, and Indian fare.

9. NALANDA

The site of the great Monastic University

"What do you think, householder? Is this town of Nalanda successful and prosperous, is it populous and crowded with people?"... "Yes, venerable sir, it is."

Upali Sutta, M. 56

The Blessed One said:
"It is by preaching the truth that the Tathagata leads men. Who will murmur at the wise? Who will blame the virtuous? Who will condemn self-control, righteousness, and kindness?"
And the Blessed One further proclaimed this verse:
"Commit no wrong but good deeds do
And let thy heart be pure.
All Buddhas teach this doctrine true
Which will for aye endure."

The Mahavagga, I, 23-24 ~ 13-14

Lying close to the village Baragaon (Nalanda District), Nalanda has the ruins of *the world's oldest university*, founded in the 5th century CE. It is approachable by road, i.e. 95 km southeast from Patna, 13 km north of Rajgir, or 13 km south from Biharsharif (population 245,000), the district headquarters. Shared taxis, mini-buses and auto-rickshaws are available from Rajgir and Biharsharif. There is a regular bus service from Patna to Biharsharif. From the bus stand or the railway station in Nalanda the ruins are at a distance of 2 km. For this distance one can take a shared *tonga*. The nearest airport is Patna (93 km), and the nearest railhead, on the Delhi-Howrah main line, is Bakhtiyarpur, 38 km, through the loop line connecting Nalanda.

Nalanda is spread out over an area of 14 hectares and has the ruins of 11 monasteries and 5 temples. Stone paved pathways criss-cross the entire site. **Sariputta's Stupa** is the most imposing structure standing in the south, a few minutes walk from the main gate. This large *stupa* was built over the mortal remains of Sariputta. Its corner towers display niches holding well modelled stucco figures of the Buddha and Bodhisattvas. A flight of steps leads to the shrine chamber which once housed a colossal image of Lord Buddha. The monastic remains show a number of small cells with wide verandas in the front, set around open quadrangular courts. Each complex had a main shrine housing a large figure of the Buddha. Huge ovens were also excavated suggesting that there was a common kitchen for students. Nalanda's main monument (Stupa/ Temple site 3) is listed in the list of **World Heritage Sites** of UNESCO. Excavations in the 1860s by Alexander Cunningham led to the discovery of the official seal with the inscription *Sri Nalanda Mahavihara Arya Bhikshu Sanghasya* (Venerable Community of Monks in the Great Vihara of Sri Nalanda).

The Buddha came to Nalanda often and stayed at Setthi Pavarika's mango grove. Two of Shakyamuni's chief disciples, Sariputta and Moggallana, came from the vicinity of Nalanda. Sariputta, who was considered the foremost in wisdom and had a very important place in the *Sangha,* attained *Nirvana* here. Although Nalanda is one of the places distinguished as having been blessed by the presence of the Buddha, it later became particularly renowned as the site of the great monastic university of the same name, which was to become the crown jewel of the development of Buddhism in India. Its name may derive from one of Shakyamuni's former births, when he was a king whose capital was here. Nalanda was one of his epithets, meaning 'insatiable in giving'. Shakyamuni stayed here on a number of occasions, for a mango grove had been offered to him by 500 merchants. The far-famed monastic establishments at Nalanda were of supreme importance in the history of latter-day Buddhism. Hsüan-tsang mentions a number of temples and *stupas* marking places where the Buddha had taught. On one visit he preached to men and gods for three months, and a *stupa* containing his hair and nail clippings of that period was erected.

Founded in the 1st century BCE, Nalanda was an ancient site of pilgrimage and teaching, which had been visited by the Buddha and Mahavira, who is reputed to have spent 14 rainy seasons on the site. Its reputation as a centre of learning dates back even further to the first millennium BCE. The Buddha first came here to study philosophy with local gurus, later attracting his own disciples. Even during his last journey from Rajagriha (Rajgir) to Pataligrama (Patna), the Buddha passed by and stopped at Nalanda. According to historical sources, Hsüan-tsang believed that the name was ascribed to it because of the Buddha's liberality in an earlier birth, and means 'charity without intermission'. According to Jain texts it was a suburb, situated to the northwest of the famous city of Rajagriha. The Pali literature contains many references to Nalanda to the effect that in the course

209

of his journeys the Buddha often halted at that place, which is mentioned as prosperous, swelling, teeming with population and containing a mango grove called Pavarika. Ashoka, the great Mauryan emperor of the 3rd century BCE, gave offerings to and worshipped the *chaitya* of Sariputta at Nalanda and erected a temple over the existing shrine. Nagarjuna, the famous Mahayana philosopher and alchemist of the 2nd century CE, had studied at Nalanda and later on became the high priest there. Suvishnu, a Brahmin contemporary of Nagarjuna, is said to have built 108 temples at Nalanda. It was at this sanctified site that the Mahavihara was first established in the reign of Emperor Kumaragupta in the 5th century AD, a tradition carried forward by his successors in the Gupta dynasty.

It is assumed that the Gupta emperors were responsible for the first monasteries. In the 7th century Hsüan-tsang spent 5 years, both as student and teacher, in the residential **Nalanda University**, which at that time had over 3,000 teachers and philosophers, over 10,000 students and monks and a **library** of over 9 million manuscripts. He received the Indian name Mokshadeva here and was remembered by the inmates of the Nalanda monastery long after he had left the place. He had studied under Shilabhadra, a great teacher and head of the monastery. The monks were supported by 200 villages, and the library attracted people from countries as far flung as Malaysia, Indonesia, China, and Korea. Great honour was attached to a Nalanda student and admission was restricted, with 7 or 8 out of 10 applicants failing to gain a place. A few years after Hsüan-tsang, another Chinese pilgrim, I-tsing reached India in 673 and studied at Nalanda. His works record very minute details about the life led by the Nalanda monks and details of the curriculum, which along with the Buddhist scriptures also included logic, metaphysics and Sanskrit grammar. During the 8th to the 12th century CE the Pala and Sena emperors ruled eastern India and continued to be liberal in their munificence to Nalanda. During the reign of Devapala at the beginning of the 9th century, Nalanda reached its zenith of fame and glory. Emissaries from around the world came with rich presents and generous donations to Nalanda, as they did to other contemporary Buddhist universities like Odantapuri and Vikramshila, in Bhagalpur district of Bihar. Under their rule Buddhism enjoyed royal patronage and the support of the laity.

Scholars converged on this blessed place, once traversed by the Buddha, thirsting for *Dhamma*. Hsüan-tsang and later his disciple Hwui-Li, who studied at this great institution in the 6th and 7th centuries, have left behind detailed descriptions. Admission was extremely coveted and only two out of ten eminent scholars were admitted. The art of debate (*vada*) and public speaking, and secular subjects like mathematics and medicine were taught here. Debating was a necessary part of monastic education, and doctrinal points were continually discussed. Among the renowned Indian scholars trained at Nalanda were Nagarjuna, Aryadeva and Asanga.

Nalanda was also very influential in the spread of Buddhism in Tibet. In the second half of the 8th century the king of Tibet invited the renowned Buddhist scholar Shantirakshita for spiritual guidance; he lived in Tibet for many years and finally died there in 762. Afterwards Padmasambhava went to Tibet from Nalanda to spread the teachings of Shakyamuni and founded the tradition of Lamaism-Buddhism there. However, Atisa Srijnana Dipankara, the head of Vikramshila University, helped to re-establish Buddhism in Tibet in the 11th century.

As narrated by Hsüan-tsang, Buddhism was slowly decaying when he visited India; however centres like Nalanda were prosperous and flourishing. He also noted the increasing impact of Tantrism, and of Brahmanic philosophy under the influence of Kumarila and Shankaracharya.

A massive fire, schisms between the different Buddhist sects and the resurgence of devotional Hinduism pushed Nalanda to the brink of destruction. Its final nemesis came with the Muslim invader Bakhtiyar Khalji, who by the turn of the 12th century brutally wiped it off the map. A few valuable manuscripts were rescued from Nalanda's famed libraries by some of the monks who were able to flee from the onslaught. According to the Buddhist teacher Taranatha "the Turks (Muslims) conquered the whole of Magadha, and destroyed many monasteries, including Nalanda". In 1235 only two monasteries survived and they too were also demolished. Thus, by the late 13th century Nalanda became a land of ruins and remains and was lost to history.

In the first quarter of the 19th century a new phase of historical upheaval started through the accounts of Buchanon-Hamilton, who described the ruins and the Hindu and Buddhist images found at Nalanda. In the 1860s Alexander Cunningham identified the place with the ancient Nalanda; and in 1915-16 the Archaeological Survey of India undertook its excavation that later resulted in the present landscape.

The greatness of Nalanda was hidden under a vast mound for centuries. The monasteries went through varying periods of occupation, and in one case 9 different levels of building have been discovered. The Buddhist monastic movement resulted in large communities withdrawing into retreats. The sanctuaries were often vast in size, as is the one here that is nearly 500 m in length and 250 m in width. Pilgrims to Nalanda today find vast and well-excavated ruins, many of which are more substantial than the mere foundations remaining in other places.

The remains of eleven monasteries and several *chaityas* (temples) built by kings of different periods, mainly in red brick, have been found, as well as a large stairway, a library, lecture halls, dormitories, cells, ovens and wells. The buildings are in several storeys and tiers on massive terraces of solid brick, with stucco decorations of the Buddha as well as Hindu divinities, and secular figures of warriors, dancers, musicians, animals and birds. Several of the monasteries are aligned south to north with a guarded entrance on the west wall; the monks' cells are disposed around a central quadrangular courtyard with a wide veranda, which was replaced by a high wall in some cases. Opposite the entrance, a shrine is found in the centre of the east wall, which must have contained an impressive image. Drains are found which carried sewage to the east and there are staircases giving access to the different storeys. The row of temples to the west of the monasteries left an open space where there were possibly smaller shrines.

The monasteries are numbered from **1** to **11** from south to north, the path from the gate entering between monasteries **1** and **4** at the south end of the site. The path goes west across an open space to the largest of the temples, **No. 3** (Fig. 75). This huge structure standing in

Fig. 75. Nalanda: Stupa / Temple site 3 (ca. late 6th century CE)

the middle of a court on the southwestern flank is surrounded by a number of votive *stupas*. Almost certainly Ashoka originally constructed it, but his *stupa* was enlarged several times. The earliest temples were small structures, completely incorporated into the successively larger mounds. It is believed that the north-facing shrine chamber on top once contained an enormous Buddha image. From the top one can have a commanding view over the remains as a whole, particularly impressive in the evening light. To the north of the *stupa* and in the same alignment, structures have been exposed, each of which consists of a temple erected directly over the remains of an earlier one (Fig. 77).

Monastery 1

Returning to the east, monasteries **1, 1A** and **1B** are the most important of the monastery group (Fig. 76). Ghosh suggests that a Sumatran king built the lower monastery in the reign of the third king of the Pala dynasty, Devapala, between CE 810-850. The excavated cells demonstrate the existence of an earlier monastery underneath, probably after earlier walls at least partially collapsed. It is possible to walk around all three of these southern monasteries. The ruins of Nalanda are entered through the passage between Monasteries 1 and 4.

Fig. 76. Nalanda, Monastery site 1 and 1A

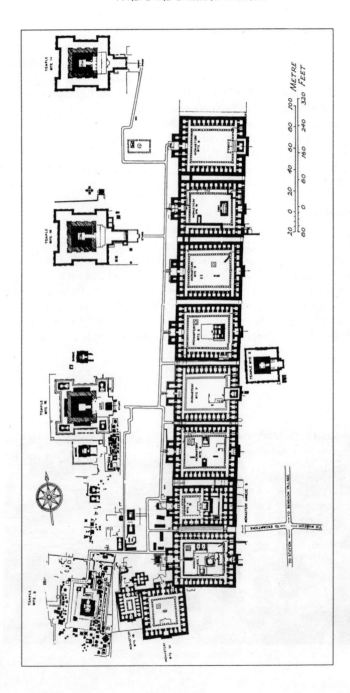

Fig. 77. Nalanda: Excavated remains (based on A. Cunningham, ASI Reports 1871, and 1920-21)

A copper plate inscription found in the veranda of Monastery 1 suggests that it was a college for students coming from Java and Sumatra. The inscription, issued by King Devapaladeva (815-54 CE) in the 39th year of his reign, mentions that King Balaputradeva of Suvarnadvipa (Java and Sumatra) had built a college at Nalanda and then, through his ambassador, had requested King Devapaladeva to grant the revenue of several villages for the use of the college. The money was to be used "for offerings, oblations, shelter, garments, alms, beds, requisites for the sick like medicine ... for writing Dhamma books and for the upkeep and repair of the monastery when damaged". King Devapaladeva agreed to the request, and the inscription ends by mentioning that he built a monastery at Nalanda for "the assembly of monks of various good qualities", and granted five villages for its support.

Monastery 1 has been built on the same site at least nine times, and what one sees now are parts of at least three or four structures superimposed upon each other. The monastery is entered through an impressive portico, the roof of which was supported by pillars and the stone bases of which can still be seen. The monastery consists of monks' cells, some with beds, arranged around a large courtyard. The stairs in the southwest corner indicate that the building was originally at least two stories high, while the thickness of the walls suggest that it may well have been higher. At the eastern end of the monastery there is a shrine that originally contained a large statue of the Buddha, of which only parts of its crossed legs and drapery survive. The platform with the stone pillars in front of the shrine was probably where teachers sat when they read their lectures to the students assembled in the courtyard (cf. Fig. 77).

Monasteries 4 to 11

Monasteries 1 and 4 to 11 were the colleges where the students of Nalanda both lived and studied, and they differ from each other only slightly. Monastery 4, immediately to the north of the entrance path, was built on an earlier collapsed monastery. Several of these monasteries have wells in their courtyards, and drains, probably used as toilets, in their northeast corners. An interesting feature of Monastery 9 is the six ovens in the courtyard. Although it is hard to picture it now, each of these monasteries was originally beautifully painted and decorated, and at least four stories high. Hsüan-tsang (638) described thus the monk-quarters as they existed at his time: "All the outside courts in which are the monks' cells are of four stories. The stories have dragon-projections and coloured eaves, the pearl-red pillars,

215

carved and ornamental, the richly adorned balustrades and the roofs covered with tiles that reflect the light in a thousand shades — these things add to the beauty of the scene."

There are several interesting features in the other monasteries; double rows of cells in **Monastery 5**, a brick courtyard and two sets of double ovens in the upper courtyard of **No. 6**, and the evidence of three successive monasteries built on the same site at **No. 7**. There is an imposing shrine and unique doorway in **No. 8**, impressive drains in **No. 9** and arched doorways in **No. 10**. The fragments of 25 stone pillars were recovered from the ruins of **No. 11**, which stood one metre apart at a height of more than 2 m (cf. Fig. 77). Ghosh suggests that fire was a recurrent hazard and every monastery was at some point of time deserted and re-occupied.

Just in front of Monastery 11 is a small shrine containing a large statue of the Buddha carved out of black stone. The statue dates to the Pala period and is now worshipped by local people as a Hindu god.

Temples

In addition to the monasteries and the main temple, four other temples have been excavated. **Temples 12, 13** and **14** are in a line stretching north from the main temple (cf. Fig. 77). They all have a square outline, and originally had large Buddha images, now kept in the museum.

The **Temple Site 12** was the largest structure at Nalanda, being approximately 52 x 50 m. Like Temple Site 3, it consisted of a central tower with four smaller ones at each of the corners, each containing a shrine that would have originally housed a statue. At the top of the stairs, on the left, are two carved pillars. Perhaps Hsüan-tsang was referring to this temple when he wrote: "The richly adorned towers and the fairy-like turrets, like pointed hill-tops, are congregated together. The observatories seem to be lost in the morning mist and the upper rooms tower above the clouds. From the windows one can see the winds and the clouds, and above the soaring eaves the conjunctions of the sun and moon may be observed." On both the north and south of Temple 12 are two smaller shrines, each containing the remains of statues of the Buddha in the earth-touching gesture (*bhumisparsha mudra*).

To the north of temple 13 the discovery of a brick-smelting furnace with metal pieces and slag in it establishes that metal objects were cast in Nalanda. The niches of the pedestal of the image in **Temple 14** contain the only example of mural paintings in Nalanda.

The **Temple Site 3** has been rebuilt, modified or renovated at least seven times over the centuries, and this together with the numerous votive *stupas* clustered around it indicates that it was the most sacred shrine at Nalanda. There is little doubt that the original structure here was the *stupa* marking Sariputta's birthplace. The first three stages of this temple are covered by later additions and cannot be seen. The temple as it appeared in later centuries consisted of a huge central tower with smaller towers at its four corners, of which three survive, not unlike the Mahabodhi Temple at Bodh Gaya. These smaller towers have niches containing stucco figures of Buddhas and Bodhisattvas dating to the Gupta period. Sadly, in recent years, the heads or faces of some of these figures have been broken off to be sold in the illegal art market. A large staircase leads to the top of the temple where there is a shrine, which must have contained a statue. The small *stupas* on the east-side of the temple are of particular interest. Several of these *stupas* have small rooms attached to them, making it possible to meditate inside them. Some of the other *stupas* were found to be built of bricks inscribed with sacred texts and were probably built in honour of the many esteemed scholars and teachers who resided in Nalanda throughout the centuries. From the top of Temple Site 3, one can get a fine view of the whole complex of Nalanda.

Temple site 2, east of monastery 7 and 8, is reached by a path between them. By far the most beautiful of all the excavated monuments, **Temple Site 2** has a stone sculpted dado with a moulded plinth and sculpted panels revealing 211 figures of Hindu gods and goddesses besides dancers, musicians, warriors, animals and birds, and panels showing a wide variety of scenes like loving couples, peacocks and geese, geometrical patterns and scenes from daily life. It is well worthwhile walking slowly around it and examining these panels. Another interesting feature of this temple can be seen by going to the main staircase. It will be noticed that the stones in this temple have been held together with iron clamps.

The panels probably date from the 6th or 7th centuries CE, and may have been brought in from another temple. In addition to the monasteries and temples there are several images, including the Buddha and Marichi's (the Buddhist goddess of Dawn).

Archaeological Museum

To the east of the monastery site 1 is the **site museum** (founded in 1917), maintained by the Archaeological Survey of India. It houses a rich collection of antiquities and relics discovered in Nalanda and its neighbourhood, including Buddha images, the *Nalanda Univer-*

sity seal, and Buddhist and Hindu images from different ages. It establishes that the university was equally famous for its prolific school of stone sculpture, bronze casting and manuscript painting. It also contains some exquisite bronzes of the 9th and 10th centuries (Pala dynasty) and other remains excavated at the site. There are many examples of pottery, coins, seals, iron objects, and stone, bronze and terracotta images of gods and goddesses of the Buddhist and some of the Hindu pantheon, mostly belonging to the Pala and Sena periods (8th-12th century). The Pala School of art is seen at its best at Nalanda. As Nalanda was also a centre of Tantrism, many images of its deities, male and female, were found along with the Buddha and **Bodhisattvas**. There are many bronze images that are placed against a square back-slab rising behind the shoulders of the deity.

One of the finest pieces is a large, almost free-standing statue of either Avalokiteshvara or Samantabhadra carved out of black stone. The left hand holds a beautiful lotus while the right hand, palms outward, bestowing blessings. On an elongated halo behind the Bodhisattva's head are three Buddhas, a fourth one being nestled on the Bodhisattva's head. Two female devotees stand at the figure's feet. The relaxed posture and the overall simplicity of this statue indicate that it dates from the late Gupta period. Unfortunately, past efforts to repair the nose detract from the beautiful expression on the Bodhisattva's face. Another interesting item in the museum is a sandal made out of ivory.

Fig. 78. Nalanda:
Avalokiteshvara

The Nalanda specimens depict the Buddha in all his characteristic attitudes, like standing and sitting in meditation under the Bodhi tree. The finest bronze image of the Buddha is one in a standing pose on a circular lotus-pedestal with a smiling and calm expression of the face. **Jambhala**, the Buddhist god of wealth, is represented in many sculptures. Images of Avalokiteshvara (Fig. 78), Tara (the saviouress), Prajnaparamita (the female personi-

218

fication of wisdom), Hariti (consort of Jambhala) and other female deities like Sarasvati, Aparajita, and Marichi are notable and worth seeing. There is a good collection of **coins** belonging to the dynasty of Shashanka of Bengal (ca. 600-20 CE), Pratihara (ca. 835-85), and Gahadavala (ca. 1114-55).

The museum is adjacent to the ruins and is open every day from 10.00 to 17.00 hr, except Fridays and Government holidays; Entrance Fee: Rs 5.

New excavations to the northeast in the **Sarai Mound** show evidence of a brick temple with frescoes of elephants and horses of the Pala period. The villages of **Bargaon** and **Begampur** to the north and **Jagadishpur** to the southwest contain several impressive Buddhist and Hindu images.

The **International Centre for Buddhist Studies**, opened in 1951, promotes the tradition of ancient Nalanda. A similar institution established in 1951, the **Nava Nalanda Mahavihara**, 2 km from the main site, is a post-graduate institute for research in Buddhism and Pali literature set up by the Govt. of Bihar; it has many rare manuscripts. It is now the site of the Indira Gandhi Open University. There is a colourful **Thai temple** built in the 1980's. Adjacent to the ruins in the village Surajpur Baragaon is an ancient **temple of Surya**, the Sun-god, attached to a tank, which attracts a great number of devotees to celebrate the *Chhata* festival (Sun worship) in the month of *Karttika* (October-November).

Nalanda Mahavihara site is open from 6 am to 5.30 pm daily and the Museum from 10 am to 5 pm. Entry fee is Rs 5 for the Museum and Rs 10 for the site. The Museum remains closed on Friday. Video-photography charges are Rs 50.

Accommodation & Food

There are no good hotels and restaurants in Nalanda, although a few *dhabas* have sprung up around the bus stand. Of course one can get cheap accommodation in the **Chinese Monastery**, or **Burmese Rest House**, beyond the museum, and also in the **Youth Hostel** and at the **Pali Institute**. However, it is better to stay at Rajgir (15 km), from where there is a regular bus service.

Excursion: Kundalpur and Pavapuri

Lying at a distance of 16 km northwest from Nalanda, **Kundalpur** is believed by folk legends and the Digambara sect of Jains to be the birthplace of Mahavira (ca. 599 BCE), the last Tirthankara and founder of Jainism. There are some Jain temples, besides two large lotus lakes called *Dirgha Pushkarini* and *Pandava Pushkarini*. King Siddhartha and queen Trishala of the small kingdom of Kundapur were the parents of Mahavira. Historically this place has not been accepted as the real birthplace. Most historians agree that the village Basadha in Vaishali district (north Bihar) is his birthplace. In the Jain literature the geographical location and account of the place are described. But this creates doubts in identification.

At a distance of 12 km east from Nalanda on the highway NH-31 is **Pavapuri** (also called Apapapuri), where Mahavira gained enlightenment, and where he also died in ca. 500 BCE. It is said that the demand for his sacred ashes was so great that a large amount of soil was removed from around the funeral pyre, creating a lotus-filled tank. According to another version, Mahavira bathed in the lotus pond and he was cremated on its bank. A marble temple, the *Jalamandir*, was later built in the middle of the tank, which is now a major pilgrimage spot for Jains. This temple is in the possession of the Svetambara sect of Jains. *Samosharan* is another Jain temple built here. There are pilgrims' rest houses of both the Jain sects Digambara and Svetambara. One can get here by bus from Rajgir or Bihar Sharif, the district headquarters.

10. VAISHALI

Where the Buddha was offered honey

When the Blessed One had remained as long as he wished at Amrapali's grove, he went to Beluva, near Vaishali. There the Blessed One addressed the brethren, and said:

"O mendicants, take up your abode for the rainy season round about Vaishali, each one according to the place where his friends and near companions may live. I shall enter upon the rainy season here at Beluva".

[...]

And the Blessed One addressed Ananda on behalf of the order, saying:

"I am now grown old, O Ananda, and full of years; my journey is drawing to its close, I have reached the sum of my days, I am turning eighty years of age".

The *Mahaparinibbana Sutta*, II, 27 - 35.

Approach

Lying 35 km north of the nearest railway station, Hajipur, and 56 km north of **Patna**, the capital of the state of Bihar, Vaishali can be approached either by road or through rail. The distance between Varanasi and Hajipur is 265 km by rail. This way from Varanasi Vaishali is at a distance of 300 km via Chapra and Hajipur, and 284 km via Patna (Fig. 79a&b). There is no local transport and visitors are advised to take their own vehicles for sightseeing. Leaving the crowded market place of this small district town, the metalled road leads to the village of Basarh, which the British archaeologist Alexander Cunningham identified as the ancient Vaishali.

The ancient remains of Vaishali are scattered over six villages. The biggest spread of ruins is in the village of Basadh, called the Raja Vishala Ka Garh, the site of the *stupa* that the Lichchhavis built over the corporeal relics of the Buddha. The other archaeological sites and the places where the artefacts were found are Kharauna tank and its associated habitation site in the village of Chakramadas; a mound in Lalpura; near the Ashokan pillar at Kolhua two earthen mounds known as Bhimasen Ka Palla; the sites near the Chaturmukha Mahadeva and two more to its west in the village Baniya; and three sites including Marpasauna mound and Chaur in village Virpur. The artefacts and

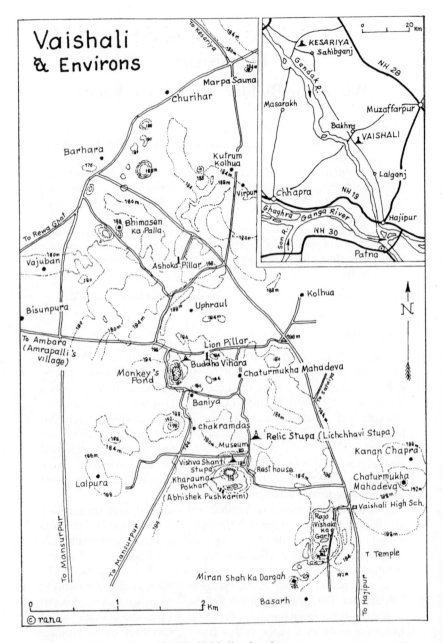

Fig. 79a. Vaishali and environs

Fig. 79b. Vaishali and environs

ancient remains found nearby at most of the sites belong to Northern Black Polished Ware (ca. 600-200 BCE). A few pieces of objects and layers at these sites belong to Painted Grey Ware (ca. 1100-800 BCE).

The historicity of the township goes to the *Ramayana* period when the mythological king Vishala founded his capital here. The *Ramayana* mentions it as the place where the gods and demons pow-wowed before churning the primordial ocean. It is situated in ancient Videha; the spread of the Vedic culture is referred to in the story of Videha Mathavya narrated in the *Shatapatha Brahmana* (1.4-11, 10.18). According to Puranic tradition, the antiquity of the ancient dynasty of Vaishali goes back to the time of Manu, the First Man; one of his descendants Sumati was ruling at Vaishali when Rama visited the place enroute to Mithila for his marriage. Later on this dynasty was replaced by a republic, which became a serious rival of Magadha during the 6th century BCE. During the 6th century BCE Vaishali was the flourishing city of the Lichchhavis. Reputedly it was one of the first cities in the world to adopt a republican form of government. The republic was subdued by king Ajatashatru of Magadha in the first quarter of the 5th century BCE, but it maintained its identity and is described as a Sangha (i.e. republic) in the *Arthashastra* of Kautilya. The Mauryas must have incorporated it within their empire, but it probably reasserted its independence in ca. 200 BCE.

According to the Buddhist tradition, five years after the Enlightenment in Bodh Gaya Lord Buddha came to Vaishali, the capital of one of the first republican states in the world. Situated on the northern banks of the Ganga, Vaishali is bound by the hills of Nepal to the north and the river Gandak to the west. The Lichchhavi nobility came to receive the Enlightened One with a cavalcade of elephants and chariots bedecked with gold. As the Lord set foot on the soil of Vaishali, loud thunder followed by a heavy downpour purged the plague-infected city. The Buddha preached the Ratna Sutra to those assembled, and eighty-four thousand people embraced the new faith.

In Vaishali women were ordained into the *Sangha* for the first time. The Buddha's foster mother, Mahaprajapati Gotami (Gautami), along with 500 Shakyan women made a pilgrimage by foot from Kapilavastu to Vaishali, seeking to join the Order. Three times the Lord refused their entreaties. Ultimately they shaved their heads, donned the orange robes and beseeched the Lord once again. The Enlightened One was finally persuaded to admit them as *bhikshunis* or nuns.

It was also at Vaishali that Amrapali, the famous courtesan, earned the respect of the *Sangha* and a place in history with her generous donations. The neighbouring village of Amvara is said to be the site of Amrapali's mango grove.

When Amrapali was sixteen years old she became involved in a love affair with the young Prince Bimbisara, but that ended in heartbreak. She gave birth to their son, Jivaka. But no one in the palace wanted to accept Amrapali and her son. Some members of the palace household even spread rumours that Jivaka was no more than an abandoned orphan that the prince had rescued from a barrel by the side of the road. Amrapali was hurt by these accusations. She endured this humiliation caused by the jealousy and hatred of others in the palace. Soon she saw that her freedom was the only thing worth guarding. She refused to live in the palace and vowed that she would never relinquish her personal freedom to anyone. She run to the Buddha for refuge.

The Buddha spoke gently to Amrapali, "Beauty arises and passes away like all other phenomena. Fame and fortune are no different. Only the peace, joy, and freedom that are the fruits of meditation bring true happiness. Amrapali, cherish and take good care of all the moments left to you in this life. Do not lose yourself in forgetfulness or idle amusements. This is of utmost importance."

The Buddha told Amrapali how she could arrange her daily life in a new way — breathing, sitting, and working in a spirit of mindfulness, and observing and practising the five precepts. She was overjoyed to receive these precious teachings. Before departing, she said, "Just outside the city of Vaishali, I own a mango grove that is both cool and peaceful. I hope that you and your monks might consider coming there for a visit. That would be a great honour to me and to my son. Please, Lord Buddha, consider my invitation."

The Buddha graciously accepted the offer. An overjoyed Amrapali returned on her chariot, raising a cloud of dust. The Lichchhavi princes going to meet the Buddha got enveloped in the dust and learnt of the Buddha's forthcoming visit to her house. The Lichchhavi princes wanted to exchange Amrapali's honour of receiving the Buddha for one hundred thousand gold coins. Amrapali steadfastly refused their offer, and after the Buddha's visit to her house she was purged of all impurities. She gifted her mango grove to the *Sangha*. Amrapali joined the Order after realising the transitory nature of all things, including beauty.

> Sweet was my singing
> Like the cuckoo in the grove
> Now my voice cracks and falters.
> Hear it, these words are true.

Amrapali: *Therigatha*

Finally the Buddha replied to the question raised by his disciple Sariputta; he said:

"Monks, when you have seen deeply and have attained the Way, the beautiful may still appear beautiful and the ugly may still appear ugly, but because you have attained liberation, you are not bound by either. When a liberated person looks at beauty, he can see that it is composed of many non-beautiful elements. Such a person understands the impermanent and empty nature of all things, including beauty and ugliness. Thus he is neither mesmerised by beauty nor repulsed by ugliness. The only kind of beauty that does not fade and that does not cause suffering is a compassionate and liberated heart. Compassion is the ability to love unconditionally, demanding nothing in return. A liberated heart is unbound by conditions. A compassionate and liberated heart is true beauty. The peace and joy of that beauty is true peace and joy. Monks, practice diligently and you will realise true beauty." (*Majjhima Nikaya* 55)

At the first incidence 51 women, under the leadership of Queen Gotami, were ordained into the *Sangha*. Venerable Sariputta arranged for them to live temporarily at Amrapali's mango grove. The Buddha also asked Sariputta to teach the nuns the basic practice. Eight days later, Bhikkhuni Mahapajapati (Gotami) paid a visit to the Buddha. She said, "Lord, please show compassion, and explain how I may best make quick progress on the path of liberation."

The Buddha answered, "Bhikkhuni Mahapajapati, the most important thing is to take hold of your own mind. Practice observing the breath and meditate on the body, feelings, mind, and objects of mind. Practising like that, each day you will experience a deepening of humility, ease, detachment, peace, and joy. When those qualities arise, you can be sure you are on the correct path, the path of awakening, and enlightenment."

The Buddha's community (*sangha*) now had four streams — the *bhikkhus* (monks), *bhikkhunis* (female monks), *upasakas* (male lay disciples), and *upasikas* (female lay disciples). (*Khuddaka Nikaya*, 10 and *Tripitaka*, 1428)

In ca. 80 BCE Vaishali, like Magadha, was probably conquered by the Kushanas. In CE 200 evidence of a Shaka ruler is suggested by two seals of Mahadevi Prabhudama found there by Spooner in 1913-14. The seals do not give the name of the husband of the great queen Prabhudama, but states that she was the daughter of Mahakshatrapa Rudrasimha and sister of Mahakshatrapa Rudrasena. The Lichchhavis, however, soon got the upper hand and founded a flourishing kingdom in CE 250, which in the time of Chandragupta I contributed to the rise of the Gupta empire. In the Gupta period Vaishali was the headquarters of a provincial administration and a large number of seals were found in the excavations of Raja Vishal Ka Garh (ASI 1903-04), which throw considerable light on the contemporary religious, social and economic conditions. The city's fortunes declined in the 7th century and its so-called fort was practically deserted at the time of the visit of Hsüan-tsang. Some Buddhist and Hindu temples were built during the Pala period outside the fort area, but the history of the city is shrouded in mystery.

The great Chinese travellers Fa-hsien (ca. CE 400) and Hsüan-tsang (CE 637) visited it and took back a piece of sculpture from one of the *stupas*. The Buddha is said to have visited Vaishali at least three times during his lifetime, where he delivered several sermons. In one of these visits several monkeys are said to have offered the Buddha a bowl of honey, the episode which was accepted as one of the main eight events in the life of the Buddha. The Buddha preached the last sermon there announcing his approaching *parinirvana*. There he had severe attacks of illness and prophesised that he would pass away in three months time (*Digha Nikaya*, II, p. 106). Following a severe illness, the Master asked Ananda to assemble all the *bhikshus*. The Great Master asked the monks to spread the *Dharma* in order to bring about the good and happiness of many (*Bahu jana hitaya, Bahu jana sukhaya*).

A century after the passing of the Buddha the **Second Buddhist Council** (*sangiti*) was held in 383 BCE at Vaishali to discuss **The Ten Points of Vinaya** (*Indulgences*), the rules of conduct under dispute due to sectarian divisions and their interpretations; this has been recorded in the *Chullavagga*. The Venerable Yasha openly declared these practices to be unlawful. At the same time some 60 *Arhats* came from the Western Country and assembled on the Ahoganga hill. About 88 monks from Avanti and the Southern Country also joined them. These monks declared the question to be hard and subtle. Finally Venerable Revata at Sahajati had declared them invalid. The dialogue continued by the Assembly of 700 monks presided by Venerable Sabbakami who also put his final mark and declared the Ten Points unlawful. The momentous results of this Council were the dispatch of missionaries to different parts of the world for the propagation of the *Dharma*.

About 1.5 km north-west of Raja Vishala ka Garh is the ancient **Coronation Tank** (*Abhisheka Pushkarni*) or Kharauna Pokhar (58.8 m high from mean sea level), which was used in the coronation of Vajjian rulers. Resembling a rustic Olympic-sized swimming pool, it contains holy water, and was used for anointing the rulers of Vaishali at their coronation — today it is used as the local Laundromat. It spreads over an area of 439 m by 203 m. On the southern side of the lake is the newly built **Vishva Shanti Stupa**, sixth in the series to be erected in India by the Nipponzan Myohoji sect of Japan, which was consecrated in October 1996. Attached to it is a Japanese Temple. The Vaishali Archaeological Museum is located near it. The *stupa* behind the museum, **Stupa I** or the **Relics Stupa**, covered with a conical tin roof, occupies a small well-landscaped garden, and is supposed to have housed the casket relic with the ashes of the Buddha. Here the Lichchhavis reverentially encased one of the eight portions of the Master's relics, which they received after the *Mahaparinirvana*. At a little distance lies the 500 m long **Lotus Tank**, said to be a picnic spot of the Lichchhavis in the 6th century BCE.

Kutagarasala Vihara is 3 km from the main town. It was built by the Lichchhavis for Shakyamuni. Known as Buddha Stupa 2, this site has revealed the extensive remains of a monastery with an open courtyard and a verandah. A large tank and the Kutagarshala Chaitya can be seen in the south. It was at Kutagarshala Vihara that a monkey took the Lord's alms bowl and climbed a tree to gather honey for him. The Buddha accepted his humble offering and the monkey in great joy, leaping from tree to tree, accidentally fell and was impaled on the stump of a tree. Dying a noble death, the monkey went to heaven.

Raja Vishala ka Garh

Going back to the town, a little way off the main road, can be seen some ruins that occupy an area enclosed by a wall about 1 km long and 2 m high, a great Vajjian assembly hall. Vaishali derived its name from this fort of the mythical King Vishala,. The moat surround-

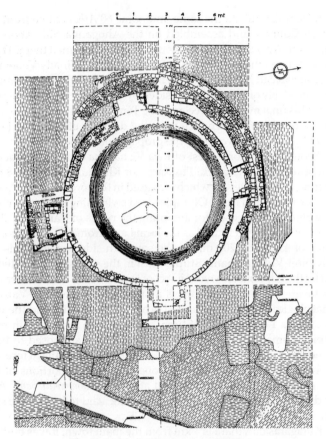

Fig. 80. Vaishali: The site plan of the Stupa

ing the ancient Parliament House, which could hold an assembly of 7,707 representatives, is 43 m wide. The Chinese pilgrim Hsüan-tsang, who visited Vaishali in January-February 637, described this site which was re-discovered by the present researches:

"The royal precincts (Raja Vishala ka Garh) are about 4 or 5 li round. There are a few people living in it ... North-west of the royal city (precincts), 5 or 6 li, is a *sangharama* with a few disciples. They study the teaching of the Little Vehicle, according to the Sammatiya school ... By the side of it is a *stupa*. It was here the Tathagata delivered the Vimalakirti sutra and the son of the householder Ratnakara and others offered parasols (to the Buddha) ... To the east of this is a *stupa*. It was here that Sariputta and others obtained perfect exemp-

Fig. 81. Vaishali: View of the main Stupa

tion. To the south-east of this last spot is a *stupa*; this was built by a king of Vaishali. After the nirvana of the Buddha, a former king of this country obtained a portion of the relics of his body, and to honour them as highly as possible, raised (this building)" (Figs. 80, 81, 82).

The rampart at Raja Vishala ka Garh belong to the ca. 1st century BCE-CE 100. Kushana coins, spear and arrow-heads and other iron implements were also found here. The Kushana period had extensive brick buildings, associated with the sprinkler and deep bowl types of pottery. The Gupta period structure, though made of broken bricks, had rooms of varying dimensions. A remarkable discovery at this site was a few pieces of the Painted Grey Ware both from the N.B.P. (Northern Black Polished) Ware level and from the mud rampart. Mention may also be made of a gold object found in a small pot, near which was another pot containing silver amulets and 121 beads of semi-precious stones. All these finds belong to the Kushana period.

The temples include the 4th century **Chaumukhi Mahadeva**, a four-faced Lord Shiva, made of black basalt at Kamman Chhapra. Another is at **Basarh**, by the ancient tank **Bavan Pokhar**, which was built in the Pala period and enshrines beautiful images of Hindu deities, mostly of basalt. Behind the Bavan Pokhar Temple is a newly built **Jain Temple** famous for enshrining an image of a *Tirthankara*, belonging to the Pala period. Jains of the Svetambara sect believe that

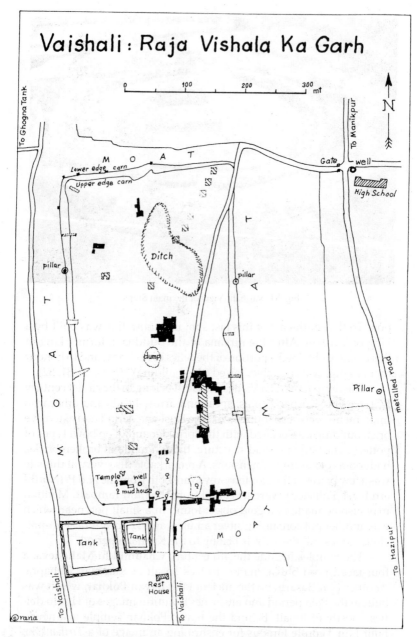

Vaishali: Raja Vishala Ka Garh

Fig. 82. Vaishali: The site plan of Raja Vishala ka Garh

Lord **Mahavira**, the 24th Tirthankara, was born here in 599 BCE in the village of **Kundupur**, 4 km from the main remains, and also spent 22 years of his initial years here. The **Harikatora Temple** at Basarh contains an image of Karttikeya, the second son of Lord Shiva.

The Ashokan Pillar

This place can be reached by rickshaw or bicycle. At Kolhua, 4 km northwest of Raja Vishala ka Garh, in a fenced-in compound stands a monolithic pillar, locally known as **Bhimasen's Lath**. This is a highly polished single piece of red sandstone, surmounted by a bell-shaped capital, 18.3 m high, that supports the seated figure of a life-size lion on a square abacus. Emperor Ashoka built this pillar to commemorate the Buddha's last sermon, in which he hinted his impending departure from the mortal world. The line of five pillars in the region is believed to have marked the stages of a royal journey from Pataliputra to Lumbini that Ashoka undertook in the 20th year of his consecration. The lion on top faces north towards Kushinagar, the direction Buddha took on his last voyage. Nearby to the south is the small tank known as **Ramakunda**, identical to *Markatahrida*, i.e. 'Monkey's Tank', which according to legends was dug by a colony of monkeys who offered the Buddha a bowl of honey.

To the northwest there is a ruined mound, at present only 5 m high and with a diameter of 20 m at the base, that is identified with the remains of the **Ashokan Stupa** mentioned by Hsüan-tsang. This was confirmed by excavations carried out between 1976 and 1978. The *stupa* was found to have been built first during the Mauryan period and rebuilt and enlarged on two other occasions. A square brick relic chamber inside contained a highly polished stone relic casket and small sheets of gold and semiprecious stones. On the summit of this mound stands a modern brick temple enshrining a medieval image of the Buddha. The two nearby Buddhist *stupas* (ca. 4th century BCE) are said to hold stone caskets containing the Buddha's ashes, the second having been excavated only in 1958. One of the ruins is the remains of a monastery where the Buddha resided.

Another Lion Pillar

Returning to the main road and proceeding for about one kilometre, the visitor will come to a large *stupa* with a stone pillar next to it. The pillar is often attributed to Emperor Ashoka, but as it differs so much from those known to be erected by him, this attribution is doubtful. The shaft of the pillar is thick and squat, in contrast to the slender shafts of Ashoka's pillars, and it also lacks the polish found on most

Mauryan stonework. The lion on the capital, while impressive, has none of the heraldic proportions of the lions from Lauriya Nandangarh (see Fig. 91), Rampurva or Sarnath. The lion sits on a plain square pedestal, while all Ashokan pillars have round pedestals, usually with a frieze around them. There is no inscription on the pillar, but there is a large amount of graffiti. Recent examination has shown that the total length of the pillar, from the base to the top of the capital, is 14.6 m, though it has sunk several metres into the ground. It is possible that this pillar dates from a little before Ashoka and was the prototype for his pillars.

The Lichchhavi Stupa

After the Buddha's passing away the Lichchhavis are said to have erected 13 *stupas* over their share of the remains of the Master, out of which only 6 are at present traced in ruins. The Buddha was equally impressed by the landscape, as is evident from his remark that the prosperity of heaven could be gauged by only looking at the prosperity of Vaishali. In his last visit, as a token of appreciation and piety, the Buddha had given to the people of Vaishali one of his alms-bowls, which remained there for a long time.

A little to the northeast of the museum are the remains of a small but extremely important *stupa*. The Lichchhavis were among those who received a portion of the Buddha's relics after his final Nirvana (cf. *Digha Nikaya*, II.164). The *stupa* they built to enshrine these relics was opened by Emperor Ashoka, who removed some of the relics and broke them into smaller pieces so he could enshrine them in the many *stupas* he was building throughout his empire. Hsüan-tsang confirms this story, adding some interesting details:

"After the Buddha's Nirvana, a former king of the country obtained a portion of the relics of his body and to honour them as highly as possible, raised this building. The records of India state: 'In this *stupa*, there was at first a quantity of relics equal to a hob'. Emperor Ashoka opened it, took away nine-tenths of the whole, leaving only one-tenth behind. Afterwards, there was a king of the country, who wished again to open the *stupa*, but at the moment when he began to do so, the earth trembled, and he dared not proceed."

The discovery and excavation of this *stupa* in 1958 provided striking confirmation of these stories. The original *stupa* was found to be made of rammed earth, proof of its very early date, and yielded a small soapstone casket containing burnt bone, one copper punch-marked coin, a small conch shell, two glass beads and a small gold plate. The *stupa* had been enlarged with bricks about 250 years after its construction, and again on two later occasions. The first and second *stupas* showed clear signs of having been opened. All the evidence points to this being the original *stupa* built by the Lichchhavis and the relics within being those of the Buddha. Despite this exciting find, the discovery of these relics, like the discovery of those at Piprahwa, caused hardly a ripple of interest in the Buddhist world, and these sacred relics now languish in the dusty storerooms of the Patna Museum.

Miranshah-ka-Dargah

A Muslim tomb, containing the relics of Sheikh Muhammad Qazin, a celebrated local saint of the 15th century CE, was built over a ruined brick *stupa* (cf. Fig. 79). This is the place from where Hsüan-tsang collected a piece of sculpture which he took back to his country. The **Jain Prakrit Research Institute** at Vaishali promotes post-graduate studies and research in Prakrit and Jainology. On similar lines the **Vaishali Sangha** is a Buddhist institution organised in 1945 to encourage studies and research relating to Vaishali.

Kutagarasala Vihara, a monastery, is open daily from 9.00 to 17.00 hr; Entry fee is Rs 2 per person.

Archaeological Museum

On the banks of the Kharauna Pokhar, in the north, is the site museum that contains a small collection of antiquities found in the area, dating from the 3rd century BCE to the 6th century CE. Just inside the main entrance is a Buddha statue, carved out of blue-black stone, in the earth-touching gesture and with one high crown on its head. The statue was originally found in a field and later enshrined in a small temple built on the top of the *stupa* next to the Lion Pillar. The inscription on the statue mentions that it was donated by "Uchaba the writer, son of Manikya". Another interesting piece is an upright post from a railing with a representation of the purchase of the Jetavana on it. The terracotta monkey heads in different styles are interesting. Open daily 9 am-5 pm, closed on Fridays. Among the precious archaeological finds is the **relic casket** containing the ashes of the Buddha now preserved in the Patna Museum. The Archaeological Museum is open from 10:00 am to 5:00 pm, closed on Fridays; Entrance Fee: Rs 5.

Facilities

Moderate accommodation is available in the Tourist Bungalow, PWD Rest House, Tourist Youth Hostel of Bihar State (Tel.: 0612-2225295), and Jain Dharmashala. There is no hotel. From Patna BSTDC tour (Rs 75), private buses, and taxis (Rs 750) go to Vaishali.

11. PATNA

An ancient Buddhist site

Postal code: 800000. STD Tel Code: 0612.

Lying at the confluence of the rivers Son, Punpun and Ganga, Patna (2 million inhabitants), the capital of the state of Bihar, is located at 240 km east of Varanasi, 350 km west of Kolkata, and 56 km south of Vaishali (Fig. 83). Patna's history can be traced back 2,600 years. The Buddhist text *Mahaparinibbana Sutta* (cf. *Digha Nikaya* II.86) mentions that the Buddha and accompanying monks, while returning from Nalanda to march towards Vaishali, had passed through the city gate of Pataligama (modern Patna), and were met by two officials from Magadha, Sunidha and Vassakara. They had been assigned by King Ajatashatru to transform Pataligama into a major city. They told the Buddha, "We plan to rename the city gate you have just passed through 'Gautamadvara'. Allow us to accompany you to the ferry landing. We will name it 'Gautama Ferry Landing'." Presently this is identified as the Gautama (Buddha) Ghat along the Ganga river (*Digha Nikaya* II.16). The tales further described that in his last pilgrimage the Buddha passed a night at this place and forecasted his future walks and the disasters the city would face, including a great fire, a flood and a war. These forecasts were proved with the passage of time. The *Vinaya Pitaka* (I. 226-230) has narrated the pre-historic mythology related to this city. The Chinese traveller of the 7th century, Hsüan-tsang has described this city as Pataliputa and Kusumpur.

Ajatashatru, the second Magadha king who ruled from Rajagriha, built a small fort at Pataligrama. Later Chandragupta Maurya founded the Mauryan Empire with Pataliputra as its capital. Buddhist histories suggest that it was here that Ashoka usurped the throne of his father, Bindusara, murdering all his rivals and starting a reign of terror, before his conversion 8 years later which marked the beginning of perhaps the greatest compassionate kingship the world has known.

The Greek ambassador Megasthenes was deeply impressed by the efficiency of Chandragupta's administration and the splendour of the city. Ruins can be seen at Kumrahar, Bhiknapahari and Bulandhi Bagh with its 75 m wooden passage. Excavations date the site back to the pre-Mauryan times of 600 BCE. In the 16th century the Pathan

Patna

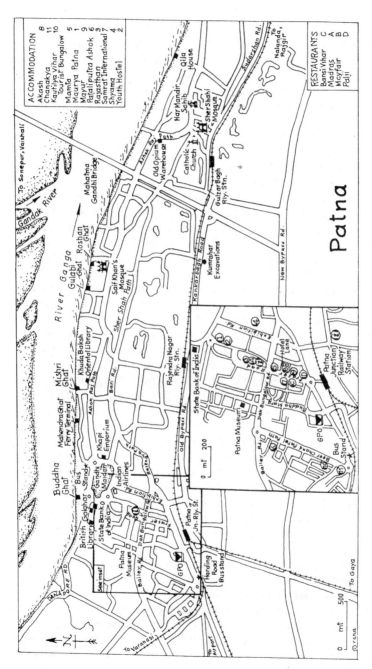

Fig. 83. Patna

235

king Sher Shah Suri established the foundations of a new Patna, building in 1540 a majestic mosque which dominates the skyline.

Modern Patna stretches along the southern bank of the Ganga for about 15 km. Divided in two by the Maidan, a large open park, it has some open suburbs, but the central city is crowded, dusty and with virtually nothing of architectural interest or merit.

Places of interest

Patna's buildings reflect its administrative and educational functions. The collectorate, Judge's court, Medical College and Hospital, Patna College, the University, the Law College and the College of Engineering are all close to the riverbanks in the western part of the city. Also on this side lies the Governor's state house (Raj Bhavan), the Maharaja's palace, the High Court and the Museum as well as the better residential quarters. To the east is Old Patna with its bazaars, the old mosques, Har Mandir and Padri-ki-Haveli or St. Mary's, the oldest Roman Catholic Church in Patna, which was built in 1775.

Golghar: The Gola or roundhouse is the extraordinary 29 m high bee-hive shaped structure between the Maidan and the Ganga. It was built of stone slabs in 1786 by Capt. John Garstin of the Bengal Engineers, as a grain store for the British army in case of a famine similar to that of 1770. It has a base 125 m wide where the wall is 3.6 m thick, with 2 brick staircases which spiral up the outside. Never completed, it was intended to hold 137,000 tons of grain. The grain was to be carried up by one side, poured in through the hole at the top and then the workforce was to descend through the other staircase to collect more. The last line of the inscription "First filled and publicly closed by –" was never completed. Although now empty, it is well worth climbing the steps for an excellent view of the city and the Ganga. Between July and September the river can be over 5 km wide at this point with a current of 8 to 10 knots at places.

Har Mandir is in the Chowk area of Old Patna. The gurdwara built by Maharaja Ranjit Singh is the 2nd of the 4 great *takhts* or thrones in the Sikh world and consecrates the birth place of the 10th Guru, Gobind Singh. The shrine of white marble with kiosks on the terrace above has a museum on the ground floor exhibiting photos, holy scriptures and personal possessions of the Guru.

Qila House or Jalan Museum, lies across the road from Har Mandir. This private house was built over the ruins of Sher Shah's fort and presently is a museum containing Chinese paintings and a valuable collection of jade and silver filigree work of the Mughal period. Prior permission must be obtained from the owner. **Saif Khan's**

Mosque or Pather-ki-Masjid is situated on the bank of the Ganga and was built in 1621 by Parwez Shah, a son of the Mughal Emperor Jahangir.

Gulzarbagh. About 8 km east of the Golghar near Kumrahar is the former East India Company's principal opium *godown* (warehouse), now a Govt printing press. Strategically placed by the river, the 3 long buildings with porticoes on each side were easily accessible to boats which would carry the opium down to Calcutta from these north Indian headquarters. The old opium *godowns*, ballroom and hall are open to visitors.

Kumrahar

Almost nothing of ancient Pataliputra can be seen today; some of it must have been washed away by the Ganga river and what was not may still lie buried under the present city. The excavations of Kumrahar at the site of the ancient capital on the bypass between Patna Sahib and Patna Junction stations have revealed ruins enclosed within a high brick pillared wall, very probably a part of King Ashoka's palace. Excavations conducted here in 1912-13 revealed brick structures dating from the Gupta period, directly below which was a thick layer of ash that formed vertical tubes in places. Below this layer of ash was a layer of silt between 2.4 m and 2.7 m thick. This is a remarkable verification of the Buddha's prediction that after Pataliputta had become a great city it would be prey to flood and fire. Towards the bottom of the silt layer and directly below the vertical tubes of ash were found fragments of polished pillars of the Mauryan type. The pillars, 4.3 m from each other, were in eight rows, seventy-two pillars altogether.

These date back to 600 BCE, the first of 4 distinct periods up to CE 600. The buildings were devastated by a fire and lay hidden in the silt. The more recent 5th phase dates from the beginning of the 17th century. The most important finds are rare wooden ramparts and a large Mauryan assembly hall with highly polished sandstone pillars that date back to 400-300 BCE. In the 5th century CE, when the Chinese pilgrim Fa-hsien visited the area, he commented on the brilliant enamel-like finish achieved by the Mauryan stone-cutters and wrote that it was "shining bright as glass". The excavations suggest that the immense pillared hall was 3-storeyed and covered an area of 77 sq. m. There were probably 15 rows of 5 pillars, each 4.6 m apart. From the single complete column found they are estimated to have been about 6 m high. Only two pillars of any length were eventually found. Spooner, who did the excavation, conjectured that the pillars, perhaps originally 12 m high, supported a wooden roof, and that at some time silt from a great flood left only about half the length of the pillars exposed. Later, a great conflagration destroyed the roof and cracked the upper ends of the pillars, which eventually sank into the soft earth dragging ash and stone fragments with them as they went. The fact that much of the building was wooden explains why so little has survived after the fire. The excavations also point to the possibility of one of the ceilings having been supported by immense *caryatid* figures which, taken together with the use of numerous columns, shows a marked similarity with the palaces at Persepolis in south Iran. The pleasant garden site has little to show today other than the remaining intact pillar. In early 1993 the site of the hall was flooded for months by a leaking water pipe, and the tiny museum had its small collection of valuable finds almost invisibly shut away in a dark room.

Today the remains of the pillared hall lie in the bottom of a large rectangular depression surrounded by a shady and well-maintained garden. Unfortunately, because of poor maintenance, the depression is full of water the whole year round and only one pillar can be seen above the surface. However, at the edge of the site a single pillar is on display. It must have fallen over before the flood that inundated the hall occurred, as it was found lying in a horizontal position, which also must have prevented its sinking into the earth. The pillar is 4.34 m long, with the entire shaft smooth and polished. The base of the pillar is smooth but not polished, and bears a number of interesting symbols thought to be mason's marks. Several of these symbols are identical with those that occur in Persian monuments of an early date, strong evidence that the Mauryan court employed Persian craftsmen. The pilgrim will notice about one and a half metre from the base of the pillar four square bosses projecting slightly from the surface. It is likely that these bosses are all that is left of rings used to hold ropes during the transport of the pillar, and which were later chipped off.

Near the remains of the pillared hall is a small museum displaying some of the terracotta found at Kumrahar and also some wooden planks found during the excavation. Beyond the museum are the remains of a monastery dating from the Gupta period and named, according to a sealing found at the site, Arogya Monastery.

The archaeological park at Kumrahar is about 7 km from Patna Junction railway station and is open from 09.30 to 17.30 hr every day except Mondays.

Patna Museum

The Patna Museum contains a fine collection of Buddhist sculptures, and despite its rather shabby appearance and poor lighting, is well worth a visit. The most famous piece in the museum is the statue of a *cauri* bearer dated to the Mauryan period. This figure was probably one of a pair that may well have stood at the entrance of a palace. The statue is life-size, realistically carved and highly polished. The anklets and bangles on the arm are large and chunky, not unlike those still worn by Indian women. The right hand holds a *cauri*, a ceremonial flywhisk. In ancient India, to be accompanied by two *cauri* carriers was a sign of power and status.

A statue of Avalokiteshvara and another of Maitreya, which were found placed on both sides of a Buddha statue (also in the museum, Acc. No. 1752), are particularly beautiful. Both the statues are carved out of grey granite, are seated in the one-leg-folded posture (*ardhaparyanka*), and date from the eleventh century. The faces perfectly express the ideal that these two Bodhisattvas embody: active and involved compassion. The statues have their right hands in the gesture imparting fearlessness, they wear jewellery on their arms, wrists and around their necks, and they have locks of hair lightly draped on their shoulders. Maitreya, distinguished by the *stupa* nestled in his head-dress, holds a *nagakeshara* flower while Avalokiteshvara, with a Buddha in his head-dress, holds a large blooming lotus. These two Bodhisattvas and their accompanying Buddha were found at Vishnupur near Sobhnath.

The gallery on the second floor of the museum contains a large collection of *thangkas* that the famous Indian Buddhist monk Rahula Sankrityayana acquired during his travels in Tibet during the 1930s. Sadly, the *thangkas* have not fared well in the heat and humidity, and inept attempts at restoration have ruined many. Another second storey gallery contains most of the famous bronzes discovered at Kurkihar in 1930.

Another object of particular interest to Buddhists is to be found in the terracotta gallery, also on the second floor. It is a round terracotta plaque called the Kumrahar Plaque depicting what seems to be the Mahabodhi Temple at Bodh Gaya. The plaque gives the pilgrim a good idea of what the great temple might have looked like shortly after it was built. Some things clearly recognisable on the plaque can still be seen on the modern temple, the main inward sloping spire, the railing around the temple, and so on. But the plaque also makes it clear that the temple has undergone major changes. The arched chamber is now completely different, and four corner spires have been added. This interesting plaque was found at Kumrahar. The museum also contains Buddhist sculptures from Nalanda, Gandhara, Orissa and Negapatarn in South India.

The Patna Museum is in Buddha Marg near the city centre, and is open from 10.30 am to 16.30 hr, closed on Mondays and Public holidays.

Hotels

There are three luxury hotels: **Maurya Patna** (80 rooms), Fraser Rd, South Gandhi Maidan (Tel: 2203040, Fax: 2203060; Email: maurya2@dte.vsnl.net.in), modern, clean, 2 restaurants, excellent pool, poolside barbecue, being renovated floor by floor, is Patna's top hotel, tariff: Rs 3000/ 6000; **Pataliputra Ashok**, Bir Chand Patel Path, Tel 2226270 (56 rooms); and **Chanakya** (90 rooms), Beer Chand Patel Marg (Tel 2220590, Fax: 2220598; Web: www.chanakyapatna.com), restaurant, clean and modern, much used by political clientele, tariff: Rs 1500/ 3000.

The middle grade hotels include: **Satkar International**, Fraser Rd, Tel 2220506 (50 rooms), central a/c, minimal spending on maintenance, mainly business clientele; **Republic** (35 rooms), Lauriya Bagh, Exhibition Road (Tel 2685021, Fax: 2685024, Email: lovelysen@ sancharnet.net.in), some a/c, dining hall, exchange, roof garden, tariff: Rs 600/ 1200; **Marwari Awas Griha**, Fraser Rd, Tel 231866 (42 rooms), some a/c, virtually all Indian guests, small but very good vegetarian dining hall — according to some, "the best veg. food in Bihar"; **Avantee**, opp. Dak Bungalow, Fraser Rd, Tel 2220540 (40 rooms), some a/c, restaurant; **President**, off Fraser Rd, Tel 2220600 (36 rooms), some a/c, restaurant, travel; **Rajasthan**, Fraser Rd, Tel 225102 (20 rooms), some a/c good vegetable meals; **Mayur**, Fraser Rd, Tel: 2224149, basic, clean rooms, restaurant; **Chaitanya**, Exhibition Rd, Tel 255123 (48 rooms), some a/c, restaurant; **Anand Lok**, just opp. Patna Jn. Rly Station, Tel 2223960 (43 rooms), some a/c; **Jayasarmin**, Kankarbagh Rd, 5-min walk Patna Junction station; and **Kautilya Vihar** (BSTDC), Bir Chand Patel Path, Tel 2225411 (44 rooms), some a/c cheap dormitory. Also several inexpensive hotels are especially on Fraser Rd and Ashok Rajpath. Some have a restaurant and few, a bar. Avoid *Railway Retiring Rooms*.

Tourist Office, day rooms for half-day use, slightly run-down maintenance, helpful management, and good food, though sometimes slow service.

EXCURSIONS

The 7.5 km Mahatma Gandhi Bridge, one of the world's longest river bridges, crosses the Ganga to the east of Patna. Note that even recent maps often do not show this road connection, opened in 1983. Bihar is divided by the Ganga, but the new bridge has made both the road route to Nepal and short excursions to the north of the river much more practicable by bus or car.

Sonepur is 22 km across the Ganga, near its confluence with the Gandak. Sonepur has a station on the NE Railway. Sonepur witnesses Asia's biggest cattle market that begins on Karttika Purnima, the first full moon after Divali/ Dipavali (Oct/Nov). The month-long fair which accompanies the trading in livestock and grain draws thousands to the magic shows, folk dances and contests of skill and stalls selling handicrafts and handlooms. According to legend Sonepur was the site of a battle between Gaja (elephant), the lord of the forest, and Graha (crocodile), the lord of the waterways. Elephants (as well as camels, horses and birds) are still bought and sold at this fair but their numbers are dwindling. The Harihar Kshetra Mela commemorates the coming together of devotees of Shiva and Vishnu who perform their *puja* at Hariharanatha (the twin-form god representing half Vishnu, Hari, and half Shiva, Hara) Temple, after bathing in the river on the full moon day of *Karttika* (Oct/ Nov).

Vaishali is 56km north of Patna, about 1 hour by car or bus. Even including Sonepur it makes a comfortable excursion.

12. KESARIYA (KESSAPUTTA)

Where the Buddha handed over his alms-bowl to the people

At Kessaputta, in the neighbourhood of Vaishali, the Blessed One said to Ananda:
"Eat your food to satisfy your hunger, and drink to satisfy you thirst. Satisfy the necessities of life like the butterfly that sips the flower, without destroying its fragrance or its texture.

It is through not understanding and grasping the four truths, O brethren, that we have gone astray so long, and wandered in this weary path of transmigration, both you and I, until we have found the truth.

Practise the earnest meditations I have taught you. Continue in the great struggle against sin. Walk steadily in the roads of saintship. Be strong in moral powers. Let the organs of your spiritual sense be quick. When the seven kinds of wisdom enlighten your mind, you will find the noble, eightfold path that leads to Nirvana.

Behold, O brethren, the final extinction of the Tathagata will take place before long. I now exhort you, saying: 'All component things must grow old and be dissolved again. Seek ye for that which is permanent, and work out your salvation with diligence'."

The *Mahaparinibbana Sutta*, III, 46 - 63.

While returning from Vaishali, one meets Daudnagar from where, following 50 km of road towards the north running parallel to the Gandak river, one encounters Sahibganj. About 1 km before Sahibganj, from village Salempur a road goes to the west on which passing about 5 km one will meet a village called Manohar Chapra. From here at a distance of 500 m to the northeast is Deura, the site encompassing a Buddhist *stupa*, ruins and mounds (84° 52.6′ E of longitude and 26° 19.8′ N of latitude). Deura is a hamlet site and is situated at the southern part of the block-headquarters of Kesariya (East Champaran District, Bihar). If you come from Kushinagar to Vaishali and Patna, following the highway NH 28, one will pass through Gopalganj, the district headquarters town near the Gandak river; then cross the river. About 10 km from this place, there is a market village Berwa (*Pali*: Beluvagamba) from where a road goes to Kesariya, lying southeast at a distance of 15 km. One will pass the village of Rampur Khajuriya,

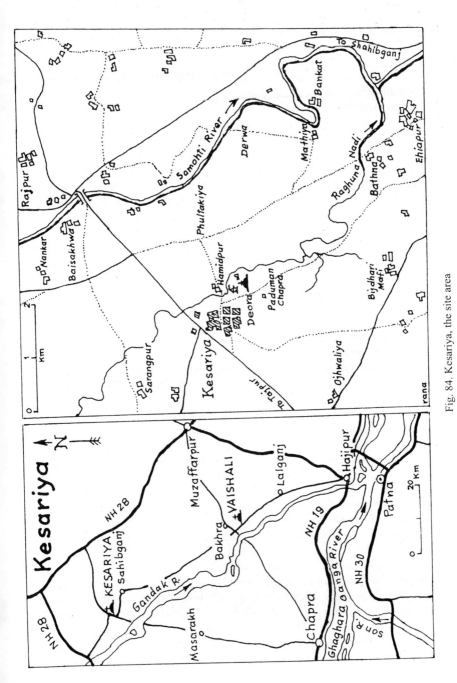

Fig. 84. Kesariya, the site area

and after reaching Kesariya, 3 km south from there is Deura. At present Deura occupies a tall mound of brick and earthen debris (Fig. 84).

After his last discourse at Vaishali the Buddha set out for Kushinagar, but the Lichchhavis kept following him. The Buddha addressed the assembly of monks at Mahavana Kutagarasala and re-minded them that his whole teachings consisted of the thirty-seven *Bodhipakshiya dhamma*, classified under seven groups. According to historical records, after these final teachings the Buddha left Vaishali and then crossed the villages of Bhandagama, Hatthigama and Jambugama, and took rest at a place called Kessaputta. When people started following him during his last journey to Kushinagar, he handed over his alms-bowl to the people at Kessaputta (or Kakuttha; cf. *Samyutta Sutta*, XLVII.1, 9) and asked them to go back. As a mark of respect to the Buddha, his followers then built a small *stupa* with mud at Kesariya. To commemorate the Buddha's stay, Emperor Ashoka also built a *stupa* at Kessaputta. In due course of time, during the Maurya, Sunga and Kushana periods, it became a brick *stupa* with several additions and enlargements. In the 6th century CE, during the Gupta period, it was further enlarged and embellished with hundreds of sculptures. A number of similar *stupas* were built in Kashmir, Bhu-tan, Tibet and Myanmar (Burma).

A little-known, but historically and archaeologically documented event is worth mentioning in this context. After his visit to Amrapali, the Buddha continued his journey towards Kushinagar. He travelled along the eastern banks of the river Gandak (also called Narayani). A band of his devoted Lichchhavis accompanied Lord Buddha in this journey. At a spot known as Kessaputta (the present Kesariya), the Buddha took rest for a night. It was here that he chose to announce to his disciples the news of his impending *parinirvana*, and implored them to return to Vaishali. The Lichchhavis, wildly lamenting, would have none of that. They steadfastly refused to leave. Whereupon, the Buddha, by creating a 914 m (3,000 ft) wide illusionary stream flooded the space between them and himself, and compelled them to leave (Fig. 85). As a reminder and to console them he gave them his alms-bowl. This site can be identified with Deora in modern Kesariya vil-lage. The Lichchhavis, most reluctantly and expressing their sorrow wildly, took leave after builing a *stupa* there to commemorate the event. The Buddha had chosen that spot to announce his impending *parinirvana* because, as he told his disciple Ananda, he knew that in a previous life he had ruled from that place, namely, Kessaputta, as a Chakravarti Raja. According to Hsüan-tsang, it was here that the Lord

Fig. 85. Kesariya: Miracle of the flood by the Buddha to compel
the Lichchhavis to return (from Sanchi Stupa, ca. 50 BCE).

Buddha had announced that in his previous life he was a Bodhisattva
and had ruled from this place as the Chakravarti Raja Ben. The *Padma
Purana* mentions Raja Ben as a Buddhist king. But according to local
legend, Raja Ben was far more famous as a very generous emperor,
and also was one among the five great kings of north India. Hsüan-
tsang mentioned another Chakravarti Raja of the 7th century BCE,
perhaps identified as Raja Ben. Deora was developed greatly during
this period.

　　According to a legend, Raja Ben took no rent for his lands. But
the more popular legend represents him as taking only a '*sup*', or 'win-

Fig. 86. Kesariya: the Buddhist Stupa

nowing basket' of corn from each cultivator, both great and small. But afterwards he ordered that every one should give him a bit of gold the size of a grain of barley. The supernatural powers acquired by his austerities suddenly stopped. The name of Raja Ben's queen was Rani Kamalavati. She used to bathe on a lotus leaf. As she was bathing, the lotus leaf gave way under her and she was drowned. Then Raja Ben consulted his *pandits*, who told him that his Rani was drowned because he had raised the old land rent. Then Raja Ben Chakravarti built the *Deura* (or *stupa*) and going inside it with all his family, he closed the entrance by his magical powers and was seen no more.

The place known as Raja Ben's Fort was badly damaged in the earthquake of 1938. The Bihar Archaeological Survey has taken control of the relics, but this historic place was not developed till date as an important pilgrimage spot. About 750 m to the northeast of Deora was the Queen's palace, which even today is called Ranivas (Queen's Residence). The pond in which she used to take her bath was famous as the *Gangeyatal*, and was spread over an area of 278.7 sq.m as narrated in the historical documents. The excavations at the Ranivas site took place in 1862, which confirmed the existence of one of the largest Buddhist *Viharas* at the site (Fig. 86). A huge statue of Lord Buddha found here support this. A pillar surmounted by a lion capital of bold and good designs was discovered here by Capt. Markham Kittoe in 1862.

One of the Buddha's most celebrated discourses is the **Kalamasutta** (cf. *The Buddha's Charter of Free Inquiry: Kalamasutta*, Wheel No. 8) in which he advised that his teachings be accepted only after careful scrutiny and reflection. Later, a *stupa* was built on the site of this incident. The later history of the famous bowl relic is to be found in the *Middle Land Middle Way*. The recent discovery, during excavations for canals, of gold coins embossed with the seal of the famous Emperor Kanishka of the Kushana dynasty confirms the ancient heritage of Kessaputta. The two great Chinese pilgrims, Fa-hsian and Hsüan-tsang visited this *stupa* and the lion capital (Fig. 87) and left short accounts of it.

Fig. 87. Kesariya: Lion Capital head (from a drawing by Capt. Kittoe, 1862)

The **Main Stupa** was discovered for the first time in 1862 by Alexander Cunningham who found it to be 427 m (1400 feet) in circumference and 15.5 m (51 feet) high and estimated that its dome would have originally been about 21.4 m (70 feet) high. He wrote, "The excavations have disclosed the walls of a small temple 10 feet square, and the head and shoulders of a colossal figure of the Buddha, with the usual crisp curly hair." According to him this place existed from CE 200 to 700 as the capital town of the kingdom. The *stupa* rises in five huge terraces each of a different shape, therefore from the top it looks like a giant *mandala*. In each terrace are niches enshrining life-size statues of the Buddha.

In 1911, according to the British historian L.O. O'Malley, the ruins at Deora were 19 m high with a circumference of 427 m. In those days, the site was covered with wild vegetation. Basically, it must have been about 24.5 m to 27.5 m high, and its total height including the mound at the base would have been about 45.7 m.

The **Main Stupa**, perhaps once the tallest ever in the world, is said to be the prototype of the Buddhist temple of Borobudur in Java, Indonesia (Figs. 88, 89 and 90). According to the local sources, the upper portion of the *stupa* fell down in the 1934 earthquake in Bihar. It is estimated that it was 37.5 m high at that time. In halcyon days, when Buddhism thrived in India, the Kesariya Stupa was 45.7 m high, while the Borobudur Stupa is 42.1 m high. The height of the Sanchi Stupa, a World Heritage Monument, is 23.6 m, almost half of Kesariya Stupa's original height.

Fig. 88. Borobudur: Base plan of the seven-storied Vihara, dated ca. 7th century CE
(after Sir Stamford Raffles, 1872). The section length is 127.5 m.

Fig. 89. Borobudur: Elevation and section of Vihara Temple
(after Sir Stamford Raffles, 1872).

Fig. 90. Borobudur: An aerial view.

248

Significantly, both Kesariya and Borobudur Stupas have six terraces each, and the diameter of Kesariya Stupa is equivalent to the width of Borobudur. But experts feel the diameter of Kesariya Stupa could be larger as several parts are still underground and are yet to be excavated. It took three years for ASI to expose the frontal parts of the monument (1999-2001). Excavation of the full *stupa* would take a few years more. The ASI has conserved the site in a befitting manner after its excavation and has decided to acquire the surrounding area to develop it into a pilgrimage and tourist spot.

Facilities

There is no place to stay nor any restaurant. Following the NH 28, at 20 km north, after crossing the Gandak river, is Gopalganj, the district headquarters which lies 50 km northwest of Kesariya, where one can stay in a cheap hotel.

A BUDDHIST SITE NEARBY: LAURIYA NANDANGARH

A further 92 km north of Kesariya, connected by the NH 28A, is Lauriya Nandangarh. This place is 26 km from Bettiah, which is on the main road north of Patna. Bettiah is 190 km from Patna via Motihari and Muzaffarpur. From Vaishali it is 142 km north, close to the Nepalese border.

The small town of Lauriya Nandangarh has no known association with the Buddha, but from the view of the monuments in the area, it is of special significance to Buddhists in ancient times. Around the settlement there are about twenty grassy mounds in three rows, one running from east to west, and two others, parallel to each other, running from north to south. These mounds are probably the remains of ancient *stupas*, and their excavation has brought to light fragments of earthen vessels, charred human bones, and in one case, a small human figure made from thin beaten gold. The *stupas* lack any developed features, indicating that they are very early. There are two other monuments in Lauriya Nandangarh that are of interest to Buddhists.

Ashokan Pillar

It is believed that King Ashoka originally erected about 40 pillars, but only a few of these survive undamaged. Some were struck by lightning, some fell and were smashed, some were dragged to other sites, and some, like the Sanchi pillar, were broken up to provide stone for various purposes. It is only the Lauriya Nandangarh pillar that remains at its original site with its capital intact, thus giving a unique glimpse of the powerful impression that these majestic monuments once produced.

The shaft of the pillar has a gradual inward slope and rises 12.8 m though it may have sunk a few metres into the ground over the centuries. The capital is slightly more squat in comparison with the Sarnath capital, and has a spiral band below it. Above this is the drum with a frieze of geese running around it from left to right. On the drum is a single crouching lion with finely carved features, powerful and majestic (Fig. 91). Unfortunately, the face of the lion is missing, probably having been shot at by a cannon when Mir Jumla's army passed this way in 1660. Six of Ashoka's edicts issued in 244 BCE are inscribed on the Lauriya Nandangarh pillar, and because they give a good idea of the scope of his attempts to apply Buddhist values to his administration, they are worth quoting in full:

Fig. 91. Lauriya Nandangarh:
Ashoka's Lion Capital
(ca. mid 3rd century BCE)

(1) Beloved-of-the-Gods speaks thus: This *Dhamma* edict was written twenty-six years after my coronation. Happiness in this world and the next is difficult to obtain without much love for the *Dhamma*, much self-examination, much respect, much fear (of evil), and much enthusiasm. But through my instruction this regard for *Dhamma* and love of *Dhamma* has grown day by day, and will continue to grow. And my officers of high, low and middle rank are practising and conforming to *Dhamma*, and are capable of inspiring others to do the same. Mahamatras in border areas are doing the same. And these are my instructions: to protect with *Dhamma*, to make happiness through Dhamma and to guard with *Dhamma*.

(2) Beloved-of-the-Gods, King Piyadassi, speaks thus: *Dhamma* is good, but what constitutes *Dhamma*? (It includes) little evil, much good, kindness, generosity, truthfulness and purity. I have given the gift of sight in various ways. To two-footed and four-footed beings, to birds and aquatic animals, I have given various things including the

gift of life. And many other good deeds have been done by me. This *Dhamma* edict has been written that people might follow it and it might endure for a long time. And the one who follows it properly will do something good.

(3) Beloved-of-the-Gods, King Piyadassi, speaks thus: People see only their good deeds, saying, "I have done this good deed". But they do not see their evil deeds, saying, "I have done this evil deed" or "This is called evil". But this (tendency) is difficult to see. One should think like this: "It is these things that lead to evil, to violence, to cruelty, anger, pride and jealousy. Let me not ruin myself with these things". And further, one should think: "This leads to happiness in this world and the next".

(4) Beloved-of-the-Gods speaks thus: This *Dhamma* edict was written twenty-six years after my coronation. My Rajjukas are working among the people, among many hundreds of thousands of people. The hearing of petitions and the administration of justice has been left to them so that they can do their duties confidently and fearlessly and so that they can work for the welfare, happiness and benefit of the people in the country. But they should remember what causes happiness and sorrow, and being themselves devoted to *Dhamma*, they should encourage the people in the country (to do the same), that they may attain happiness in this world and the next. These Rajjukas are eager to serve me. They also obey other officers who know my desires, who instruct the Rajjukas so that they can please me. Just as a person feels confident having entrusted his child to an expert nurse, thinking: "The nurse will keep my child well", even so, the Rajjukas have been appointed by me for the welfare and happiness of the people in the country.

The hearing of petitions and the administration of justice has been left to the Rajjukas so that they can do their duties unperturbed, fearlessly and confidently. It is my desire that there should be uniformity in law and uniformity in sentencing. I even go this far, to grant a three-day stay for those in prison who have been tried and sentenced to death. During this time their relatives can make appeals to have the prisoners' lives spared. If there is none to appeal on their behalf, the prisoners can give gifts in order to make merit for the next world, or observe fasts. Indeed it is my wish that in this way, even if a prisoner's time is limited, they can prepare for the next world, and that people's Dhamma practice, self-control and generosity may grow.

(5) Beloved-of-the-Gods, King Piyadassi, speaks thus: Twenty-six years after my coronation, various animals were declared to be protected — parrots, *mynas*, *aruna*, ruddy geese, wild ducks,

nandimukhas, *gelatas*, bats, queen ants, terrapins, boneless fish, *vedareyaka*, *gangapuputaka*, *sankiya* fish, tortoises, porcupines, squirrels, deer, bulls, *okapinda*, wild asses, wild pigeons, domestic pigeons and all four-footed creatures that are neither useful nor edible. Those nanny goats, ewes and sows which are with young or giving milk to their young are protected, and so are young ones less than six months old. Cocks are not to be caponised, husks hiding living beings are not to be burnt and forests are not to be burnt, either without reason or to kill creatures. One animal is not to be fed to another. On the three Chaturmasis, the three days of Tisa and during the fourteenth and fifteenth of the Uposatha, fish are protected and not to be sold. During these days animals are not to be killed in the elephant reserves or the fish reserves either. On the eighth of every fortnight, on the fourteenth and fifteenth, on Tisa, Punarvasu, the three Chaturmasis and other auspicious days, bulls are not to be castrated, billy goats, rams, boars and other animals that are usually castrated are not to be. On Tisa, Punarvasu, Chaturmasis and the fortnight of Chaturmasis, horses and bullocks are not to be branded. In the twenty-six years since my coronation prisoners have been given amnesty on twenty-five occasions.

(6) Beloved-of-the-Gods speaks thus: Twelve years after my coronation, I started to have *Dhamma* edicts written for the welfare and happiness of the people, and so that not transgressing them, they might grow in the *Dhamma*. Thinking: "How can the welfare and happiness of the people be secured?" I give attention to my relatives, to those dwelling near and those dwelling far, so I can lead them to happiness and then I act accordingly. I do the same for all groups. I have honoured all religions with various honours. But I consider it best to meet with people personally. This *Dhamma* edict was written twenty-six years after my coronation.

These same edicts are to be found on the Topra and Meerut pillars, now in Delhi, the Allahabad pillar, and the pillars at Lauriya Areraj and Rampurva, both locations not far from Lauriya Nandangarh. As well as Ashoka's inscription, the pillar has a large amount of graffiti on it, both ancient and modern. Why Ashoka chose this site to erect a pillar is not known, but it has been suggested that in ancient times, Lauriya Nandangarh was one of the main stops on the pilgrimage route from Patna to Lumbini.

Stupa

About 1.5 km from Ashoka's pillar, behind the local sugar mill, are the ruins of what must have been one of the largest *stupas* ever built in India. Although the *stupa* is now only about 24 m high it has a circumference of nearly 457 m. The base of the *stupa* rises in a series of huge terraces, the lower ones having a polygonal plan, while the upper ones are circular. Excavation revealed that the core of the *stupa* was made of earth. At a depth of 11 m from the top a smaller complete *stupa* was found which had no relic inside it. However, beside it was a casket containing a long strip of birch bark, which proved to be a page from a Buddhist sacred book dating from about the 4th century CE. A *stupa* of such enormous proportions must have been built to enshrine some very precious relic or to commemorate some very important event, but what it was remains a mystery.

13. KUSHINAGAR

Where the Buddha entered *parinirvana*

"How transient are all component things!
Growth is their nature and decay:
They are produced, they are dissolved again:
And this is best — when they have sunk to rest."

The Mahaparinibbana Sutta

Before the Final entering into nirvana at Kushinara (Kushinagar), the Blessed One addressed the venerable Ananda, and said:
"It may be, Ananda, that in some of you the thought may arise, 'The word of the Master is ended, we have no teacher more!' But it is not thus, Ananda, that you should regard it. It is true that no more shall I receive a body, for all future sorrow has now forever passed away. But though this body will be dissolved, the Tathagata remains. The truth and the rules of the order which I have set forth and laid down for you all, let them, after I am gone, be a teacher unto you. When I am gone, Ananda, let the order, if it should so wish, abolish all the lesser and minor precepts."

The Mahaparinibbana Sutta, v, 1-14.

Once more the Blessed One began to speak: "Behold now, brethren", said he, "I exhort you, saying, 'Decaying is inherent in all component things, but the truth will remain forever! Work out your salvation with diligence!'" This was the last word of the Tathagata. Then he fell into deep meditation and entered into nirvana.

The Mahatanahasamkhya Sutta, Majjhima Nikaya, vol. 1, p. 263.

Approach & Historical Background

Population: 26,000. STD Tel Code: 05563.

Kushinagar (Kushinara, or Kasia) can be approached by bus from Gorakhpur, 55 km east on the NH 28. Some major road distances are: Lumbini 175 km, Kapilavastu 146 km, Shravasti 274 km and Varanasi 270 km. The nearest Railway Station is Gorakhpur, 51 km. No buses leave Kushinagar after 6.30 pm. All the places of worship, tourist attractions, and accommodations are on Kushinagar's main road (Fig. 92). The bus station is in the neighbouring town of Kasia, 3 km east. In the vicinity of the monuments a colony of buildings has sprung up,

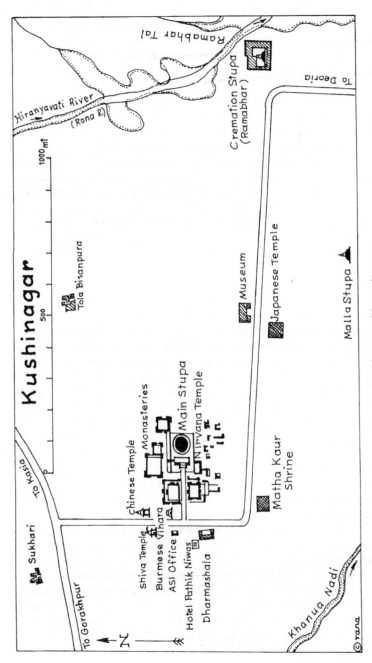

Fig. 92. Kushinagar and its environment

including a degree college with the attached high school and residential buildings and three public rest houses and *dharmashalas*, one each belonging to the Arakanese and Burmese Buddhists and the third erected by the Birlas.

In one of his last utterances, the Buddha thus named Kushinagar (*Kushinara*), the site of his *parinirvana*, as one of the chief places of Buddhist pilgrimage. Three reasons had been assigned for the Buddha's choice of Kushinagar for the final retreat: (1) it was the proper venue for the preaching of the *Maha-sudassana suttanta*, (2) to admit Subhadda to the *Sangha* before his death, as he was living there, and (3) the availability of the Brahmin Drona who would solve the problem of his relics. Moreover, it had been the site of his death in seven previous births and he beheld no other spot "where the *Tathagata* for the 8th time will lay aside his body". At this place the Buddha left his corporeal self and finally attained *mahaparinirvana*. Thus was assured its sanctity.

When he reached his eighty-first year, the Buddha gave his last major teaching — the subject was the thirty-seven wings of enlightenment — and left Vulture's Peak with Ananda to journey north. After sleeping at Nalanda he crossed the Ganga river for the last time at the place where now stands the city of Patna and came to the village of Beluva. While staying for the rainy season at this village near Vaishali, the Buddha told Ananda that he was attacked by illness and bodily pain and the effect of old age. The Buddha declared that he was going to lay down his mortal body after three months. While staying at Vaishali, the Buddha thrice mentioned to Ananda a Buddha's ability to remain alive until the end of the aeon. Failing to understand the significance of this utterance, Ananda said nothing and went to meditate nearby. Shakyamuni then rejected prolonging his own life-span. When Ananda later learned of this he implored the Buddha to live longer but his request was refused, for it had come too late. The Buddha suppressed his sickness and continued to Vaishali. He called all the monks residing in and around Vaishali to assemble at Mahavana Kutagarasala and reminded them that his whole teaching consisted of the 37 *Bodhipakshiya Dhammas* divided into 7 groups (this episode is considered as the **Third Turning of the Wheel of Dhamma**):

1. **Smrityupasthana** (Pali, *Satipatthanas*), mindfulness or awareness of what is happening in one's body (*kaya*), feeling (*vedana*), mind (*citta*), and what are his acquisitions (*dhamma*). This group of practices has been highly praised by the Buddha as the single best path (*ekayana*) for attaining emancipation.

2. Samyakaprahana (Pali, *Sammappadhanas*), right exertions, efforts, i.e. duties prescribed under the *sammayayama* of the eight-fold path, viz. to eradicate demerits, to collect merits and to preserve and increase the merits.

3. Riddhipada (Pali, *Iddhipadas*), attainment of supernormal powers by means of a strong desire for perfection, application of energy by meditation, application of mind to cultivate meditation, and discrimination of the mental factors accompanying the meditation. The Lord said that those who mastered the four powers of will, thought, energy and investigation could, if they wished, live for an aeon.

4. Indriya (Pali, *Indriyas*), dominance of forces or factors led by firm faith in the Buddha as the fully enlightened, wise, world-knower, the excellent guide of men and gods, and so forth; this faith is also extended to the *Dhamma* and *Sangha*. The dominance of faith is supported by the predominance of energy, memory, thoughts, and intellect.

5. Balas, internal strength, or prowess. The five attributes constitute the *Balas*; they are the same as the *Indriyas*, viz. Faith, Energy, Memory, Meditation, and Knowledge. The main difference between Indriyas and Balas is that the former is actively operating and does not necessarily remain the same for all times while the latter is the result of the activity of the faculty. The latter one is steady and makes the adept firmly established in the dominant faculty, i.e. the dominating faculty changes into the steady strength or prowess.

6. Sambodhyanga (Pali, *Sambojjhangas*), acquisitions leading to full enlightenment, destroying impurities and hindrances, and leading to attain knowledge and emancipation. The condition precedent to the acquisition of *sambojjhangas* is that the adept must be perfect in moral precepts (*shila*).

7. Marga (Pali, *Magga*), the '*Middle Way*' between extreme asceticism and worldly life. The Buddha was insistent that his Truth was none of the two extreme views, viz. *Shashvata* (eternal) and *Uccheda* (annihilation). By the realisation of the origin and decay of *vedana* (feelings) the Buddha had become free without any support and had found out the Ultimate Truth that was deep and subtle and beyond dialectics. (*Digha Nikaya*, I. 30)

Bearing all the ailments with fortitude, the Buddha proceeded with Ananda to Kushinagar passing by the village Pava and rested near a village through which a caravan had just passed. Coming to Pava, the metalsmith's son Kunda offered him a meal that included meat. It is said that all the Buddhas of this world eat a meal containing meat on the eve of their passing away. Buddha accepted, but directed that no one else should partake of the food. The Buddha asked Kunda to bury the rest so that others would not be harmed by it. Later it was learned that the meat was bad. Kunda was overcome with grief and guilt when he realised that his offering was the cause of the Master's fatal illness. But the Buddha consoled him saying that the merit created by offering an enlightened one his last meal is equal to that of offering food to him just prior to his enlightenment. The owner of the caravan, a Malla nobleman, came and talked to the Buddha. Deeply moved by Shakyamuni's teachings, he offered the Buddha two pieces of shining gold cloth. However, their lustre was completely outshone by Shakyamuni's radiance. It is said that the Buddha's complexion becomes prodigiously brilliant on both the eve of his enlightenment and the eve of his death.

The next day, when they arrived at the banks of the Hiranyavati river south of Kushinagar, there, between two pairs of unusually tall *shala* trees (*shorea robusta*), the Buddha lay down on his right side in the lion posture with his head to the north. The Buddha spoke to Ananda his memorable words on the doctrines of the faith, some rules of discipline to be followed by the monks, including instructions about the disposal of his body:

"Ananda, you speak from faith, while the Tathagata has direct knowledge. The Tathagata knows that all the monks here possess deep faith in the Three Gems. Even the lowest attainment among these monks is that of a Stream-Enterer."

The Buddha-looked quietly over the community and then said, "Bhikkhus, listen to what the Tathagata now says. *Dhammas* are impermanent. If there is birth, there is death. Be diligent in your efforts to attain liberation! I declare to you that all conditioned things are of a nature to decay — strive on untiringly."

The Buddha closed his eyes. He had spoken his last words. The earth shook. Sal blossoms fell like rain. Everyone felt their minds and bodies tremble. They knew the Buddha had passed into nirvana. (*Mahaparinibbana Sutta*, D.16).

The Lord had instructed that his body should be disposed of in the same way as that of a king of kings: the body should be wrapped in new cloth and corded cotton-wood, placed in an iron-vessel, which should be covered by a similar vessel, and cremated. And finally, *stupas* should be erected at the four crossroads. As desired by the Buddha, the Mallas of Kushinagar came and paid their respects to him. At this last discourse, Subhadda, a Brahmin mendicant of 120 years of age, converted to Buddhism, and soon passed away with the honour of being the last of Buddha's converts. Finally, the Buddha uttered his last words: "Behold thee, brethren, I exhort thee, saying, decay is inherent in all component things! Work out your salvation with diligence." Subhadda then sat nearby in meditation, swiftly fell into a trance and attained *parinirvana* on the full-moon night of the month of *Vaishakha* (April-May), shortly before the death of the Buddha.

Lord Buddha preached his doctrine for over 45 years travelling from place to place. It is believed that he died of an illness brought on by some error in diet. According to another version he became ill through eating *Sukara-maddavam*, prepared for him by a lady adherent named Cundo, the mother of Kunda. The commentator explains the word as meaning 'hog's flesh'. Some scholars define this as something which wild boars are fond of and say that it has something of the nature of a truffle. Some says that it is not boar's flesh but *Sukarakanda* or hog's root, a bulbous root found chiefly in the jungle and which Hindus eat with great joy. It is a pure nature-given fruit (*phalahara*) which is eaten on days of fasting.

As the third watch of the night approached, the Buddha asked his disciples thrice if there were any remaining doubts concerning the doctrine or the discipline. After giving his last preaching the Buddha passed away. The earth shook, stars shot from the heavens, the sky burst forth in flames in the ten directions and the air was filled with celestial music.

For the next six days, during which the body laid down flat, the Mallas made preparations for a befitting funeral under the directions of Aniruddha, a cousin and follower of the Buddha. On the 7th day, they honoured the body with perfumes, garlands and appropriate music. The last ceremony of cremation was performed by Mahakasyapa, the most celebrated of Buddha's disciples, at the Makutabandhana-chaitya (Rambhar Stupa), the sacred shrine of the Mallas. The master's body was washed and robed once more, then wrapped in a thousand shrouds and placed in a casket of precious substances. After the cremation had been completed the ashes were examined for relics. Only a skull bone, teeth and the inner and outer shrouds remained. The relics of the body were then collected by the Mallas and taken ceremoniously to Kushinagar with a view to enshrining them in *stupas*. Today not much remains of this *stupa* except a large brick mound rising to a height of almost 15 metres set within a well-kept park.

The Mallas of Kushinagar first thought themselves most fortunate to have received all the relics of the Buddha's body. However, representatives of the other eight countries that constituted ancient

India also came forth to claim them; that turned into a war-like situation, which is represented as one of the main scenes in the stone slabs (Fig. 93). To avert a conflict, the Brahmin Drona suggested an equal, eight-fold division of the relics between them. Some accounts state that in fact the Buddha's remains were first divided into three portions — one each for the gods, *nagas* and men — and that the portion given to humans was then subdivided into eight. Each of the eight peoples took their share to their own countries and eight great *stupas* were built over them. In time these relics were again subdivided when Ashoka decided to build 84,000 *stupas*. Today they are contained in various *stupas* scattered across Asia.

Fig. 93. A scene showing a war-like situation to get the relics of the Buddha
(from Sanchi, ca. 50 BCE)

For two centuries after the Great Decease, however, Kushinagar did not rise much in importance. Lastly, by the visit of the great Mauryan Emperor **Ashoka** (r. 270-232 BCE), Kushinagar was rejuvenated. In course of time Ashoka erected *stupas* and pillars at this site. This is testified to by the descriptions of the Chinese pilgrims Fa-hsien (CE 399-414) and Hsüan-tsang (629-644), who visited this site (in January 637?) and mentioned three *stupas*, two pillars and several holy spots; of course most of the area was deserted. Hsüan-tsang did see an Ashoka *stupa* marking Kunda's house, the site of Buddha's last meal. Commemorating the *mahaparinirvana* was a large brick temple containing a recumbent statue of the Buddha. Beside this were a partly ruined Ashoka *stupa* and a pillar with an inscription describing the event. Two more *stupas* commemorated former lives of the Buddha at the place. Both Chinese pilgrims mention a *stupa* where Shakyamuni's protector Vajrapani threw down his sceptre in dismay after the Buddha's death, some distance away a *stupa* at the place of cremation, and another built by Ashoka where the relics were divided. Another Chinese pilgrim, I-ching (672-693) gives a little factual information about the monuments at Kushinagar, however a more flourishing condition was described by him. According to an inscription dated to the 10th-11th centuries, in the times of a local chief of the Kalachuri dynasty, a monastery with a chapel attached to it enshrining a colossal statue of the seated Buddha was constructed. After a silence of more than a millennium, the ruins received attention by Buchanan, an officer of the East India Company. For the first time in modern times, in 1854 H.H. Wilson suggested the identity of Kushinagar and Kasia. However, it was Alexander Cunningham, the Archaeological Surveyor, who in the course of his visit to this area in 1861-62 firmly identified Kushinagar. In 1876-77 his assistant A.C.L. Carlleyle did extensive digging and completely exposed the great central *stupa*, and right at the front the famous reclining *parinirvana* statue of the Buddha. During 1904-1907 under J. Ph. Vogel and in 1910-1912 under Hirananda Shastri major excavations were performed, which showed numerous brick buildings, monuments and inscriptions. It is strange that none of these records makes any direct mention of the name Kushinagar or any of its equivalents. The renovation and restorations were largely due to the efforts of Bhikshu Mahavira who lived here during 1890-1920. The annual fair on the occasion of the birth anniversary of the Buddha, instituted by Maha Thera Chandramani, has become very popular and attracts numerous visitors.

Kushinagar (Fig. 94) was rediscovered and identified before the end of the 19th century. Excavations have revealed that a monastic tradition flourished here for a long time. The remains of ten different monasteries dating from the 4th to the 11th centuries have been found. Most of these ruins are now enclosed in a park, in the midst of which stands a modern shrine housing a large recumbent figure of the Buddha. This statue was originally made in Mathura and installed at Kushinagar by the monk Haribhadra during the reign of King Kumaragupta (415-56 AD), the alleged founder of the Nalanda Monastery. When discovered late in the 19th century the statue was broken, but it has now been restored. Behind this shrine is a large *stupa* dating to the Gupta age. The Burmese restored this early in this century. Not far away a small temple built on the Buddha's last resting place in front of the *shala* (teak) grove has also been restored. Some distance east a large *stupa*, now called Ramabhar, remains at the place of the cremation.

The Nirvana Stupa

Directly behind the Nirvana Temple is a *stupa* built over the very place where the Buddha attained final Nirvana between the twin *sala*

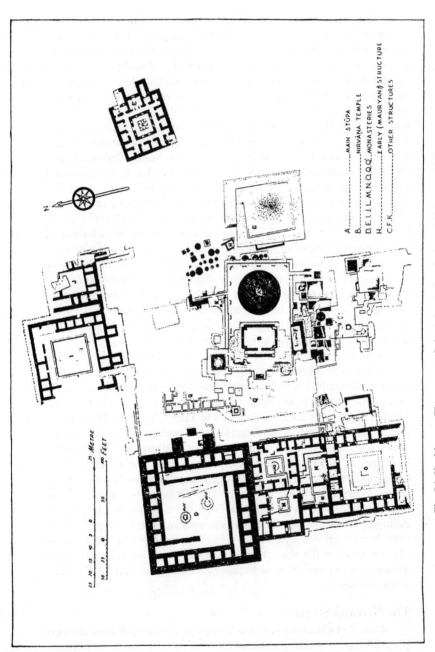

Fig. 94. Kushinagar: The excavated site (after A. Cunningham, ASI Report 1871)

A .... MAIN STŪPA
B .... NIRVĀṆA TEMPLE
D.E.I.J.L.M.N.O.P.Q. MONASTERIES
H .... EARLY (MAURYAN?) STRUCTURE
C.F.K. .... OTHER STRUCTURES

25 METRE
80 FEET

trees. Like most *stupas*, this
one consists of several
stupas, one inside the other.
Inside the earliest *stupa*,
which was perfectly pre-
served, were found pieces of
charcoal and blackened
earth, no doubt from the funeral pyre. The Main Stupa
was excavated and exposed
by Carlleyle in 1876. It was
then a huge mass of brickwork in a tottering condition
(Fig. 95). This represents the

Fig. 95. Kushinagar: the main Stupa

core of what must once have been a grand structure, which, inclusive
of its pinnacle, may once have reached the height of nearly 45.72 m.
The plinth on which the *stupa* and the temple were erected was 2.74 m
higher than the ground level. Above it stood the cylindrical neck of
the *stupa* to a height of 5.5 m fringed along its top with the remnants of
a row of decorative and miniature pilasters. On this neck was the dome
proper with only its broken brick shell exposed, its top about 19.8 m
above the ground level. The inscription on the copper vessel found
here contained the text of the *Nidana-sutra* in Sanskrit. The text is concluded with the statement that the plate had been deposited in the
nirvana-chaitya by one Haribala who, it may be added, also installed
the great **Nirvana statue of Buddha** in the nearby temple (CE 413-
455). The *stupa* was also enlarged by Haribala. It also stated that the
remains of the Buddha were deposited here. In 1927, the *stupa* was
completely restored out of the donations of U Po Kyu and U Po Hlaing
of Myanmar (Burma).

Nirvana Temple

On the same plinth of the Main Stupa stands the Nirvana
(*Mahaparinirvana*) Temple (Fig. 96). In 1876 Carlleyle had exposed the
site and discovered the great statue lying on a broken pedestal. Many
of its broken parts were then missing, however he found many of
them buried in the core of the pedestal itself. With their help he restored and repaired the statue and the pedestal almost to their original forms and shapes, though some of the broken fragments of the
statue were still missing. The statue measures 6.1 m in length and is
executed out of single block of reddish sandstone of mixed reddish
colour, probably from Chunar. It represents the Dying Buddha reclin-

ing on his right side with his face turned towards the west. It is placed on a large brick pedestal with stone posts at the corners.

The Buddha statue lies peacefully on its right side with the head towards the north; the right hand is placed under the head, and the left hand rests on the thigh. The plinth on which the statue lies has three small niches on its west side, each containing a small figure. The figure on the left is that of a woman with long hair, obviously distraught and probably representing the grief of the Mallas. The figure in the centre shows a monk meditating with his back to the viewer. The figure on the right is again of a monk, but this time he rests his head on his right hand overcome with grief. These two figures no doubt represent the monks who remained calm at the Buddha's final Nirvana and those who cried. This image of the *Reclining Buddha* is draped in mustard coloured silk and lulled by the rhythmic chanting of his present disciples. The Buddha's expression changes depending on the approaching angle of the beholder. To facilitate circumambulation and gathering to the pilgrims, changes were made along the platforms and finally the present temple structure was made in 1956 by the Government of India on the occasion of Buddha's 2500th birthday celebrations.

Fig. 96. Kushinagar: The Nirvana Temple

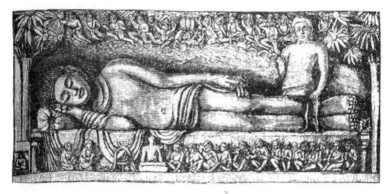

Fig. 97. Parinirvana of the Buddha (from cave 26 at Ajanta)

An inscription at the pedestal dates the statue to the 5th century. This inscription, partly damaged, reads: "This image is the meritorious gift of Haribala, a monk from the Great Monastery and was fashioned by Din ......". It tells us that in the reign of Kumargupta (CE 413-455), a devout Buddhist named Haribala installed the Nirvana statue (Figs. 97 and 98). From the evidence of the later plaster repairs to the statue, it is likely that the original temple might also have undergone changes in the succeeding centuries. The statue is the one seen by Hsüan-tsang during his visit, and judging by the style of the letters in the inscription it dates to the fifth century CE. When Carlleyle excavated the Nirvana Temple in 1876, he found this Buddha statue completely smashed and evidence of attempts to repair it. It is notable that this is one of the very few representations of the Buddha's final Nirvana ever found in northern India.

Fig. 98. The Buddha in the posture of nirvana in the Nirvana Temple

Matha-kuar Shrine

About 200 m southwest of the Main Stupa, leaving the archaeological park and proceeding south down the main road, is the Matha-kuar Shrine, where a colossal statue of the Buddha is installed. According to local legends, it is believed that this is the place where the Buddha died after he delivered his last sermon. This statue is locally called as *Matha-kuar*, which means the 'dead prince'. A black stone image of the Buddha measuring 3.05 m in height in the *bhumisparsha mudra* ('gesture of touching the Earth') was recovered here, dated to ca. the 5th century CE. The statue, when found during Carlleyle's excavations, was broken into two and must have originally been in the shrine of a large monastery, the foundations of which can still be seen. In this pose the Buddha is seated in meditation and touches the earth with his right hand. This posture symbolically expresses the supreme moment in the Buddha's life just before his Enlightenment, when he called upon the Mother Earth to bear witness to the pieties performed by him in his previous births and of his victory over Mara. The large size statue was found broken into two pieces and was repaired and restored to its original position in the chapel and the existing temple built to shelter it in 1927. The shrine was built by Burmese pilgrims in 1927 to shelter the statue. It is believed that the last sermon of the Lord was given here.

The Cremation Stupa

About 1.6 km east of the Matha-kuar shrine stands a mound facing the road from Kasia to Deoria that marks the site of the Cremation Stupa (cf. Fig. 99), or the **Makutabandhana-chaitya** of Buddhist tradition where the Buddha was cremated. Nearby is the Ramabhar Lake, that is why the monument is called **Ramabhar Stupa**. This *stupa* has a huge circular drum, 34.14 m in diameter, and rests on a circular plinth that consists of two or more terraces 47.24 m in diameter at the base. The *stupa* rises to a height of 15.4 m. With respect to dimensions the *stupa* appears to have been double the size of the Main Stupa of the main site.

Fig. 99. Kushinagar, the Old Stupa: Funerary structure to protect the relics of the Buddha

266

Fig. 100. Kushinagar, the New Stupa: An archetype of the cosmos

The other excavated ruins represent the usual minor *stupas* raised by pilgrims from time to time. A replica of the Cremation Stupa has been recently built which is based on the archetypal principle of the cosmos, representing the five gross elements of the organic life, representing the earth (the square base), air (the sphere), flame (the triangular upthrust), water (the crescent) and the ether (the conical drop) (Fig. 100). The **Kunwarkakot Matha**, about 2.4 km west of Ramabhar Stupa, is a temple with a huge seated Buddha.

The lush gardens that surround the *stupas*, the ruins and the neighbourhood sublimate the entire area. A golden Buddha sits majestically in the **Myanmar Temple**, built in a large water tank opposite the tourist office. A beautiful statue of the Buddha is a special attraction in the **Chinese Temple**. The **Japanese Temple** enshrines an *astha dhatu* (eight metals) statue of the Buddha. There are numerous Buddhist monasteries, including the modern Indo-Japan-Sri Lanka Buddhist Centre. On one side of the park a former Chinese temple has been reopened as an **International Meditation Centre**. On the southern side of the park is a small **Tibetan monastery** with *stupas* in the Tibetan style beside it. Thus also at Kushinagar one can see Buddhist activities alive even today. On the occasion of the Buddha Purnima (the full-moon day of *Vaishakha*), every year a grand celebration takes place.

In the near future the dates for the Buddha Purnima are: 16 May 2003, 4 May 2004, 23 May 2005, 13 May 2006, 2 May 2007, 20 May 2008, 9 May 2009, and 27 May 2010.

There are several new monasteries and temples. The Sri Lanka-Japan monastery has also an *ashta dhatu* (eight metals) statue of the Buddha flanked by Japanese style portraits of his ten principal *bhikshus*. The oldest monastery in Kushinagar is the large Burmese **Chandramani Bhikshu Dharamasala**. Near to it is the Chinese Temple that enshrines the marble images of the Buddha and the White Tara.

Next to the meditation centre of the Sri Lanka Japanese Foundation is the new **Kushinagar Museum**.

Information & Facilities

STD Code: 05563. Central Bank of India on NH 28 - Kasya Rd (Tel. 271089), and State Bank of India (Tel. 271024); however they do not cash traveler's checks. UP Government Tourist Bureau on Buddha Marg. Sub Post Office at main crossing (Tel. 271029); **Postal code**: 274403. Community Health Centre on Deoria Rd at Kasia. Government Ayurvedic Hospital on the Buddha Marg. STD/ISD booths on the Buddha Marg, next to the Buddha Dwar.

Accomodation & Food

Hotel Nekko Lotus (Tel. 271039), International Buddhist Guest House, Hindu Birla Buddha Dharmashala, Nepali Dharmashala, Hotel Pathik Niwas (Tel. 271038), Chandramani Bhikshu Dharmashala, UP State Tourist Bungalow, and Ashok Traveler's Lodge (ITDC). Cheaper accommodations are also provided by the Linh-Son Chinese Temple and the Myanmar Buddhist Temple & Guest House (Tel. 271035). Next to the Myanmar Buddhist temple, on Buddha Marg is Yama Kwality Café that serves the best food in the area including Indian, Thai, Burmese, Chinese, Tibetan and Nepalese.

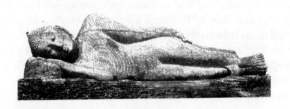

268

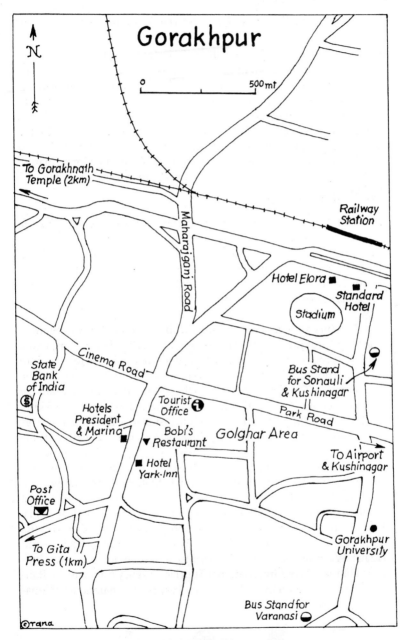

Fig. 101. Gorakhpur

Excursion and Link Station: Gorakhpur

Population ca. 1 million; STD Tel Code: 0551.
This is the last major Indian town travellers bound for Nepal pass through. The British and the Gorkha armies clashed near the town in the early 18th century. Later it became the recruitment centre for Gorkha soldiers enlisting into the British and Indian armies. It is a delightful centre and a major railway maintenance town (Fig. 101). It is also a pilgrimage centre due to the Gorakhnath Temple, an important centre for the adherent ascetics (*sannyasis*) of the Gorakhpanthi sect. On the NH 28 at 55 km east of Gorakhpur is Kasia, from where 3 km southwest is Kushinagar.

Hotels. Mainly for the budget traveller are: *Ganges*, Cinema Chowk, well managed with some a/c rooms and a good restaurant and ice cream parlour; and *Bobina*, Gatashanker Chowk, Nepal Road. The other reasonable hotels are: *Modern*, near the bus station; *Standard*, opposite the bus station; *York* in the City Centre; and *Gupta Tourist Lodge*, opposite the Railway Station.

The **bus** station is a 3 minutes walk from the Railway Station. The buses provide service to Lucknow, Varanasi (205 km, 6 hr), Patna and other regional towns. Many travellers choose buses to cross into Nepal. About 5 km out of Gorakhpur city the road passes the Gorakhanath Temple, moving a further 7 km after Campierganj (29 km) turn left for Nauwgarh (32 km) and proceed to **Lumbini** (65 km), the birthplace of the Buddha, which is just across the Nepalese border. This border crossing may be closed so you may have to continue to Sonauli (59 km). The shortest route is to go north to Pharenda crossing the Nepalese border at Sonauli. Buses for Nautanwa (95 km, 4 hr) run from the Bus Stand near the Railway Station. At Nautanwa you can hire a rickshaw to take you through the customs and to Bhairawa (6 km) in Nepal, then to Pokhara (departure: mornings only at 10 hr). From Gorakhpur, frequent buses to Sonauli just over the border (Rs 40, 3hr) and from there to Pokhara (Rs 100, 10.00 am) or Kathmandu (12 hr). **Warning**: Beware of ticket touts. Some demand excessive 'luggage charge'. Avoid International Tourism Agency opposite the Railway Station; their buses to Pokhara are very poorly maintained. Nepalese buses from Sonauli are OK.

14. SANKISA

Where the Buddha descended
from the *Tuṣhita* heaven

"Four places are always determined in advance: where the Buddhas shall
attain Buddhahood; where they shall begin to preach; where they shall
expound the law and refute heretics; and where they shall descend from
the Tushita Heaven after having preached to their mothers. Other places
are chosen according to circumstances."

Fa-hsien

The most westward and perhaps most obscure of the eight important places of Buddhist pilgrimage is **Sankasya**, whose name may
derive from a *stupa* built there by Suddhodana, the Buddha's father,
which was dedicated to his son. Sankasya (Pali, *Sankissa*; present
Sankisa-Basantpur) is a small village 37 km west of Fatehgarh in
Farrukhabad district (Figs. 1 and 102). Situated on the banks of the
river Kali, Sankisa is at a distance of 180 km west of Lucknow, and 80
km north of Kannauj. Sankasya is 12 km from the railway station
Pakhna, on the Shikohabad-Lucknow railway track. It is most easily
accessible from Agra which is 175 km away on the Agra-Mainpuri
road.

This place is associated with one of the Buddha's **Great Miracles**, where the Buddha is said to have descended to the earth from
the Tushita, 'Trayastrimsha', heaven ('Heaven of the 33 Gods') where
he went to preach the *Abhidhamma* to his mother and other gods. This
event is said to have occurred after the Great Miracle was performed
at Shravasti, as it was an immutable law that all Buddhas should resort to the Heaven of the 33 Gods after they had performed their greatest miracles. According to Buddhist legend, after giving a discourse
to his mother, Mayadevi, the Lord came down by a triple ladder, accompanied by the gods Brahma and Indra.

The excellent scene of the great Ladder by which the Buddha
descended at Sankisa from the Trayastrimsha heaven is distinctly represented in the Bharhut bas-relief (dated ca. 100-80 BCE)(Fig. 103).
The Ladder is represented as a triple flight of solid stone steps, similar
in all respects to the single flight of steps, which was found at the

271

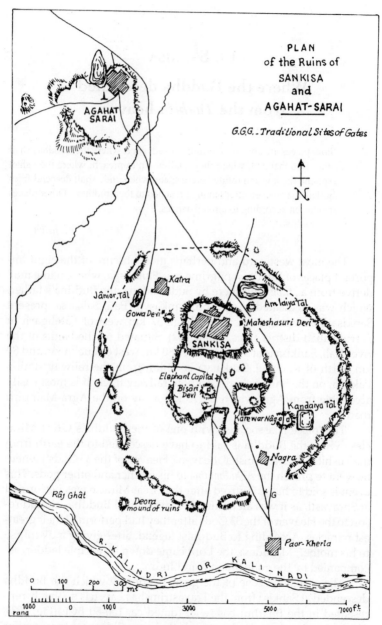

Fig. 102. Sankisa and Agahat Sarai, the ruins and archaeological site
(based on A. Cunningham, ASI Report 1872)

272

Fig. 103. Bas-relief showing the Great Ladder by which the Buddha descended from the Tushita heaven at Sankisa (from Bharhut, ca. 100-80 BCE)

Western Gateway of the Stupa. The legend of the Sankisa Ladder is narrated by both the Chinese pilgrims, Fa-hsien and Hsüan-tsang, as well as by the Pali annalists of Ceylon. According to ancient legends, the Buddha visited the Trayastrimsha heaven to preach his doctrine to divinities as well as to his mother Mayadevi. At the end of three months, his purpose having been accomplished, he determined to visit the earth at the city of Sakaspura (i.e. Sankassa or Sankisa in Pali, and Sankasya in Sanskrit). Then Sakra (Indra) reflected that he (Buddha) had come from the earth with three steps, but that it would be right to celebrate his departure with special honours. He therefore caused a Ladder of gold to extend from Mahameru to Sakaspura.

At this time there appeared a threefold precious Ladder. The Buddha standing above the middle Ladder, which was made of the seven precious substances, began to descend. Then the king of the *Brahma kayikas* (i.e. Brahma) caused a silver Ladder to appear, and took his place on the right hand, holding a white *chauri* (umbrella) in his hand; whilst the divine Sakra (Indra) caused a bright golden Ladder to appear, and took his place on the left hand, holding a precious parasol in his hand. Innumerable divinities were in attendance while the Buddha descended. After he had accomplished his return the three Ladders all disappeared in the earth, except seven steps which still continued to be visible. These Ladders were more than 80,000 *yojanas* in length. The steps in the Ladder of the Buddha were alternately of gold, silver, coral, ruby, emerald, and other gems, and they were beautifully ornamented. The whole appeared to the people of the earth like three rainbows. The account of the later pilgrim Hsüan-tsāng is substantially the same as that of Fa-hsien.

When the Buddha went up to the Trayastrimsha heavens to say *bana* (message of consonance) for the sake of his mother, after three months he descended at this place (Sankisa). At the appointed time the great kings of the eight kingdoms, and all the ministers and people, not having seen the Buddha for so long, greatly desired to meet him. They flocked, therefore, in great crowds to this country to await the return of the world-honoured one. Then the Bhikshuni Utpala began to think thus, "Today the king, ministers, and people are all going to meet the Buddha and render homage to him, but I, a woman, how can I contrive to get the first sight of him?" The Buddha immediately by his divine power changed her into a holy Chakravarti Raja, and in that capacity she was the first to reverence him on his return. The Buddha was now about to descend from the Trayastrimsha heaven.

In the Bharhut bas-relief (ca. 100-80 BCE), the triple Ladder occupies the middle of the scene with a Bodhi tree and a Vajrasan at its foot. There is one footprint on the top step and a second footprint on the bottom step of the middle Ladder. These are, of course, intended for the footprints of Buddha, and in his absence they form the visible objects of reverence. A number of spectators on all sides are intended to represent the crowd of kings, ministers, and people who flocked to Sankisa to await the return of the Buddha. Although the Buddha is never represented in person in the Bharhut sculptures, the triple Ladder shows that as early at least as the time of Ashoka the legend had already appropriated the Brahmanical gods Indra and Brahma as the attendants of Buddha's descent from heaven.

The Buddha bathed immediately after his descent, and later a bathing house and a *stupa* were built to mark the site (Fig. 104, as represented at Amravati). *Stupas* were also raised at the spot where he cut his hair and nails, and where he entered *samadhi* (a state of super-consciousness) and finally disappeared. The Chinese pilgrims describe further *stupas* and a *chankramana* where Shakyamuni and the previous Buddhas walked and sat in meditation. This incident forms a favourite motif in Buddhist art, and is represented by a scene depicting a ladder touching the earth. It is identified with a site near the present temple of **Bisahari Devi** in Sankisa. It appears that there was an old statue of this goddess here which has since been replaced by a modern one.

Fig. 104. The Stupa of Sankisa as represented in the monument of Amravati

From the description of the Chinese pilgrims Fa-hsien and Hsüan-tsang, it appears that during the 7th century, both Buddhism and Shaivism were flourishing at Sankisa. There were a number of big monasteries and temples. The Mauryan emperor Ashoka, and after him several other kings, erected a number of beautiful buildings in the town. The present day Sankisa abounds in sculptural and terracotta remains. Emperor Ashoka erected a pillar with an elephant capital to mark this holy spot. This, to which the Chinese pilgrim Hsüan Tsang made a reference, has been remounted on a 3 m high pillar beneath a stone canopy. And its capital, with an elephant's figure whose head has fallen (Fig. 105), is preserved near the Bisahari Devi temple. The capital bears decorative patterns of lotus flowers and leaves of the Bodhi-tree (holy fig).

The present village of Sankisa is situated on a high mound. The long chain of other mounds is spread outside the village, locally called 'the fort' (*kila*). It is 12.5 m high and is spread over an area of 457.2 m x 305 m. About 400 m to the south is another **mound** composed of solid brickwork and surmounted by a temple dedicated to Bisahari Devi. Other mounds containing masses of brickwork may be seen scattered around and there are also the remains of an earthen rampart over 5.5 km in circumference. To the east of the village Sankisa, at about 400 m is a place called **Chaukhandi**. Here were found a large number of ancient bricks of large size. To the northeast of this site was found a **railing pillar** (0.84 m high) of Mathura sandstone. Nearby is a temple called Terha Mahadeva; attached to this is a holy pond called **Nagasara** ('pool of the snakes'). Pilgrims visiting Sankisa go round this pond.

Fig. 105. Sankisa: Elephant capital (from a drawing by A. Cunningham, 1865)

This is the only one of the eight places of pilgrimage directly associated with the Buddha himself (*ashta-mahasthanani*), where today there is no temple, monastery or even a solitary monk. Perhaps the wildness and isolation of the area are the causes. With or without a dragon's aid, it may be hoped that this will change.

Accommodation

The only accommodation available is a Tourist Bungalow, UPSTDC. The nearest town is Mainpuri, or better proceed to Agra (175 km) by following the NH 2, or to procced 58km further north from Agra to Mathura on the NH 2. Lucknow in 180 km southeast.

15. Mathura

The capital of Surasena
which was visited by the Buddha

Mathura has five disadvantages. What five? The ground is uneven, there is a lot of dust, the dogs are fierce, there are evil yakkhas, and it is difficult to get alms-food.

Anguttara Nikaya, III. 256.

Population: ca. 350,000, STD Tel Code: 0565.

Mathura is 145 km from Delhi and 58 km from Agra on the National Highway 2, and has a railway station between the two cities. The Government Museum is about 1 km from the railway station.

Mathura, earlier spelled Madhura, was at the Buddha's time the capital of the kingdom of Surasena, and was situated on the banks of the Yamuna River. Being on the outer edge of the Middle Land, the Buddha came to Mathura only on a few occasions, and he does not seem to have had a very good impression of the place. When Maha Kachchhana came here, he preached the *Mathura Sutta* to the king, refuting the Brahmins' claims to be superior to other castes (cf. *Majjhima Nikaya*, II.83). Despite these minor associations with the Buddha and his direct disciples, Mathura developed into a great centre of Buddhism in later centuries. During the Kushana and Gupta periods, the stone masons of Mathura produced an enormous number and variety of works of art to adorn local shrines as well as those in many other parts of India.

Ptolemy already mentioned the town, and it asumed the importance of a capital city during the 1st to the 2nd century. When Fahsien visited Mathura he found 20 monasteries and up to 3,000 monks. There were *stupas* honouring Sariputta, Maha Moggallana and Ananda, and also *stupas* honouring the *Suttas*, the *Vinaya* and the *Abhidhamma*. Once a year, after the rains retreat, there was a great religious festival in which the whole population participated.

"All the monks come together in a great assembly and preach the *Dhamma*, after which offerings are presented to the *stupa* of Sariputta, with all kinds of flowers and incense. All through the night, lamps are kept burning and skillful musicians are employed to perform... The nuns for the most part make their offerings to the *stupa* of Ananda because it was he who requested the World-Honoured One to allow females to renounce their families. The novices mostly make their offerings to Rahula. The professors of the Abhidhamma make their offerings to it; those of the Vinaya to it."

Hsüan-tsang (CE 634) mentioned seeing this same festival during his stay in Mathura. He also saw three *stupas* built by King Ashoka. In 1017 Mahmud of Ghazni sacked the city and desecrated its temples. This was followed by the destructions of Sikander Lodi in 1500. In the late 17th century, by the order of the bigoted Mughal emperor Aurangzeb, all the major temples were devastated. Jats and Marathas faught over the city as the Mughal Empire declined, but at the beginning of the 19th century it came under British control. They laid out a cantonment in the south and left a cemetery and the Roman Catholic Sacred Heart Cathedral (1870). Presently there are no pre-Muslim monuments of any significance, and some of the finest buildings have been badly scarred by decay, neglect and misuse.

The vitality of Buddhism in Mathura is testified by the fact that well over a hundred years of digging in and around the town have brought to light a great number of Buddhist antiquities. In 1836 Col. L.R. Stacy found a statue of a full-busted girl, standing on a crouching dwarf, with a bird on her shoulder and a birdcage in her right hand. This charming sculpture, now in the Indian Museum in Kolkata, attracted much attention, and amateur archaeologists began digging in the mounds around the town looking for more. Cunningham explored the area in 1853 and again in 1862 and 1871. In 1860, while the court house was being built, a great deal of sculptures were found, including images, railing stones, pillars, votive *stupas* and stone umbrellas. It was here that the famous 'Mathura Buddha', perhaps the most beautiful Buddha statue ever produced in India, was unearthed. It is now kept at Rastrapati Bhavan in New Delhi and cannot be viewed by the public.

Among the Mathura Buddha images two postures are very common. From the Katra mound a seated stone image of the Buddha shows him preaching (dated to the 2nd century CE), while Sariputta and Moggallana are standing in the back (Fig. 106). The other usual posture shows the Buddha standing and preaching (dated to the 4th century CE); the Buddha is wearing a silk cloth (Fig. 107).

The last of a string of extraordinary archaeological finds from Mathura took place in 1976 on the western outskirts of the city, just near the water-works (cf. Fig. 108). A vast treasure of sculptures from

Fig. 106. The Buddha in preaching pose, Gandhara art, Mathura

the Kushana and Gupta periods was found, including two life-size statues of the Buddha, both of great beauty and inscribed with the name of the artist who made them. Unfortunately, none of Mathura's numerous temples and shrines can be seen today, as the modern city has grown up over them. To see Mathura's past glory it is necessary to visit the city's museum.

The Government Museum

The Government Museum is undoubtedly one of India's best museums, and because of its large collection of Buddhist sculpture is of particular interest to the Buddhist pilgrim. The most beautiful piece in the museum is a standing life-size Buddha statue. The statue dates from the mid-fifth century CE, and an inscription on the pedestal states that it was dedicated by a monk named Yasadinna. The right hand, now missing, was

Fig. 107. The Buddha in standing pose, Gandhara art, Mathura

raised in the gesture of bestowing fearlessness while the left hand holds the fringe of the robe. The belt around the waist can be seen under the robe, making the drapery appear light and semi-transparent. Two small devotees kneel in adulation at either side of the Buddha's feet. The hand, face and the halo have been carved with great delicacy, making the whole statue alive and unique in Indian sculpture.

Another fine sculpture is the small seated Buddha found at Katra, a few km from Mathura. The statue, which is perfectly preserved, sits cross-legged on a pedestal supported by three lions. It dates from the second century CE, and the inscription on the pedestal records that it was dedicated by the Buddhist nun Amoha-asi "for the welfare and happiness of all beings." Two crowned attendants peep from behind the Buddha, while two *devas*, the one on the left carrying a bowl of gems and the one on the right raising its hand in a gesture of respect, fly towards the halo. The leaves and branches of the Bodhi Tree can be clearly seen behind the Buddha's head. The Buddha's eyes are wide open, and the left hand placed firmly on the knee gives the impression of vigour and alertness.

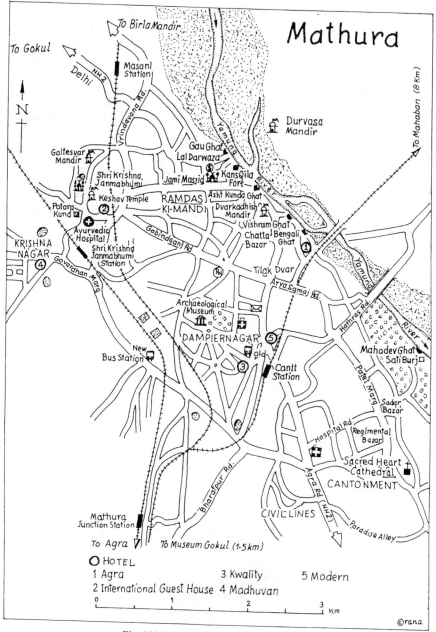

Fig. 108. Mathura: The City and Environs

Historically speaking, the most important sculpture in the museum is the portrait of King Kanishka, one of the few portraits of an historical personage to survive from ancient India. Although the head is missing, the splayed feet, the left hand touching the mace, and the right hand grasping the huge sword makes it clear that Kanishka was a no-nonsense monarch. The inscription on the statue reads: "Great King, King of Kings, the Son of God, Kanishka". Despite the military prowess that this portrait conveys, Kanishka was also a lover of the arts, and did more to promote Buddhism than any other Indian king except Ashoka.

The Government Museum is open during 1 July to 30 April: 10.30 to 17.00 hr, and 1 May to 30 June: 07.30 to 12.30 hr, and is closed on Sundays, Mondays, and second Saturday every month. Between the 16th April and 30th June, the timings are 7.30 am to 12.30 pm; Entry Fee: Rs 5.

Hotels

Madhuvan (28 rooms), Krishna Nagar, Tel 2420064, Fax 2420684, some rooms a/c with bath, restaurant, exchange, travel, pool; **Radha Ashok** (Best Western, 21 rooms), Masani By-pass Road, Chatkara, 4 km north from centre, Tel 2530395, Fax 2530396, bwra@vsnl.com, rooms, modern hotel, good restaurant, pool — highly recommended; **Mansarovar Palace** (22 rooms, most a/c), State Bank Crossing, Tel 2408686, Fax 2401611, restaurant; **Agra**, near Bengali Ghat, Tel 2403318. Some aircooled rooms, traditional, friendly; **Tourist Bungalow** (UP Tourism, 14 rooms), Civil Lines, Bypass Road, Tel 2407822, restaurant, bar; **International Guest House**, Katra Keshav Deo, Tel 2405888, some air-cooled rooms, restaurant; **Quality**, Tel 2406195, with a restaurant, and **Modern**, Tel 2404747, both near the Old Bus Stand.

Further Reading (Bibliography)

Abhinishkramana Sutta 1875. **The Romantic Legends of Shakya Buddha**. Translated from Chinese by Samuel Beal. Pali Text Society, London. Reprinted by Low Price Publs., Delhi, 1985.

Agrawala, V.S. 1992. **Sarnath**. 5th Ed. Archaeological Survey of India, Calcutta.

Ahir, D.C. 1986. **Buddhist Shrines in India**. Indian Book Centre, Delhi.

— **Buddha Gaya Through the Ages**. Sri Satguru Publs., Delhi.

Allchin, B. and Allchin, F.R. 1982. **The Rise of Civilisation in India and Pakistan**. Cambridge University Press, Cambridge.

Allen, Charles 2002. **The Buddha and the Sahibs**. Murry Books, London

Arnold, Sir Edwin 1879/ 1999. **The Light of Asia or The Great Renunciation**. Reprinted by Srishti Publ., New Delhi.

Asher, Fredrick M. 1989. **Gaya : Monuments of the Pilgrimage Town**. *Marg* (Bombay), vol. 40 (No.1): pp. 45-60.

Ashvaghosha 1883. **The Life of Buddha**. Translated from Sanskrit into Chinese by Dharmaraksha: **The Fo-Sho-Hing-Tsan-King** (CE 420). From Chinese translated into English by Samuel Beal. Vol. XIX of the Sacred Books of the East. Clarendon Press, Oxford.

Badiner, Allan H. 2003. **The Buddha Land**. Parallax Press, Berkeley, USA.

Bapat, P.V. 1956. **2500 Years of Buddhism**. Publication Division, Ministry of Information and Broadcasting, Govt. of India, New Delhi.

Barua, Beni Madhab, 1931-34. **Gaya and Bodh-Gaya. Early History of the Holy Land**. 2 vols. (I, 1931; II 1934). Indian Research Institute, Calcutta.

Barua, Dipak K. 1981. **Buddha Gaya Temple. Its History**. Buddha Gaya Temple Management Committee, Buddha Gaya, 2nd Ed.

Beal, Samuel, 1906. **Buddhist Records of the Western World. (Travels of Hiuen Tsang)**. 2 Vols. Kegan Paul, Trench, Trubner & Co., London.

Bechert, Heinz, ed. 1995. **When Did the Buddha Live**. Bibliotheca Indo-Buddhica Series No. 165. Sri Satguru Publs., Delhi.

Bhattacharya, Tarapada 1966. **The Bodh-Gaya Temple**. 2nd ed. Firma K.L. Mukhopadhyaya Publs., Calcutta.

Brown, Percy 1962/ 1996. **Hindu Architecture – Hindu and Buddhist Periods**. Taraporewala, Bombay.

Buchanan, Hamilton, 1811-12. **Patna-Gaya Report**. 2 Vols. Bihar & Orissa Research Society, Patna.

Carus, Paul 1902/ 1997. **The Gospel of Buddha**; (compiled by Paul Carus and illustrated by Olga Kopertzky). Bodleyhead, London.

— 1907. **The Dharma, or The Religion of Enlightenment**. 5th ed. Aldine Publs., Chicago.

Chakrabarti, Dilip K. 1995. **The Archaeology of Ancient Indian Cities**. Oxford University Press, Delhi.

Chakravarty, Kalyan Kumar 1997. **Early Buddhist Art of Bodh Gaya**. Munshiram Manoharlal Publs., New Delhi

Chandra, Pramod 1985. **The Sculptures of India, 3000 BC–AD 1300**. Harvard University Press, Cambridge, MA.

Choudhary, R.K. 1958. **History of Bihar**. Bihar Research Society, Patna.

Coomaraswamy, Anand K. 2001. **The Origin of the Buddha Image**. Munshiram Manoharlal Publs., New Delhi.

Cowel, E.B. (translated and edited) 1893. **The Buddhacarita of Ashvaghosha**. Clarendon Press, Oxford.

Cunningham, Alexander 1871/ 1996. **The Ancient Geography of India**. Reprinted by Low Price Publs., Delhi.

— 1879/ 1998. **The Stupa of Bharhut: A Buddhist Monument**. Wm. Allen & Co., London. Reprinted by Munshiram Manoharlal Publs., New Delhi.

— 1892/ 2001. **Mahabodhi or the Great Buddhist Temple under the Bodhi Tree at Buddha Gaya**. W.H. Allen & Co., London. Reprinted by Munshiram Manoharlal Publs., New Delhi.

Cunningham, Alexander & H.B.W. Garrick, 1883. **Report of the Tour in North and South Bihar**. Government Printing Press, Calcutta.

Devahuti, D. 2001, ed. **The Unknown Hsüan-tsang**. Oxford University Press, New Delhi.

Dhammika, S. 1992. **Middle Land, Middle Way. A Pilgrim's Guide to the Buddha's India.** Buddhist Publication Society, Kandy (Sri Lanka). (This book has been used as a main reference)

— 1996. **Navel of the Earth: The History and Significance of Bodh Gaya.** Buddhist Publ., Singapore.

Dutt, N. & Bajpai, K. D., 1956. **Development of Buddhism in Uttar Pradesh.** Publication Bureau, Govt. of Uttar Pradesh, Lucknow.

Fa-Hsien 1886. **The Travels of Fa-Hsien. A Records of Buddhist Kingdoms.** Translated from Chinese by James Legge. Pali Text Society, London. Reprinted by Low Price Publs., Delhi, 1990.

Fausbölli, V. 1877-97 / 1962-64, ed. **The Jatakas;** (together with commentary). Pali Text Society, London. Reprinted by Luzac & Co. Ltd., London.

Fergusson, James 1875 / 1910. **History of Indian & Eastern Architecture.** Murry, London. Reprinted by Low Price Publs., Delhi, 1997.

Forbes, Duncan 1999. **The Buddhist Pilgrimage.** Buddhist Tradition Series 37. Motilal Banarasidass Publ., Delhi.

Ghosh, A. 1986. **Nalanda.** 6th Ed. Archaeological Survey of India, Calcutta.

Grierson, George A. 1892. **Notes on District of Gaya.** Government Printing Press, Calcutta.

Hanh, Thich Nhat 1991 / 1998. **Old Path White Clouds. Walking in the Footsteps of Buddha.** Drawings by Nguyen Thi Hop. Parallax Press, Berkeley CA. Reprinted by Full Circle, New Delhi.

Hazra, Kanai Lal 1983. **Buddhism in India as Described by the Chinese Pilgrims, AD 399–689.** Munshiram Manoharlal Publ., New Delhi.

— 1995. **The Rise and Decline of Buddhism in India.** Munshiram Manoharlal Publ., New Delhi.

Heruka, Tsang Nyön 1982/1995, **The Life of Marpa, the Translator: Seeing Accomplishes All.** Transl. from the Tibetan by the Nalanda Translation Committee under the direction of Chogyam Trungpa. Prajña Pree, Boulder CO, USA. Repr. by Shambhala, Boston & London.

HMG 1976. **Lumbini Development Project.** The Lumbini Development Committee, His Majesty's Government, Babar Mahal (Kathmandu).

285

Hwui Li, Shaman 1911/ 2001. **The Life of Hiuen-Tsang.** Introduction by Samuel Beal. Kegan Paul, Trench, Trübner & Co., London. Reprinted by Low Price Publ., Delhi.

Jha, Satyendra Kumar 1998. **Beginnings of Urbanisation in Early Historic India.** Novelty & Co., Patna.

Johnson, E.H. 1936/ 1972. **Ashvaghosha's Buddhacarita.** Edited & translated. Reprinted by Low Price Publs., Delhi.

Kuraishi, M. H. 1975. **Rajgir.** Revised by A. Ghosh. 6th Ed. Archaeological Survey of India, Calcutta.

Lahiri, Latika 1986. **The Chinese Monks in India.** Munshiram Manoharlal Publ., New Delhi.

Lal, R.B. 1953. **Bodh Gaya: Past and Present.** Bihar Research Society, Patna.

Law, Bimala Churn 1932/ 1979. **Geography of the Early Buddhism.** Kegan Paul, Trench, Trübner & Co., London. Reprinted by Oriental Books Reprint, New Delhi.

Legge, James 1886/ 1998. **A Record of Buddhist Kingdoms. Being an Account by the Chinese Monk Fa-hsien of his Travels in India and Ceylone (A.D. 399-414) in Search of the Buddhist Books of Discipline.** Reprinted by Munshiram Manoharlal Publ., New Delhi.

Leoshko, Jania 1988. Ed. **Bodh Gaya, the Site of Enlightenment.** Taraporewala, Bombay.

Lhalungpa, Lobsang P. 1979. **The Life of Milarepa.** Far West Edition, Inc., San Francisco. Reprinted by Book Faith India, Kathmandu.

Michell, George 1989. **Penguin Guide to the Monuments in India.** Vol. 1. Penguin, Middlesex.

Mitra, Rajendralal , 1878. **Buddha Gaya. The Great Buddhist Temple, the Hermitage of Sakya Muni.** Bengal Secretariat Press, Calcutta. (with 51 plates).

Mookerji, Radhamumud 1928/ 1962. **Ashoka.** 3rd edition. Motilal Banarasidass Publs., Delhi.

O'Malley, L.S.S. 1901. **Gaya and the Gayawal.** Bengal Secretariat Press, Calcutta.

— 1906. **Bengal District Gazetteer,** vol. XII **GAYA.** Bengal Secretariat Press, Calcutta.

Patil, D. R. 1981. **Kusinagara**. 2nd Ed. Archaeological Survey of India, New Delhi.

Paul, Debjani 1995. **The Art of Nalanda. Development of Buddhist Sculpture AD 600–1200**. Munshiram Manoharlal Pub., New Delhi.

Rahula, Walpola Sri 1959/2001. **What the Buddha Taught**. The Gorden Fraser Gallery Ltd., Bedford. Reprinted by Oneworld, Oxford.

Rhys Davids, T. W. 1890. **Buddhism**. (Series of Non-Christian Traditions). Pali Text Society, London.

— 1896/ 1999. **The History and Literature of Buddhism**. Reprinted by Munshiram Manoharlal Publ., New Delhi.

— 1903/ 1999. **Buddhist India**. T. Fisher Unwin, London. Reprinted by Munshiram Manoharlal Pub., New Delhi; in 2002 by Low Price Publ., Delhi.

Rhys Davids, T. W. and Carpenter, J. Estlin, eds. 1890/ 1958. **The Digha Nikaya**. Nalanda Devanagiri Pali Series. Pali Text Society, London. Reprinted by Bihar Government Board, Patna.

Rinpoche, Thrangu, 1999. **Ten Teachings from the 100,000 Songs of Milarepa**. Translated by Peter Roberts. Sri Satguru Publs., Delhi.

Roychaudhary, P. C. 1958. **Gaya. District Gazetteer.** Government Printing Press, Patna.

Sangharakshita 1964. **Anagarika Dharmapala, A Biographical Sketch**. Buddhist Publication Society, Kandy (Sri Lanka).

Schotsman, Irma (ed. & trans.) 1996. **The Buddha Charita**. Institute of Higher Tibetan Studies, Sarnath (Varanasi).

Sharma, R. S. 1987. **Urban Decay in India (ca. 300–ca. 1000)**. Munshiram Manoharlal Publ., New Delhi.

Singh, J. R. 1980. **Sarnath. Past and Present**. Atmatosh Prakashan, Varanasi.

Singh, Rana P. B. 1993. Ed. **Banaras (Varanasi). Cosmic Order, Sacred City, Hindu traditions**. Tara Book Agency, Varanasi: "Sarnath": pp. 235 – 256.

Singh, Rana P. B. & Lata, Prem 1991. **Sarnath. Cultural Heritage, Museum, Tourism**. Tara Book Agency, Varanasi.

Singh, Rana P. B. & Rana, P. S. 2002. **Banaras Region. A Spiritual and Cultural Guide**. Indica Books, Varanasi.

Sinha, B. P. & Roy, Sita Ram 1969. **Vaisali Excavations, 1958–1962**. Directorate of Archaeology & Museums, Bihar, Patna.

Si-Yu-Ku 1884. **Buddhist Records of the Western World**. Translated from Chinese by Samuel Beal. Pali Text Society, London. Reprinted by Low Price Publs., Delhi, 1981.

Snelling, John 1991. **The Buddhist Handbook**. Inner Traditions, Rochester, VT.

Srivastava, K. M. 1986. **Discovery of Kapilavastu**. Books & Books, New Delhi.

Strong, John S. 1983. **The Legend of King Ashoka: A Study and translation of** *Ashokavadana*. Princeton University Press, Princeton.

Takakusu, J. 1966. **A Record of the Buddhist Religion as Practiced in India and the Malay Archipelago AD 671–695**. Reprinted by Oriental Publishers, Delhi.

Tulku, Tarthang 1994. **Holy Places of the Buddha**. Ed. Elizabeth Cook. Shambhala, Berkeley.

Valisinha, Devapriya 1960. **A Guide to Bodh Gaya**. Firma K.L. Mukhopadhyaya, Calcutta.

Venkataramayya, M. 1981. **Shravasti**. 2nd Ed. Archaeological Survey of India, Calcutta.

Vidyarthi, L. P. 1978. **The Sacred Complex in Hindu Gaya**. 2nd ed. Concept Publ. Co., New Delhi.

Watters, Thomas 1905/ 1996. **On Yuan Chwang's Travels in India AD 629-645**. (vol. I & II). Royal Asiatic Society, London. Reprinted by Munshiram Manoharlal Publ., New Delhi.

APPENDICES

APPENDIX 1

Major historical events related to Buddhism

Year	Events
563 BCE	Birth of the Buddha, Siddhartha Gautama, at Lumbini, son of Suddhodana, a Kshatriya chief of the Shakya clan, and his consort Mayadevi.*
547	Siddhartha Gautama married to his maternal cousin Yashodhara.
534	After the birth of his son, Rahula, one day Siddhartha left his wife Yashodhara and son, and proceeded to an unannounced march.
528	After six years of wandering and self-mortification, Siddhartha realised that penance does not lead to enlightenment. On the 49th day of meditation at Bodh Gaya under a Holy Fig tree he received enlightenment and was given the name of 'Buddha'.*
544-493	Rule of Bimbisara, a king of the Haryanka dynasty at Rajgir, who later became a Buddhist and a close friend of the Buddha.
529	The Buddha's First Sermon, Dharmachakra Parivartana, at Sarnath, near Varanasi.
483	Death of the Buddha at Kushinagar.*
483	After 6 months of the Buddha's death, under the guidance of the monk Kashyapa the First Buddhist General Council held at Sataparni cave, Vaibhara hill, Rajgir.
383	Ven. Kakavarna convened the Second Buddhist General Council held at Vaishali.
270	Ashokavardhana (Ashoka, 304–232 BCE) became the third Mauryan emperor.
259	Ashoka promoted and established Buddhism.
258-257	Ashoka's edicts inscribed in rocks in four scripts: Greek & Aramic in Afghanistan, Kharoshti in present-day Pakistan, and Brahmi elsewhere.
256-255	Ashoka's further rock inscriptions containing the Kalinga Edicts, referring to his conversion to Buddhism.
250	Mahinda (Mahendra), son of Ashoka, became a Buddhist monk, and embarked on a mission to Sri Lanka.

249 Ashoka's pilgrimage to the Buddhist places, like Kapilavastu, Kushinagar, Bodh Gaya and Sarnath.

240 Under Ashoka's patronage the Third Buddhist General Council was convened at Pataliputra (Patna).

232 Ashoka died, and his son is crowned emperor.

187-151 Rule of Pushyamitra, founder of the Shunga dynasty, who promoted Brahmanism and Buddhism.

100 BCE The Buddhist Sangha ('Order'), funded largely by rich merchants and craftsmen, built cave temples, especially in the Deccan.

CE 78-101 Rule of emperor Kanishka, known as the 2nd Ashoka and the greatest of the Kushana rulers; later in his life he became a Buddhist and a patron of the *Sangha*.

101 Emperor Kanishka presided over the Fourth Buddhist General Council, convened in Kashmir.

106-119 Kanishka's son Huvishka succeeded the crown and promoted the Gandhara School of Art of making images of the Buddha and the Bodhisattvas.

357 A Buddhist mission is dispatched to China, the first in a series of ten.

383 The Indian Buddhist monk Kumarajiva arrived in China to set the new standards in the translation of Buddhist scriptures into Chinese.

399 Fa-hsien (374-462), a Chinese monk, arrived in India in search of Buddhist texts.

404-14 Chih-meng, a Chinese pilgrim, travelled in India.

412 Fa-hsien returned to China.

606-647 Rule of Harsha, who built a large number of *stupas*.

630 Hsüan-tsang (603-664), a Chinese Buddhist monk, was made a courtier by Harsha Vardhana and became a royal chronicler.

638-42 Yuan-chan, a Chinese pilgrim, visited India, also again in 665.

645 Hsüan-tsang returned to China.

664 Hsüan-tsang died in the Wu Li monastery in China.

671-85 I-tsing (634-713), a Chinese pilgrim, travelled in India.

770-890 Pala dynasty, under which the Buddhist art and architecture reached to its most mature stage.

1033 Hui-wen, a Chinese pilgrim, visited India by the order of His Imperial Majesty T'ai Tsung.

1070 First major restoration and renovation of the Maha Bodhi temple by the Burmese (Myanmar), under the patronage of King Anawrahta (CE 1044-1077).

1197 Allauddin Khilji, a Muslim king, sacked Nalanda and massacred all the Buddhist monks.

1234-61 Dharmasvamin (1196-1263), a Tibetan monk, visited the Buddhist places; he died in Tibet.

1861-85 Alexander Cunningham (1814-1893), became the founding director of the Archaeological Survey of India, and excavated many Buddhist sites.

1871 Under the patronage of king Min-donmin the Fifth Buddhist General Council convened at Mandaley (Myanmar).

1881 Foundation of the Pali Text Society at London by T.W. Rhys Davids.

1885 Edwin Arnold (1833-1904), an Englishman, visited Bodh Gaya; he died in 1904.

1891 Anagarika Dharmapala (1864-1933) visited Sarnath, founded the Mahabodhi Society at Colombo, and finally died in Sarnath.

1949 Bodh Gaya Temple Management Act enacted by the Govt. of Bihar, constituting a management committee of 4 Hindus and 4 Buddhists.

1954 The Sixth Buddhist General Council inaugurated at Rangoon (Myanmar), on *Vaishakha Purnima*, 17 May.

1956 The Concluding ceremony of the Sixth Council on the occasion of the 2500th anniversary of the Buddha's nirvana, at Rangoon, on *Vaishakha Purnima*, 24 May.

1959 Being exiled from China in April, the 14th Dalai Lama Tenzin Gyatso (b. 5 July 1935), head of the Gelugpa or Yellow Hat Sect and renowned as Tibet's god-king, settled in Dharmashala, India.

* On the day of *Vaishakha* (April-May) Purnima (Shukla 15th), waxing, Full Moon. In the near future the dates for the **Buddha Purnima** are: 16 May 2003, 4 May 2004, 23 May 2005, 13 May 2006, 2 May 2007, 20 May 2008, 9 May 2009, and 27 May 2010.

APPENDIX 2

The Dates of Rajgir Festivals
The Malamasas
(Intercalary months), *Samvata* 2058-2100: CE 2001 – 2044

Se	Hindu month, *masa*	Hindu Samvata	Planetary Lord (*Shukla Paksha*)	Light-half, waxing (*Krishna Paksha*)	Dark-half, waning	Roman Year, CE
1.	Ashvina	2058	Moon	18 Sept-2 Oct	3 Oct-16 Oct	2001
2.	Shravana	2061	Sun	18 July-31 July	1 Aug-16 Aug	2004
3.	Jyeshtha	2064	Moon	17 May-31 May	1 June-15 June	2007
4.	Vaishakha	2067	Mars	15 Apr-28 Apr	29 Apr-14 May	2010
5.	Bhadrapada	2069	Venus	18 Aug-31 Aug	1 Sept-16 Sept	2012
6.	Ashadha	2072	Saturn	17 June-2 July	3 July-16 July	2015
7.	Jyeshtha	2075	Sun	16 May-29 May	30 May-13 June	2018
8.	Ashvina	2077	Mercury	18 Sept-1 Oct	2 Oct-16 Oct	2020
9.	Shravana	2080	Mercury	18 July-1 Aug	2 Aug-16 Aug	2023
10.	Jyeshtha	2083	Jupiter	17 May-31 May	1 June-15 June	2026
11.	Chaitra	2086	Venus	16 Mar-30 Mar	31 Mar-13 Apr	2029
12.	Bhadrapada	2088	Moon	19 Aug-1 Sept	2 Sept-16 Sept	2031

13.	Ashadha	2091	Mars	17 June- 1 July	2 July- 15 July	2034
14.	Jyeshtha	2094	Mars	16 May- 29 May	30 June- 13 June	2037
15.	Ashvina	2096	Venus	19 Sept- 2 Oct	3 Oct- 17 Oct	2039
16.	Shravana	2099	Saturn	18 July- 1 Aug	2 Aug- 15 Aug	2042

The Hindu almanac follows the lunar calendar of time, which is shorter than the solar. When this gap accumulates to one lunar cycle, or 29.53 days approximately, an additional month bearing the same name as the month to come is added. This is known as *Purushottama-masa* and is popularly called the *Malamasa* (polluted month), i.e. intercalary month of the leap year. On average the month that separates this lunar year from the others will fall after a period of 32 months, 16 days and 4 hours (i.e. every third year). According to an ancient astrological Hindu text, in a period of 432,000 mean solar years of the Kali Yuga there will be 159,330 *Malamasas*. During CE 1945–2044, there fall 37 *Malamasas*.

APPENDIX 3
List of Maps and Figures

APPENDIX 4

Airlines Schedules

Web: www.indian-airlines.com ; www.indian-airlines.nic.in

From GAYA (since 18 Dec. 2002)

To	Day	Fl. No.	Air Craft	Dep.	Arr.	Stop	Fares, Y, INR
Bangkok	3	IC 729	320	11.00	15.30	1	
Kolkata	6	IC 730	320	16.25	17.20	0	2750

From BANGKOK (since 18 Dec. 2002)

To	Day	Fl. No.	Air Craft	Dep.	Arr.	Stop	Fares, Y, INR
Gaya	6	IC 730	320	14.10	15.40	1	
Kolkata	6	IC 730	320	14.10	17.20	0	
Kolkata	3	IC 732	320	16.20	17.20	0	

From KOLKATA (since 18 Dec. 2002)

To	Day	Fl. No.	Air Craft	Dep.	Arr.	Stop	Fares, Y, INR
Gaya	3	IC 729	320	09.15	10.10	0	2750
Bangkok	3	IC 729	320	09.15	15.30	1	
Bangkok	6	IC 730	320	09.15	13.10	0	
Patna	1, 7	CD 7412	737	06.30	08.35	1	3210
Patna	3, 5	CD 7412	737	09.30	11.35	1	3210
Kathmandu	1	IC 747	300	11.15	12.45	0	3225
Kathmandu	6	IC 747	300	11.00	12.30	0	3225

From DELHI (since 1 October 2002)

To	Day	Fl. No.	Air Craft	Dep.	Arr.	Stop	Fares, Y, INR
Patna	D	IC 809	320	09.45	11.10	0	4675
Patna	2,4,6	CD 7891	737	05.55	07.20	0	4675
Patna	2,4,6	CD 7411	737	16.00	18.15	1	4675
Patna	7	CD 7411	737	17.00	19.15	1	4675
Varanasi	D	IC 806	320	08.40	11.00	1	4155
Varanasi	1,3,5	CD 7407	737	12.15	15.10	2	4155
Varanasi	D	J-9W723	320	10.30	11.40	0	4550
Varanasi	D	S2-513	320	12.05	14.15	0	4350

From VARANASI (since 1 October 2002)

To	Day	Fl. No.	Air Craft	Dep.	Arr.	Stop	Fares, Y, INR
Agra	1,3,5	CD 7408	737	15.40	17.20	1	3590
Delhi	D	IC 805	320	16.00	18.15	1	4145
Delhi	1,3,5	CD 7408	737	15.40	18.40	2	4145
Delhi	D	J-9W724	320	14.30	15.50	0	4550
Delhi	D	S2-514	320	14.45	17.00	0	4350
Khajuraho	1,3,5	CD 7408	737	15.40	16.20	0	2670
Lucknow	D	IC 805	320	16.00	16.45	0	2370
Mumbai	D	IC 805	320	16.00	20.55	2	7115
Kathmandu	2,4,6	IC 752	320	11.55	13.05	0	2500

From KATHMANDU (since 1 October 2002)

To	Day	Fl. No.	Air Craft	Dep.	Arr.	Stop	Fares, Y, INR
Varanasi	2,4,6	IC 751	320	13.25	14.45	0	2500

From MUMBAI (since 1 October 2002)

To	Day	Fl. No.	Air Craft	Dep.	Arr.	Stop	Fares, Y, INR
Varanasi	D	IC 806	320	06.00	11.00	2	7115

From PATNA (since 1 October 2002)

To	Day	Fl. No.	Air Craft	Dep.	Arr.	Stop	Fares, Y, INR
Delhi	1, 7	CD 7412	737	09.05	11.20	1	4675
Delhi	3, 5	CD 7412	737	12.05	14.20	1	4675
Delhi	2,4,6	CD 7892	737	13.00	14.25	0	4675
Delhi	D	IC 810	320	14.50	16.15	0	4675
Kolkata	2,4,6	CD 7411	737	18.45	20.50	1	3210
Kolkata	7	CD 7411	737	19.45	21.45	1	3210
Lucknow	1,7	CD 7412	737	09.05	10.00	0	3305
Lucknow	3,5	CD 7412	737	12.05	13.00	0	3305
Mumbai	D	IC 810	320	14.50	18.55	1	7025

Days: D Daily, 1 Monday, 2 Tuesday, 3 Wednesday, 4 Thursday, 5 Friday, 6 Saturday, 7 Sunday.

J Jet Airways; **S2** Sahara Airlines; **CD** and **IC** Indian Airlines.

APPENDIX 5

The Buddhist Circuit:
Package Tour, U.P. Tourism

Varanasi – Kushinagar – Lumbini – Kapilavastu – Shravasti –
Ayodhya – Kaushambi – Allahabad – Sarnath – Varanasi
(cf. Fig. 109)

Dep.	Arr.	From	To	Activity	Km
1st Day: Varanasi to Kushinagar					
—	08.30	*START* at Varanasi	Tourist Bungalow	Assembling, introduction	—
09.30	13.30	Varanasi	Dohrighat	Lunch	160
14.30	17.00	Doharighat	Kushinagar	Sight scene, halt, Hotel Pathik Niwas	114
2nd Day: Kushinagar to Sonauli					
08.00	13.30	Kushinagar hotel	Ruins and temples	Sight scene, Lunch	3
14.30	18.30	Kushinagar	Sonauli Nepal border	Halt, Hotel Niranjana	155
3rd Day: Sonauli to Lumbini – Kapilavastu and Balrampur					
08.00	09.30	Sonauli	Lumbini	Sight scene	26
11.00	13.30	Lumbini	Kapilavastu	Sight scene, Lunch	93
14.30	15.30-19.00	Kapilavastu (walk 10km)	Balrampur	Sight scene, halt, Tourist Bungalow	140

4th Day: Balrampur to Shravasti – Ayodhya – Allahabad					
08.00	08.30	Balrampur	Shravasti	Sight scene	17
10.30	13.30	Shravasti	Ayodhya	Lunch, sight scene	115
15.00	19.00	Ayodhya	Allahabad	Halt, Tourist Bungalow	166

5th Day: Allahabad to Kaushambi – Sarnath					
08.00	10.00	Allahabad	Kaushambi	Sight scene	48
11.00	12.30	Kaushambi	Allahabad	Return, Lunch	48
14.30	18.30	Allahabad	Sarnath	Halt, Hotel Mrigadaya	135

6th Day: Sarnath to Varanasi					
05.30	06.00	Sarnath	Varanasi	boat ride, Sunrise	12
08.00	08.45	Varanasi	Sarnath	BF, Sight scene, ruins	12
14.00	17.30	Sarnath	Varanasi	City tour	12
17.30	18.15	Varanasi	Sarnath, CONCLUDED	Hotel Mrigadaya	12

\# For information on this Circuit, U.P. Tourism, see Appendix 12.

Dep. Departure time, hrs; Arr. Arrival time, hrs.

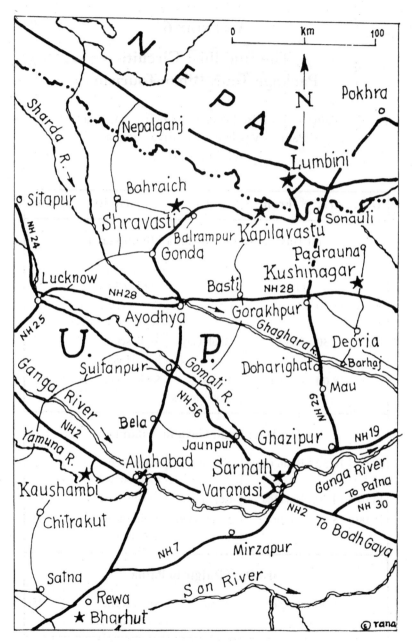

109. The Buddhist Circuit, Uttar Pradesh

APPENDIX 6

The Buddhist Circuit:
Package Tour, Bihar Tourism

Patna – Gaya/ Bodh Gaya – Rajgir – Nalanda –
Patna – Vaishali – Kesariya – Patna
(cf. Fig. 110)

Dep.	Arr.	From	To	Activity	Km
1st Day: Varanasi to Gaya / Bodh Gaya					
—	08.00	**START** at Patna	BTIC	Assembling, introduction	—
09.00	11.30	Patna	Gaya	Sight scene, in route see Barabar Caves	100
13.00	13.30	Gaya	Bodh Gaya	Sight scene, halt, Hotel	13
15.00	18.00	Bodh Gaya	Temple, monasteries	Sight scene	5
2nd Day: Bodh Gaya to Nalanda					
08.00	10.30	Bodh Gaya	Nalanda	Sight scene, monasteries	85
14.00	14.30	Nalanda	Rajgir	Lunch, hotel	12
16.00	18.30	Rajgir	Sight scene	Sight scene, halt, Hotel	4
3rd Day: Rajgir to Patna					
08.30	11.00	Rajgir	Patna	Sight scene, City tour, halt	105

4th Day: Patna to Vaishali and / or Kesariya					
08.00	11.30	Patna	Vaishali	Sight scene, Lunch	56
14.30	15.45	Vaishali	Kesariya	Sight scene	58
16.45	19.00	Kesariya	Patna	Return to Patna, halt,	114
—	19.00	Patna	CONCLUDED	Hotel, Dinner	—
OR, in case of continuation of journey for rest of the Buddhist places					
16.45	19.00	Kesariya	Kushinagar	halt	102
5th Day: Kushinagar to Lumbini ; **now follow the itinerary as in App. 5**					

For Bihar Tourism Information, see **Appendix 13.**

Dep. Departure time, hrs; Arr. Arrival time, hrs.

NOTE:

Both the Circuits, U.P. and Bihar, can be linked together for a period of 9/ 10 days; one should start from Patna and on the 4th day from Kesariya continue to Kushinagar via following the NH 28 (passing through Gopalganj), which covers a distance of 102 km.

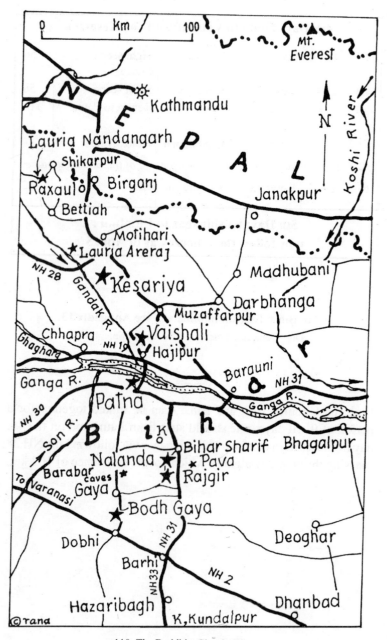

110. The Buddhist Circuit, Bihar

APPENDIX 7

Varanasi : Railway Time Table

July 2002-June 2003

To South & West, DN			← From Varanasi Jn. (Cantt.) →	To East & North, UP		
Arv.	Dep.	TNo	Day] ← To (Name of the Train) → To [Day	TNo	Arv.	Dep.
10.45	11.05	1028	D] Dadar (Kashi Express) Gorakhpur [D	1027	12.55	13.20
03.30	04.00	1032	4,7] Pune (Darbhanga-Pune Exp) Darbhanga [4,5	1031	21.25	21.40
—	15.50	1072	D] Kurla (Kamayani Exp) Varanasi [D	1071	19.25	—
—	11.30	1094	D] Mumbai (Mahanagri Exp) Varanasi [D	1093	04.10	—
—	13.30	1108	D] Gwalior (Bundelkhand Exp) Varanasi [D	1107	10.25	—
21.15	21.35	1452	1] Nagpur (Dikshabhumi Exp) Gaya [7	1451	04.44	05.00
—	16.30	2053	D, no 7] Lucknow (Jan Shatabdi) Varanasi [D, no 7	2054	12.05	—
—	20.25	2166	2, 5, 7] Kurla (Kurla Superfast) Varanasi [2, 5, 7	2165	07.20	—
21.10	21.20	2317	2] Amritsar (Akal Takht Exp) Sealdah [4	2318	01.45	02.05
21.10	21.20	2319	7] Amritsar (Matribhumi Exp.) Asansol [3	2320	01.55	02.05
19.35	19.45	2381	3, 4, 7] New Delhi (Poorva Exp) Howrah [2, 3, 6	2382	04.50	05.00
15.00	15.15	2401	D] New Delhi (Shramajivi/Rajgir) Patna/Rajgir [D	2402	02.35	02.50
01.15	01.25	2435	1,3,4,7] N. Delhi (Rajdhani Exp.) Guwahati [1,4,5,6	2436	22.15	22.25
07.00	—	2560	D] New Delhi (Varanasi Exp.) Varanasi [D	2559	—	18.45
09.50	10.05	3005	D] Amritsar (Panjab Mail) Howrah [D	3006	16.35	16.50
10.15	10.30	3009	D] Dehradun (Dehra-Howrah Ex) Howrah [D	3010	16.00	16.15
01.55	02.05	3013	3] Dehradun (Upasana Exp.) Howrah [5	3014	01.55	02.05
08.25	08.45	3049	D] Amritsar (Amritsar –Howrah Ex) Howrah [D	3050	19.00	19.30
14.35	14.45	3073	3,6,7] Jammu Tabi (Himagiri) Howrah [1,2,5	3074	20.55	21.10
21.55	—	3133	D] Varanasi (Varanasi-Sealdah Exp.) Sealdah [D	3134	—	09.25
02.35	02.50	3151	D] Jammu Tabi (J.Tabi-Sealdah Ex) Sealdah [D	3152	01.30	01.40
06.25	06.40	3307	D] Firozpur (Ganga-Sutlaj Express) Dhanbad [D	3308	20.20	20.35
—	05.00	4227	D] Lucknow (Varuna Express) Varanasi [D	4228	23.15	—
—	14.10	4257	D] New Delhi (Kashi Vishvanath) Varanasi [D	4258	05.25	—
—	17.25	4853	1,3,6] Jodhpur (Marudhar via Faiz.)Varanasi [2,5,7	4854	09.30	—
—	18.35	4863	2,4,5,7] Jodhpur (Marudhar)Varanasi [1,3,4,6	4864	08.15	—
12.45	12.55	5008	D] Maruadih (Krishak Exp.) Gorakhpur [D	5007	16.10	16.30
04.30	04.50	5004	D] Kanpur (Chaurichaura) Gorakhpur [D	5003	23.55	00.15
17.00	17.10	5105	5, 7] Baijnath Dham (BD-Kashi Ex) Varanasi [4, 6	5106	20.40	21.00
20.30	21.00	5110	1,3,5] Sarnath (Buddha Poornima) Rajgir [2,4,6	5109	08.10	08.45
12.15	12.30	5160	D] Durg (Sarnath Express) Chapra [D	5159	16.10	17.00
14.40	15.00	5205	D] New Delhi (Lichchhavi) Muzaffarpur [D	5296	05.10	05.25
—	17.45	6040	1, 3] Chenai (Ganga-Kaveri) Varanasi [1, 3	6039	08.00	—
20.50	21.35	6360	2] Cochin (Patna-Ernaklm Express) Varanasi [2	6359	04.40	05.20
20.50	21.35	7092	3, 5] Sikandarabad (Sikandarabad) Varanasi [3, 5	7091	04.45	05.20
07.27	07.37	8475	1, 3, 6] New Delhi (Neelanchal Exp) Puri [2, 5, 7	8476	19.55	20.10
07.50	08.05	8609	2] Pune (Gyananga Express) Hatia [7	8610	21.25	21.40

Days: 1 Monday, 2 Tuesday, 3 Wednesday, 4 Thursday, Friday, 6 Saturday,
7 Sunday; D- Daily; Arv-Arrival; Dep-Departure; TNo-Train Number

APPENDIX 8

Mughalsarai : Railway Time Table

July 2002-June 2003

To West & N / S, UP			← From Mughalsarai →	To East & N / S, DN		
Arv	Dep	TNo	Day] ← To (Name of the Train) To → [Day	TNo	Arv	Dep
03.12	03.32	1159	2, 3, 5, 7] Gwalior (Chambal) Howrah [2, 3, 5, 7	1160	19.35	19.45
16.20	16.40	2142	1,2,4,6] L.T. Mumbai (LT Exp) Patna/RN [1,2,4,6	2141	01.25	01.45
00.33	00.45	2301	2,3,5,6,7] New Delhi (Rajdhani) Howrah [1,3,4,5,7	2302	02.07	02.19
20.25	20.40	2303	1, 2, 5, 6] New Delhi (Poorva) Howrah [1, 4, 5, 7	2304	04.05	04.25
00.25	00.45	2305	1, 4] New Delhi (Rajdhani) Patna-Howrah [2,6	2306	02.07	02.27
09.50	10.10	2307	D] Jodhpur (H-J-Bikaner Express) Howrah [D	2308	16.50	17.10
00.35	00.55	2309	2, 7] New Delhi (Rajdhani Exp.) Patna [1, 5	2310	02.22	02.37
06.10	06.40	2311	D] Delhi (Kalka Mail) Howrah [D	2312	20.00	20.30
01.03	01.15	2313	1,2,5,6] New Delhi (Rajdhani Exp) Sealdah [3,4,6,7	2314	01.50	02.05
01.05	01.35	2315	6] Ajmer (Ananya Express) Sealdah [2	2316	01.50	02.10
08.10	08.30	2321	D] Mumbai (Howrah-Mumbai Mail) Howrah [D	2322	00.02	00.17
04.55	05.15	2323	2, 6] New Delhi (N Delhi-Howrah) Howrah [1, 4	2324	19.10	19.30
18.45	19.05	2381	3, 4, 7] New Delhi (Poorva) Howrah [2, 3, 6	2382	04.05	04.25
22.25	22.45	2391	D] New Delhi (Magadh Express) Patna [D	2392	07.25	07.45
00.43	00.55	2421	1, 4] New Delhi (Rajdhani) Bhuvaneshwar [2, 6	2422	02.22	02.34
00.35	00.55	2423	2,5,6] New Delhi (Rajdhani) Patna-Guwahati [2,4,6	2424	22.57	23.17
01.03	01.15	2439	3] New Delhi (Rajdhani Exp.) Ranchi [2	2440	01.50	02.02
16.40	17.00	2801	D] New Delhi (Purushottam) Puri [D	2802	09.55	10.15
04.35	04.50	2815	2, 4, 5, 7] New Delhi (Nilanchal) Puri [1, 3, 4, 6	2816	18.00	18.15
01.40	02.00	3007	D] Sri Ganganagar (Udyan Abha) Howrah [D	3008	01.05	01.25
13.45	14.05	3039	D] Delhi (Janta Express) Howrah [D	3040	11.50	12.10
11.45	12.05	3111	D] Delhi (Lal Qila Express) Sealdah [D	3112	13.40	14.00
20.50	21.00	3133	D] Varanasi (M-S Ex.) Sealdah [D	3134	10.05	11.00
04.20	04.40	3201	D] Kurla (K-P Express) Patna [D	3202	03.25	03.55
18.45	19.05	3447	2, 5, 7] Dadar (Shramashakti) Guwahati [1, 3, 5	3448	10.15	10.35
17.20	17.40	4055	D] Delhi (Brahmaputra) Dibrugarh [D	4056	08.45	09.05
03.40	04.00	4083	D] Delhi (Mahananda) Katihar [D	4084	21.00	21.20
08.00	08.20	5621	D] New Delhi (Northeast Superfast) Guwahati [D	5622	18.15	18.35
18.45	19.05	5646	3, 5] Dadar (D-G Express) Guwahati [3, 6	5645	10.15	10.35
18.45	19.05	5648	4] Dadar (Shramashakti) Guwahati [5	5647	10.15	10.35
19.50	20.05	6360	2] Ernakulam (Ernakulam Exp) Patna /RN [2	6359	06.00	06.15
19.50	20.05	7092	3, 5] Secunderabad (Sec.-Patna/RN) Patna/RN [3, 5	7091	06.00	06.15
06.30	06.50	8475	1, 3, 6] New Delhi (Nilanchal) Puri [2, 5, 7	2816	21.10	21.50
01.10	01.30	8605	3, 5, 7] Delhi (Jharkhand) Hatia [2, 5, 7	8606	06.30	06.50
19.20	19.40	9048	2, 7] Surat (Surat-Bhagalpur Ex) Bhagalpur [1, 6	9047	08.30	08.45
16.20	16.40	9050	3] Valsad (Valsad Express) Patna/ RN [3	9049	01.25	01.45
03.12	03.32	9306	1, 3, 6] Indore (Shipra) Howrah [3, 5, 7	9305	19.35	19.45

Days:1 Monday, 2 Tuesday, 3 Wednesday, 4 Thursday, 5 Friday, 6 Saturday,
7 Sunday; D-Daily; Arv-Arrival; Dep-Departure; TNo-Train Number

APPENDIX 9

Gaya : Railway Time Table

July 2002-June 2003

To West & N / S, UP			← From Gaya →	To East & N / S, DN		
Arv	Dep	TNo	Day] ← To (Name of the Train) To → [Day	TNo	Arv	Dep
00.03	00.11	1159	2, 3, 4] Gwalior (Chambal) Howrah [3, 5, 7	1160	22.20	22.28
00.03	00.11	1181	7] Agra (Chambal Express) Howrah [2	1182	22.20	22.28
—	17.00	1452	1] Nagpur (Dikshabhumi Exp) Gaya [7	1451	08.55	—
09.35	—	2023	D] Gaya (Gaya-Howrah Express) Howrah [D	2024	—	15.00
22.04	22.10	2301	1,2,4,5,6] N.Delhi (Rajdhani) Howrah [2,3,4,6,7	2302	04.16	04.20
06.34	06.39	2307	D] Jodhpur (H-J-Bikaner Express) Howrah [D	2308	20.38	20.43
02.49	02.53	2311	D] Delhi (Kalka Mail) Howrah [D	2312	23.15	23.20
01.00	01.15	2313	1, 4, 5, 7] NewDelhi (Rajdhani) Sealdah [2, 3, 5, 6	2314	03.59	04.03
05.14	05.19	2321	D] Mumbai (Howrah-Mumbai Ml) Howrah [D	2322	03.00	03.05
01.50	01.55	2323	2, 7] New Delhi (Delhi-Howrah) Howrah [1, 4	2324	22.00	22.05
16.00	16.05	2381	3, 4, 7] New Delhi (Poorva) Howrah [1, 2, 5	2382	08.36	08.40
22.11	22.16	2421	3, 7] New Delhi (Rajdhani) Bhuvaneshwar [1, 5	2422	04.32	04.36
22.27	33.31	2439	3] New Delhi (Rajdhani) Ranchi [1	2440	05.59	04.03
13.30	13.38	2801	D] New Delhi (Purushottam) Puri [D	2802	13.00	13.10
01.30	01.39	2815	2, 3, 4, 6] New Delhi (Neelanchal) Puri [2, 4, 5, 7	2816	21.00	21.06
04.55	05.09	3009	D] Dehradun (Dehradun Exp) Howrah [D	3010	21.15	21.27
11.45	12.05	3151	D] Jammu Tabi (Sealdah JT Exp) Sealdah [D	3152	06.10	06.17
02.10	02.16	3307	D] Firozpur (Ganga-Sutlej Exp) Dhanbad [D	3308	00.45	00.55
02.26	02.50	3329	D] Patna (Ganga Damodar Exp) Dhanbad [D	3330	01.25	01.47
20.50	20.15	3347	D] Patna (Barkana Palamau Exp) Barkana [D	3348	22.30	22.50
03.40	03.55	5109	2, 4, 6] Sarnath (Buddh Purnima) Rajgir [2, 4, 6	5110	01.15	01.28
03.25	03.32	8475	2, 3, 5] New Delhi (Neelanchal Exp) Puri [1, 3, 6	8476	24.00	00.10
21.15	21.25	8605	1, 3, 5, 7] New Delhi (Jharkhand) Hatia [2, 4, 7	8606	09.30	09.40
03.38	03.43	8609	2] Mumbai LT (LT Hatia Mail) Hatia/ Ranchi [5	8610	01.28	01.35
03.10	03.40	8624	D] Patna (Rajendranagar-Hatia Exp) Hatia [D	8623	23.30	23.50
13.10	13.45	8626	D] Patna (Rajendranagar-Hatia Exp) Hatia [D	8625	12.15	12.40
00.03	00.11	9306	1, 4, 6] Indore (Kshipra Exp.) Howrah [1, 4, 6	9305	22.20	22.28

Days: 1 Monday, 2 Tuesday, 3 Wednesday, 4 Thursday, 5 Friday, 6 Saturday,
7 Sunday; D-Daily; Arv-Arrival; Dep-Departure; TNo-Train Number

APPENDIX 10
Patna : Railway Time Table
July 2002-June 2003

To West & N / S, UP			← From Patna →	To East & N / S, DN		
Arv	Dep	TNo	Day] ← To (Name of the Train) To → [Day	TNo	Arv	Dep
21.30	—	2023	D except 7] Patna (Shatabdi) Howrah [D except 7	2024	—	06.00
12.50	13.00	2142	1,2,4,7] Patna/RN (Terminus) Mumbai/LT [1,2,4,7	2141	06.00	06.10
16.55	17.08	2303	1, 2, 5, 6] New Delhi (Poorva) Howrah [1, 4, 5, 7	2304	07.47	08.02
21.05	21.15	2305	3, 7] New Delhi (Rajdhani) Patna-Howrah [2, 6	2306	05.35	05.45
—	21.15	2309	2, 6] New Delhi (Rajdhani Exp.) Patna [1, 5	2310	05.45	—
21.46	22.02	2315	6] Ajmer (Ananya Express) Sealdah [2	2316	06.10	06.25
10.02	17.17	2317	3] Amritsar (Akal Takht Exp) Sealdah [7	2318	06.10	06.25
10.02	17.17	2319	7] Amritsar (Asansol-Amritsar Exp) Asansol [3	2320	06.10	06.25
—	18.55	2391	D] New Delhi (Magadh) Patna [D	2392	11.25	—
—	18.20	2393	D] New Delhi (Sampooma Kranti) Patna [D	2394	08.45	—
—	11.10	2401	D] New Delhi (Shramjeevi Express) Patna [D	2402	07.20	—
21.05	21.15	2423	1, 5, 6] N. Delhi (Rajdhani) Patna-Guwahati [3, 4, 7	2424	02.25	02.35
04.58	05.13	3005	D] Amritsar (H-Amritsar Mail) Howrah [D	3006	21.40	21.55
20.52	21.02	3007	D] Sri Ganganagar (Udyan Abha) Howrah [D	3008	06.50	07.00
21.46	22.01	3013	2] Dehradun (Upasana Exp) Howrah [6	3014	06.10	06.25
08.10	08.20	3039	D] Delhi (Janta Express) Howrah [D	3040	17.05	17.15
02.15	02.30	3049	D] Amritsar (H-Amritsar Exp) Howrah [D	3050	01.45	02.05
10.05	10.20	3073	1,4,7] Jammu Tabi (Himgiri Exp) Howrah	3074	02.05	02.15
06.30	06.40	3111	D] Delhi (Lal Qila Express) Sealdah [D	3112	18.40	18.50
13.35	13.45	3133	D] Varanasi (Varanasi Express) Sealdah [D	3134	16.00	16.10
—	23.20	3201	D] LT Mumbai (Patna-LT Terminus Exp) Patna [D	3202	10.25	—
07.30	07.55	3231	D] Danapur (D – Howrah Exp) Howrah [D	3232	20.15	20.45
19.20	20.00	3288	D] Tatanagar (South Bihar Exp) Patna/ RN [D	3287	06.45	07.10
22.35	22.45	3330	D] Dhanbad (Ganga Damodar) Patna/ RH [D	3329	05.15	05.25
19.50	20.00	3348	D] Patna (Barkana Palamau Exp) Barkana [D	3347	04.50	05.00
11.05	11.35	3401	D, not 7] Danapur (Intercity) Bhagalpur [D, not 7	3402	16.35	16.50
14.40	15.05	3447	2, 5, 7] Dadar (Shramashakti) Bhqagalpur [1, 3, 5	3448	14.32	14.44
18.00	18.55	3467	D] New Delhi (Vikram Shila) Bhagalpur [D	3468	11.25	11.50
13.10	13.24	4055	D] Delhi (Brahmaputra Mail) Dibrugarh [D	4056	12.55	13.05
23.40	23.55	4083	D] Delhi (Mahananda Express) Katihar [D	4084	01.18	01.33
04.16	04.31	5621	D] New Delhi (Northeast Superfast) Guwahati [D	5622	22.15	22.25
14.50	15.05	5646	3, 7] Dadar (D-G Express) Guwahati [1, 5	5645	14.32	14.44
14.50	15.05	5648	2] Dadar (D-G Express) Guwahati [7	5647	14.32	14.44
—	13.20	6310	4] Ernakulam (Er.-Patna Express) Patna [3	6309	22.55	—
16.05	16.15	6360	2] Ernakulam (RN/Patna-Ern. Exp) Patna/ RN [2	6359	09.30	09.40
14.35	14.45	6596	4,7] Yesvantpur (Sanghamitra Exp) Patna/ RN [4,7	6595	09.00	09.10
16.05	16.15	7092	3,5] Secunderabad (Secunderabad) Patna/ RN [3,5	7091	09.30	09.40
06.33	06.38	8184	D] Tata (Tata – Danapur Exp) Danapur [D	8183	18.30	18.35
—	09.00	8450	3] Patna (Baidyanath Dham Exp.) Puri [1	8449	10.05	—
21.05		8623	D] Hatia (Hatia – Patna Express) Patna [D	8624	06.00	—
09.45	09.55	8625	D] Hatia (H-Rajendra Nagar) Patna/ RN [D	8626	16.20	16.30
15.20	15.35	9048	2, 7] Surat (Tapti-Ganga) Bhagalpur [1, 6	9047	13.10	13.25

APPENDIX 11

Train Service to the Buddhist Circuit

July 2002-June 2003

Sarnath/ Varanasi - Gaya - Patna - Nalanda - Rajgir

Patna-Rajgir Expr.	New Delhi-Rajgir Expr.	Baidya-nath Dham Exp.	Buddh Purnima Exp.	Train Name	New Delhi-Rajgir Expr.	Baidya-nath Dham Expr.	Patna-Rajgir Expr.	Buddh Purnima Exp.
3234	2402A	5106	5110	↓Train No.↑	2401A	5105	3233	5109
II	3A,SL,II	SL,II	SL,II	*Class of accommodation*	3A,SL,II	SL,II	II	SL,II
D	D	6, 7	1, 3, 5	*Days of operation*	D	1, 7	D	2, 4, 6
—	—	—	20.20	Sarnath	—	—	—	09.00
—	02.35	20.40	20.30	Varanasi	15.15	17.10	—	08.45
—	03.25	22.00	21.50	Mughalsarai	14.30	16.05	—	07.25
—	—	—	01.28	Gaya	—	—	—	03.55
09.15	07.20	02.00	03.30	Patna	11.10	12.30	17.45	01.00
11.09	09.57	—	05.27	Nalanda	07.52	—	15.27	22.42
11.30	10.15	—	05.50	Rajgir	07.40	—	15.15	22.30
—	—	07.20	—	Baidyanath Dham	—	07.40	—	—
D	D	1, 2	2, 4, 6	*Days of operation*	D	1, 2	D	1, 3, 5

The train time refers to the Departure; most of the trains stop around 10/ 15 minutes.

Class of accommodation: II, 2nd Class; 3A, 3-Tier AC reserved; SL, Sleeper reserved.

Days: 1 Monday, 2 Tuesday, 3 Wednesday, 4 Thursday,

5 Friday, 6 Saturday, 7 Sunday; D-Daily.

311

APPENDIX 12

Government of India Tourist Offices

INDIA

Agra
191, The Mall Agra 282001
Tel: (0562)-2363959, 2363377

Aurangabad
Krishna Villas, Station Road
Aurangabad 431005, Maharashtra
Tel: (02432)-2331217

Bangalore
KFC Building, 48, Church Street
Bangalore 580001, Karnataka
Tel/Fax: (080)-25585417

Bhubaneshwar
B/21, B.J.B. Nagar,
Bhubaneswar 751014, Orissa
Tel: (0674)-2412203

* Mumbai (Bombay)
123, M Karve Road,
Opp. Church Gate
Mumbai 400020, Maharashtra
Tel: (022)-22014496
Email: gitobest@bom5.vsnl.net.in

* Kolkata (Calcutta)
'Embassy', 4, Shakespeare Sarani
Kolkata 700071, West Bengal
Tel: (033)-22421402, 22421475,
22425813 Fax: (033)-22423521
Email: caltour@cal2.vsnl.net.in

Kochi (Cochin)
Willingdon Island
Tel: (0484)-2668352

* Guwahati
B.K. Kakati Road, Ulubari
Guwahati 781007 Assam
Tel: (0361)-2547407

Hyderabad
3-6-369/A-30 Sandozi Building
2nd Floor, 26 Himayat Nagar
Hyderabad 500029, Andhra Pradesh
Tel: (040)-27630037

Imphal
Old Lambulance, Jail Road
Imphal 795001, Manipur
Tel/Fax: (03852)-2221131

Jaipur
State Hotel, Khasa Kothi
Jaipur 302001, Rajasthan
Tel/Fax: (0141)-2372200

Khajuraho
Near Western Group of Temples
Khajuraho 471606, Madhya Pradesh
Tel: (07686)-22047, 22048

* Chennai (Madras)
154, Anna Salai
Chennai 600002, Tamil Nadu
Tel: (044)-28524295, 28524785,
28522193
Fax: (044)-28522193
Email: goirto@md3.vsnl.net.in

Naharlagun
Sector C, Naharlagun 791110
Arunchal Pradesh
Tel: (03781)-24328

*New Delhi
88, Janpath, New Delhi 110001
Tel: (011)-23320342, 23320005,
23320109, 23320008, 23320266
Fax: (011)-23320342
Emil: rdnorth@ndf.vsnl.nat.in

Domestic Airport Counter
Tel: (011)-23295296
International Airport Counter
Tel: (011)-23291171
Panaji (Goa)
Sh. Syed Iqbal
Communicade Building
Church Square, Panaji 403001
Tel: (0832)-2223412
Patna
Sudama Palace, Kankar Bagh Road
Patna 800020, Bihar
Tel/Fax: (0612)-2345776
Port Blair
VIP Road, 189, Lind Floor,

Junglighat PO, Port Blair 744103
Andaman & Nicobar Islands
Tel: (03192)-221006
Shillong
Tirot Singh Sylem Road
Police Bazar
Shillong 793001, Meghalaya
Tel/Fax: (0364)-2225632
Thiruvananthapuram
Airport Counter
Tel: (0471)-2451498
Varanasi
15-B, The Mail
Varanasi 221002, Uttar Pradesh
Tel: (0542)-243744

OVERSEAS

Argentina (Buenos Aires)
950, Cordoba Avenue, 9th A
(1054) Buenos Aires, Argentina
Tel: 0054-11-4326 5391
Fax: 0054-11-4326 5143
Email: turindia@vianetworks.net.ar
* Australia (Sydney)
Level 2, Piccadilly,
210, Pitt Street,
Sydney, New South Wales 2000
Australia, Tel: 0061-2-92644855
Fax: 0061-2-92644860
Email: indtour@ozemail.com.au
Web: www.tourisminindia.com
Canada (Toronto)
60, Bloor Street, West Suite
1003, Toronto, Ontario
M4 V3, BC, Canada
Tel: 001-416-962-3787 & 3788
Fax: 001-416-962-6279
Email: india@istar.ca
Web: www.tourindia.com

France (Paris)
11-13, Bis Boulevard Haussmann,
F-76009 Paris, France
Tel: 0033-145233045
Fax: 00331-45233345
Email: goitopar@aol.com

* Germany (Frankfurt)
Basolar Strasse 48, D-60329,
Frankfurt AM MAIN – 1, Germany
Tel: 0049-69-2429490
Fax: 0049-69-24294977
Email: info@india-tourism.com
Web: www.india-tourism.com

Israel (Tel Aviv)
Sharbat House, E-5,4 Kaufman
Street, Tel Aviv 68012, Israel
Tel: 00972-3-5101407
Fax:00972-5100894
Email: goitota@netvision.net.il
Web: www.tourisminindia.com

Italy (Milan)
Via Albricci 9, Milan 21022, Italy
Tel: 0039-2-8053506
Fax: 0039-2-72021681
Email: turismo.info@cnn.it

* Japan (Tokyo)
Pearl Building, 7-9-18, Ginza
Chuo-Ku, Tokyo 104, Japan
Tel: 0081-33-671-5197,
571-5196, 571-5062/63
Fax: 0081-33-471-5235
Email: indtour@blue.ocn.ne.jp
Web: www.tourindia.com

The Netherlands (Amsterdam)
9-15,1012, K.K. Amsterdam,
Tel: 0031-20-6208991
Fax: 0031-20-6383059
Emails: info.nl@india-tourism.com
director.nl@india-tourism.com
Web: www.india-tourism.com/nl

Russia (Moscow)
20, Petrovskia Unni, Building 1,
Suite 32, Moscow 103051, Russia
Tel: 007-096-2003581/2000570
Fax: 007-095-2003071
Email: goito@com2.com.ru

Singapore
20-Kraniat Line, #01-01A
United House, Singapore - 228773
Tel: 0065-235-3900
Fax:0065-235-8677
Email: tourgoito.sing@pacific.net.sg

South Africa (Johannesburg)
P.O. Box 412542, Craig Hall 2024
Johannesburg - 2000, South Africa
Tel: 0027-11-3250880
Fax: 0027-11-3250881
Email: goito@global.co.az
Web: www.goirto.com

Spain (Madrid)
Avenida Pio XII, 30-32
Madrid 28016
Spain. Tel: 0034-1-3457339
Fax: 0034-1-3457340
Email: turindia@accesnet.es

Sweden (Stockholm)
Sveavagen, 9-11, 8th floor,
S-1 1, 157, Stockholm, Sweden
Tel: 0046-8-101197
Fax: 0046-8-210186
Email: info.se@india-tourism.com
Web: www.india-tourism.com

* UAE (Dubai)
Post Box 12856, NASA Building,
Al Maktoum Road, Deira, Dubai, UAE
Tel: 00-971-4-274848, & 274199
Fax: 00-971-4-274013
Email: goirto@emirates.net.ae
Web: www.goirto.com

United Kingdom (London)
7, Cork Street, London, W1X2 AB, UK
Tel: 0044-1711-437-3677,
0044-171-734-6613
Fax: 0044-171-494-1048
Email: info@indiatouristoffice.org
Web: www.indiatouristoffice.org

U.S.A. (Los Angeles)
3350, Wilshire Boulevard, Room No.204
Los Angeles, California 90010 ,USA
Tel: 001-213-380-8855, 477-3824
Fax:001-213-380-6111
Email: goitola@aol.com

* U.S.A. (New York)
1270, Avenue of the Americas, Suit
1808, New York 10020-1700, USA
Tel: 001 -212-586-4901/2/3
Fax: 001 -212-592-3274
Email: andy@tourindia.com

* GOI Regional Office

APPENDIX 13

U.P. Tourism Offices
Contact for the Buddhist Circuit Tour Package

* U.P. Tourism,
  Chandialok Building. 36,
  Janpath **New Delhi** – 110001.
  Tel. : 011-23322251
  Fax : 011-23711296

* U.P. Tourism,
  38, World Trade Centre
  Cuffe Parade, Colaba,
  Mumbai, MR 400005
  Tel.: 022-22185458,
  Fax : 022-22155082

* U.P. Tourism,
  SCO 1046-47, 1st Floor, Sector
  22-B, **Chandigarh**-160022.
  Tel. : 0172-2707649
  Fax : 0172-2707649

* U.P. Tourism,
  28, Commander-in-Chief Road
  Chennai, TN 600001,
  Tel. : 044-28283276
  Fax : 044-28283276

* U.P. Tourism,
  6, Smriti Kunj,
  Opposite Asia English School,
  Navrang Pura, **Ahmedabad**, GJ
  Tel. : 079-26560752
  Fax : 079-26564245

* U.P. Tourism,
  2nd Floor, 12A, Netaji Subhash
  Road, **Kolkata**, WB 700001.
  Tel. : 033- 22207855
  Fax : 033-22206798

* UP Tours, Hotel Gomti,
  6, Sapru Marg
  Lucknow, UP 226001.
  Tel. : 0522-2212659,
  Fax : 0522-2212659

* UP Tours, Tourist Bungalow,
  Raja Ki Mandi, **Agra**, UP.
  Tel. : 351720,
  Fax : 0562-351720

* Tourist Bungalow,
  Parade Kothi
  Varanasi, UP 221001.
  Tel. : 0542-2342018, 2343413

* Hotel Mrigadava, Sarnath
  Varanasi, UP 221008.
  Tel. : 0542-2386965

UTTAR PRADESH
U.P. State Tourism Development Corporation Ltd.
3, Naval Kishore Road Lucknow, UP 226001. INDIA
Tel.: (0522)-2228349, 2225165, Fax: +091-522-2221776
Email: upstdc@lwl.vsnl.net.in
Website: http//www.up-tourism.com

315

APPENDIX 14

Bihar Tourist Information Centres, BTIC, Govt. of Bihar

* BTIC, Frazer Road, **Patna**, BH 800001.
  Tel.: 0612-2225295.
* BTIC, Patna Junction, **Patna**, BH 800001.
  Tel.: 0612-2221093.
* BTIC, Hotel Pataliputa, **Patna**, BH 800001.
  Tel.: 0612-2226270.
* BTIC, Main Road, Sethia Compound,
  Ranchi (Jharkhand).
  Tel. 0651-230046.
* BTIC, Railway Station, **Raxaul**
  Tel.: 06225-262393.
* BTIC, **Vaishali**
  Tel. 062344-222392.
* BTIC, 216-217 Kanishka Shopping Plaza, 19 Ashoka Rd,
  New Delhi 110001.
  Tel.: 011-23723371.
* BTIC, 26 Bamae Street, Nilkanth Bhavan,
  Kolkata, WB.
  Tel.: 033-22803304.
* BTIC, Englishia Lane, JL Nehru Market,
  Varanasi, UP 221010.
  Tel.: 0542-2343821.

INDEX

A

abhayamudra 44, 134
abhidhamma 145, 271, 277, 278
Adi Gaya 105
Adinatha, temple of 199
Adittapariyaya Sutta 115
Agahat Sarai 272
Airlines Schedule 298
Ajapala Nigrodha tree 97
Ajatashatru 116, 192, 200
— Fort 196
Ajivika faiths 164
Ajivika sect 120
Akbar 130, 131, 183
Akshayavata 107, 112, 114, 185
All Japan Buddhist Nursery 94
All Saint's Cathedral 186
Allahabad 8, **183-189**
— Fort 181, 183
— Museum 187
— pillar 252
— University 182, 187
— University Archaeological Museum 187
Amrapali 224, 225
Amravati 16, 275
Ananda 18, 20, 23, 145, 254, 256, 257, 277
Anandabodhi tree 164, 171
Anandakuti 164
Anathapindika 145, 164
Anattalakkhana Sutta 124, 140
Anawrahta 292
ancestors-rites 107, 118
Andhaka 137
andhakasuravadha 137
Angulimala 145, 162, 163, 168
Anguttara Nikaya 27, 62, 114, 122, 277
Animeshalochana Stupa 79
Aniruddha 259

anjalimudra 44
Anotatta Lake 134
antaravasaka 44
Anuradhapura 86, 134
Anuruddha 26, 145
Appelbaum, David 11
Araurakot 55
Archaeological Survey of India, ASI 39, 126, 217
arhats 129
Arnold, Sir Edwin 5, **40-41**, 77, 87, 283, 292
Arogya Monastery 238
Asher, Fredrick M., 107, 283
Ashoka 21, 24, **28-30**, 71, 81, 86, 88, 120, 129, 139, 166, 181, 210, 213, 231, 232, 249, 252, 260, 275, 278, 281, 286, 288, 290
—'s edicts, six of 250
Ashokan Column 139
— Lion-Capital 133, 250
— Lion-pillar 139
— pillar 29, 49, 51, 53, 57, 79, 177, 179, 183, 223, 231, 249, 252
— Stupa 231
Ashokavandana 81
ashtamahasthana 135
ashtamahashthanani 24, 276
Ashvaghosha 140, 158, 283, 284, 286
Ashvina 109
ASI, *see* Archaeological Survey of India
Asita Kaladevela, see Kaladevela, Asita
Assaji 78, 129, 146
Astabhuja Devi 114
Atthamahathanani 24. *See also* ashtamahashthanani
Avalokiteshvara 167, 169, 170, 218
Aurangzeb 152
axis mundi 183

Index

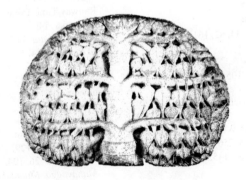

THE AUTHOR

Prof. RANA P. B. SINGH (b. 1950), MA, PhD, Professor of Cultural Geography at Banaras Hindu University, Varanasi, UP 221005, India. He has been working in the areas of cultural geography, cultural astronomy, peregrinology, literary images and sacred geography. He has been involved in studying, performing and promoting heritage planning and eco-tourism in the Varanasi region for the last two decades, as consultant, project director, collaborator and organiser. He has been Visiting Professor of Geography at Virginia Tech (USA), Japan Foundation Scientist at Okayama, Indo-Swedish Visiting Professor at Karlstad, Ron Lister lecturer at University of Otago, NZ, and Linnaus-Palme Visiting Professor at Karlstad University, Sweden. As visiting scholar he has given seminars at many universities in Australia, Belgium, Denmark, Germany, Finland, Japan, Nepal, Netherlands, New Zealand, Norway, Singapore, Spain, Sweden, Switzerland, USA (including Hawaii), and USSR. He is the *Founding President* of the (a) Society of Pilgrimage Studies, SPS (fd. 1989), (b) Society of Heritage Planning & Environmental Health, SHPEH (fd. 1989), (c) Indo-Nordic Cultural Association, INCA (fd 1992), and (d) Indo-Japanese Friendship Association, Banaras, IJFAB (fd. 1989). He is a member of the SASNET (Sweden), JASNET (Japan) and AASNET (Australia). He is a Life Member of the NAGI, NGSI, SPS, and EMS. During 1985-95, he has served as Assoc./ Executive Editor of the *National Geographical Journal of India*. He has also served as Chief Co-ordinator to international projects, like (a) UNO-CHBP, New York on "Rural development in Indian Environment; case of Varanasi", 1977, (b) SAI Heidelberg (Germany) project on "Visualising Sacred Space and Religious Cartography of Varanasi", 1999-2002; and (c) "Xerox Co. Project on Crossings: Kashi and Cosmos", 2000-01. Eight students have obtained PhD degrees under his supervision. His publications include 9 monographs, 22 books, and over 140 research papers, including articles in journals like GeoJournal, Architecture & Behaviour, Erdkunde, Geoscience & Man, Pennsylvania Geographer, The Ley Hunter, and Place. His recent publications include *Environmental Ethics* (1993), *Banaras (Varanasi): Cosmic Order, Sacred City, Hindu Traditions* (1993), *The Spirit and Power of Place* (1994), *Banaras Region: A Spiritual & Cultural Guide* (2002, with P. S. Rana), *Towards the Pilgrimage Archetype: The Pancakroshi Yatra of Banaras* (2002), *Where the Buddha Walked: A Companion to the Buddhist Places of India* (2003). He is presently working on *Cultural Landscapes and the Lifeworld: Literary Images of Banaras* and *Kashi & Cosmos: Sacred Geography and Ritualscape of Banaras.*

E-mail: ranapbs@satyam.net.in ; ranapbs@bigfoot.com
Web site: http://ecoclub.com/experts/singh.html

Pilgrimage and Cosmology Series

1. *Banaras Region. A Spiritual and Cultural Guide*
   Rana P. B. Singh and Pravin S. Rana, 2002, 2006

2. *Benares, A World Within a World*
   Richard Lannoy, 2002

3. *Towards the Pilgrimage Archetype.*
   The Pancakrosi Yatra of Banaras
   Rana P. B. Singh, 2002

4. *Banaras in the Early 19th Century: Riverfront Panorama*
   Text by Rai Anand Krishna, 2003

5. *Where the Buddha Walked:*
   A Companion to the Buddhist Places of India
   Rana P. B. Singh, 2003, 2009

6. *Cultural Landscapes and the Lifeworld: Literary Images of Banaras*
   Rana P. B. Singh, 2004

7. *Luminous Kashi to Vibrant Varanasi*
   K. Chandramouli, 2006

8. *Banaras, the Heritage City of India.*
   Geography, History and Geography
   Rana P. B. Singh, 2009

Also published by **Indica Books**

* *A History of Pali Literature* by Bimala Churn Law

* *A Buddhist Spectrum* by Marco Pallis

* *A Pilgrimage to Kashi. Banaras, Varanasi, Kashi*
  colour comic by Gol

* *The Ganga Trail. Foreign Accounts and Sketches of the River Scene*
  by Jagmohan Mahajan

* *Varanasi Vista. Early Views of the Holy City*
  by Jagmohan Mahajan